Grow Your Heart Centred Business

From Passion to Profit

Chris and Karene Lambert-Gorwyn

Wow! This book is a BEAST! Inside you'll find everything you'll ever need to know about starting and growing a heart centred business. Marketing, sales, mindset, systems, it's all here in one place. Get stuck in and read it cover to cover. You'll be glad you did.

Nick James,
Founder and Creator of Expert Empires.

Chris and Karene are Rockstars in helping those with a passion to help others get to the top. Follow their advice closely and you will see your dreams come true!

Kane and Alessia Minkus,
Number One Global Business Mentors

Chris and Karene are the definition of a power couple. The way they support and complement each other, and bring their combined brilliance to the world is really a sight to behold. Their integrity shines through everything and their teachings, while surprisingly accessible, are mission critical steps in the growth of any business.

Oliver Codrington,
Serial Entrepreneur and Owner of the London Wellness Centre

Chris and Karene have written this book not only from their experience but from their hearts. They have poured you a glass of their best work, their most valuable tools and concepts that have helped so many thousands before. I hope you enjoy it, more importantly I hope you integrate it and find success with it.

Kevin Paetz,
Global Business Advisor

Chris & Karene are truly exceptional role models, both in business and in raising their daughter. Inspiring and heart centred people like them are rare. Take this opportunity to learn from them and create your own personal and business success.

David Gil Cristobal,
Switzerland's Number One I Fitness Business Mentor

An inspiring read, Chris and Karene share the ways in which readers may empower change in their lives so as to understand themselves, identify their dreams and work with others towards achieving their goals.

David Lewis,
Sunseeker London

This book is both insightful and practical and provides a brilliant 'how-to' manual that will transform any heart-centered business into a profitable enterprise. A veritable gold mine of information - you have to read this book.

Laura Hurren, Executive Director BNI London,
UK & Co-National Director BNI Italy

Exclusive Offer

We would love for you to get the most out of this book and along with your Bonus Chapter of 100 Ways to Get More Clients, we have some additional training materials and support lined up for you.

Visit www.heartcentredbusiness.com/book/offers to access free marketing support, sales and money mindset training and a FREE Business Strategy Session with our Coaching Team valued at over £1000!

We wrote this book to help you succeed!

Click on the link now and let's make that happen!

www.heartcentredbusiness.com/book-offers

ISBN: 978-1-8380061-0-5

On the flipside, if you do everything we say in this book and build a massively successful business and fulfilling life as a result, we demand the right to interview you on stage and to make you a star! Ok, we're joking about that last bit, but we'd love to hear from you.

Thank you!

Dedication

To our wonderful daughter Mya, who inspires us to be better. You make our world complete!

To our parents, you have provided the support and impetus for us to create the life and businesses of our dreams. Thank you.

To Tom Elphick. For always being there, for always having my back and accepting me as I am whilst challenging me to become more, we love you and thank you. You are family and always have a place in our home and our hearts.

To Ruth Beadle. You have been a constant in my life since I moved to the UK. You are part of our family and always will be. We love you.

To Philip Aarons. You inspired me all those years ago as an Osteopathic student to step outside the norm and seek better results. Our conversations and friendship continue to do the same today. I love you and thank you for being all that you are.

To Kevin and Stephanie Paetz. For having the biggest hearts and gentlest souls of anyone we have ever met, thank you. You are and always will be part of our family!

To David Gil Cristobal. Your humility and unwavering commitment to creating excellence in this world inspires us every day. We are truly blessed to have you as our friend and business partner.

To Oliver Codrington. For your willingness to learn, your loyalty to friends and family, and your joy of the entrepreneurial adventure, thank you. Your friendship and our business partnerships mean more to us than you know.

To David Roylance. Thank you for always challenging yourself to become more, whilst already being the gold standard for humility, excellence and absolute commitment to serving and supporting your clients, your friends and your family! Thank you for bringing your love and brilliance to our business and our clients. We love you and are ever grateful for your friendship!

To Anna Goodwin. Having you join our company was one of the smartest business decisions we've ever made. Not only did you bring your brilliance to our business and our clients, we grew a family-wide friendship that makes us feel we gained a sister and extended our family. We love you more than you know. Thank you

To Sylvia Cohen. Thank you for your drive, your commitment to overcoming self-doubt and passion to change the world. We are honoured by your friendship.

To Patrick Nairne. You have made us look fabulous in photos at our events, in our personal life and at our wedding. Thank you for your friendship and your expertise.

To our Passion to Profit Mentorship Client Community, we love you all. You drive us to become more than we are, so we can serve you better. Thank you.

To our 6 Figure Practitioner Event Team. You Rock! The best Event Team we have ever witnessed and still getting better every time. Your willingness to be challenged, your commitment to growth and customer service, and the absolute love you bring to our events have made them the world class experience they are today!

Amy, Simon, Hayley, Tara, Koosje, Anni, Graham, Sarah, Maite, Ian, Jane, Jules, Yves. Thank you! We love you all!

To Reid Nelson. You started our journey into personal development and showed us a different way to view money and success. For your kindness, your heart and your willingness to share your expertise, thank you.

To Kane and Alessia Minkus. Without you, none of this would have happened. You put me on the road to success when I was drowning financially and had no idea how to be the father, the husband, or the man I wanted to be. The ripple effect your input has had in our lives continues to expand through us and is impacting more people every day. For your teaching, your coaching, your love and your friendship, we are ever grateful.

To Mark Dalton & Lindsay Hopkins. You turned my property knowledge into tangible results that are our financial foundation for everything Chris and I have now been able to create. Thank you for sharing my journey and for teaching me the principles of the slight edge through your actions.

To Gill Fielding. Not only have you sparked the fire of financial freedom and education in me through your work and our business partnership, your inspiration continues through the work Chris and I do with our clients.

To Nick James. Your passion and directness inspire us to reach ever higher, whilst your knowledge and expertise provides the framework to make that happen. Thank you.

To Sir Richard Branson. Meeting you in Singapore was a pivotal moment in my business and personal development. Witnessing your playfulness and passion first-hand whilst having the opportunity to speak with you privately, allowed me to step into a bigger vision for the impact I wanted us to have in the world. Thank you.

To Robert & Kim Kiyosaki. Rich Dad, Poor Dad was the book that started this all for us. From Karene meeting you backstage in Stockholm, Kim; to us both being at dinner with you in London, Robert; you have made a bigger impact in our lives than you could ever know, thank you.

To Tony Robbins. The impact you have had on us is profound. From meeting you in the Solitaire Lounge at UPW, to walking on fire, you have always inspired us to be more.

To Dr Tony Quin. Thank you for opening my eyes and my mind to another way of living and being. The impact you've had is still evolving and I'm excited at what comes next.

To Randi Zuckerberg. Presenting alongside you on stage in Stockholm opened our eyes to a different way of thinking around global impact. Your shoes, books and singing also made a huge impression on our daughter Mya, thank you.

To Kevin Harrington. Presenting on stages alongside you on four different continents, opened my eyes to a different level of success in areas I had never even dreamed of. Thank you for always striving to be more and inspiring me to do the same.

To David Goggins. For being vulnerable enough to share your story and pain with the world, thank you. Spending private time with you and getting to see the heart and humility that underpin your story has inspired us to challenge our mindset around what's possible.

To Les and Ona Brown. Whilst short, our time spent speaking with you in London had a profound shift on how we show up for our clients. Thank you for your hugs and your on-going passion and drive to impact the world!

To Teens Unite Fighting Cancer. Through your work supporting teenagers with cancer, you have given me a way to pay it forward and use my own experience of teenage cancer to positively impact others. Thank you Debbie Pezzani and Karen Millen for founding the charity and making such a difference in so many lives.

To Francis Holland Sloane Square School, Lucy Elphinstone and all the wonderful teachers. Thank you for sharing our values and raising the bar of education in order to create children who can think, who can bounce back and who are set up to change the world rather than just excel academically.

To everyone who has touched and influenced our journey. You are too numerous to mention individually and yet our thanks and appreciation for having you in our lives is undiminished.

And to you, dear reader, we hope this book provides you with the knowledge, the inspiration and the nudge for you to create whatever you want in your life, your business and your finances. If nothing else, we want to give you the belief that anything is possible and a roadmap for making that happen!

A Note from the Authors

It's good to have money and the things that money can buy, but it's good, too, to check up once in a while and make sure that you haven't lost the things that money can't buy.

– George Lorimer

This book has been a long time coming, however, the actual writing of it was rather accelerated. When Chris first had a vision of this book and started writing a few bits well over a year ago, I was lukewarm at best. I wasn't sure I wanted to share my story with the world. However, I realised if I didn't tell people what we've learnt and experienced, I was holding myself back and remaining invisible. I was also selfishly limiting who had access to all of our system for transforming life, business and finances.

Our clients typically increase their income by £50,000-£100,000 within 12 months of them implementing what we teach. This book is our gift to you so you can create the same results. It contains our insights and strategies; the knowledge we've gained from building our own businesses; and our experience of working with thousands of business owners just like you. If you can just implement a fraction of what we've included in this book, your business and income will grow massively. However, if you read it carefully, put it in action, and follow our system; your life and finances will transform more than you can currently imagine.

We've had an interesting journey to get to where we are now, and it is by no means over! If you'd told us that 9 years after meeting in a yoga studio, we would have built a number of 5, 6 and 7 figure businesses together; that we'd have a nationwide property portfolio; have a beautiful daughter; have helped thousands of people to understand what's possible for them and to have the systems and tools to create the life of their dreams....we'd have had a hard time believing it could be possible. We may have even had a good chuckle! Looking back now, we're definitely chuckling....mostly at how many mistakes we've made along the way simply because we didn't believe in ourselves enough. Today, still laughing when we make mistakes, we feel we're just starting to build real momentum.

Chris had cancer as a teenager and coming through this traumatic experience connected him early on with his passion for health and helping people. He trained as an Osteopath and spent many years honing his expertise and helping his clients solve their health challenges. He also managed to get himself massively into debt and had no idea how to run a business. When he finally learnt how to be successful, he decided what he really wanted to do was apply his talent for solving problems and his experience of overcoming financial hardship to helping other health practitioners to get more clients, so they could make a difference for more people.

My journey was somewhat different to Chris'. At school, I learnt to be an overachiever as a reaction to being bullied. This drive to succeed and prove my worth culminated in a career as a Management Consultant, where I spent many years working with large brands and corporations in Australia, Singapore, the UK and Europe. Like Chris, I was always clear about helping people, yet I wasn't wasn't as clear as he was on what I was truly passionate about. It is only now that I am connected with the change I can be in the world that I am clearer as to what this passion looks like for me.

When the opportunity presented itself to join Chris' journey helping health practitioners to get more clients and make more money, I jumped at it. Working with your life partner on something that makes a difference in people's lives, what could be better? And together, we realised we could apply our business models and success strategies to more than just health practitioners. We started supporting other experts and service-based businesses to grow their businesses because anyone selling their expertise is a practitioner. It doesn't matter whether they are an architect or acupuncturist, lawyer or massage therapist, accountant or osteopath. All these practitioners have exactly the same business challenges underlying their different expertise. And we've found the most successful and fulfilling way to solve these challenges is by building a Heart Centred Business.

Training practitioners how to succeed has magnified the impact and ripple effect we can have in this world, as all those different businesses now help more people. Having worked hard to create our own financial success in multiple areas, we've had the privilege of making growing other people's businesses our main focus. This book takes everything we've learnt and taught our clients over the last number of years and gives it to an even wider audience allowing even greater ripples of impact.

Whenever we're doing something new and need a new skill, or want to take something to the next level, we find someone who has done it before. Someone who has failed and then created success, so we can learn a shortcut based on their experience. We've worked with many different mentors in our business and personal lives and always created great results. From growing Chris' clinic revenue from £20,000 to over £100,000 in just 10 months; to teaching our daughter Mya how to play the flute or ride a bike; to building our property investment business to a £3million+ portfolio and £250,000 cash flow. Mentors are a key aspect of any success and it's by being mentors for our own clients that we've built a 7 figure Training Company helping thousands of business owners to succeed in their own lives. If you want to succeed more quickly in anything, find an expert in that area who has a system to teach you, so you can learn from their mistakes.

By sharing what's possible for you in this book and highlighting the right actions to take in the right order, we will help you avoid the pitfalls we fell into and help you step into the life, the business and the financial reality of your dreams!

Contents

Introduction

"Expect the best. Prepare for the worst. Capitalise on what comes"
– Zig Ziglar

We're passionate about making a difference in the world. We know this sounds like a cliché but it's just the way it is. By supporting other people to succeed, you never know how far the ripple effects of that action will go. From personally training thousands of business owners at our various events, we've seen the difference this is making in the world. Yet we've realised we're still only scratching the surface of our vision. Putting our great Training into this book allows us to talk to even more people who want to turn their passion into profit and grow a heart centred business.

The thing is, we teach our clients how to build successful heart centered businesses live from stage. We're professional speakers who teach using a microphone and a flip chart. We are not natural writers! So, instead of writing a book, we're going to have a conversation with you as though you were seated in front of us at one of our events. This means we're focused on maximising your personal results whilst keeping things simple and perhaps even having a little fun along the way.

In order to give you as much insight as possible, we're going to be totally open about our successes and failures in life and business. If you can take on board what we share, you'll rapidly achieve the vision you have for yourself and your business. By talking candidly with you about what worked and what didn't in building our multiple 5, 6 and 7 figure businesses, you'll be able to avoid making the same mistakes we did and progress much quicker. If you pay attention to the tried-and-tested strategies we've taught to thousands of clients, ranging from start-ups to six and seven figure businesses, you'll have the opportunity to achieve more than you ever imagined. And we'll also share the insights we've learnt from working with our Private Clients who we charge £100,000 per year to work with us.

Our clients typically increase their income by £50,000-£100,000 within 12 months of implementing our 3 Step Success System – Knowledge, Mindset, and Community.

Would you like £100,000 growth this year in your business?

No? You want more? Great! However, typically, just reading something isn't going to be enough. Making changes in life and business can be challenging and sometimes, no matter how hard we work at it, the changes just don't stick. This is why we use our 3 Step Success System to ensure your success. Our System has developed from over two decades working with some of the best coaches, mentors, gurus, experts and geniuses in the world. Countless hours of reading, researching and applying the knowledge of books, audios and videos, as well as attending endless days of training events and seminars. We also bring the practical experience of working with thousands of clients, growing multiple 5, 6 and 7 figure businesses of our own, and making thousands, if not hundreds of thousands of mistakes.

In this book, we aim to move you much further than just minor tweaks and changes. We want you to transform, so you don't revert backwards. To do this requires your participation in our 3 Step Success System.

Step 1, is Knowledge.

We're going to pack this book with as much great information as possible, so you have the tools to grow your business whatever stage it's at. We'll focus on teaching you the right things in the right order so you know what to do, and more importantly how and when to do it. As most experts and practitioners have never been trained how to make money from their expertise, it's unsurprising so many struggle in business. We'll start with the right foundations and build up to more advanced business strategies once the basics are in place. If you're already further along in business and enjoying good success, congratulations! We find most practitioner businesses share the same basic challenges no matter what size they are, so you'll enjoy even greater growth by focusing first on the fundamentals.

Step 2, is Mindset.

The right mindset enables you to take action and use the knowledge you have. Why do men get lost more often than women? Because we men often have a mindset that says it's not manly to ask for directions or look at a map. This is a great example of a self-sabotaging mindset and many of us do this sort of thing in our business and finances without even realising. I'll admit, along with not asking for directions when I'd get lost driving my car, I was also guilty of not asking for directions when I was lost in my business. It took me a long time to realise the discomfort of asking for help was far less than the discomfort of staying lost! I know Karene, and our bank balance, are definitely happier now I've moved past that particular self-sabotaging mindset.

To support you upgrading your mindset, so it works for you rather than against you, we have a couple of approaches. We'll share lots of stories from our clients to help you realise: if they can do it, so can you. We will share our own challenges and failures so you can see how we overcame them and how you could do this in your own life. We will also explore and help you identify where exactly your mindset might be holding you back. Awareness, after all, is the first step to changing these beliefs.

Step 3, is Community.

When it comes to a supportive community, most of us don't necessarily have people who talk us up. Instead, most people are surrounded by people who talk them down, even if only subconsciously. We'll discuss this a lot later in the book, but it is our community and people we spend time with, who either help us succeed in life and business, or who help us stay stuck. Having a peer group who share their values and are similarly driven to succeed, is one of the key reasons our clients grow their businesses and incomes so quickly.

If you don't a supportive community, we would encourage you to join ours. Sharing challenges and successes with other growth oriented heart centred business owners will accelerate your journey. Please join us at

www.facebook.com/groups/HeartCentredBusiness/

10 Keys to Creating Success in Life & Business... and how to get the most out of this book

How you get the most out of this book, in our experience, is also how you will get the most out of your life. The degree to which you choose to apply these principles, is the degree to which things will change for you.

1. Get Multiple Points of View

It really helps to see things from different perspectives. We see, interpret and experience the world differently based on filters and meaning we have developed through our own lives.

Chris and I have very different backgrounds and experiences. We've read different books, learnt from different experts, and had very different careers. We have experienced different levels of success and failure and grew up on opposite sides of the world. As well as having the obvious gender difference, we're just different people with very different viewpoints and mindsets. Our collective insights and experience will give you better results than if just one of us had contributed to this book.

Similarly, we use this same principle in our Client Mentorship Programme and Training Events. We always have a team of Coaches and Trainers who are the best at what they do, working alongside us, so our clients can benefit from these multiple viewpoints as well as our own. In this book, we've done the same. We will share from our personal experiences and also add and share from our observations of each other's experience's. Our writing style might therefore chop and change from 'We' to 'I' however, we will make it obvious who is talking each time.

We will also share some of our client's perspectives about the challenges they have faced and overcame. It might just be that hearing about what someone else has done unblocks something for you. If they can do it, so can you. Everything written in this book and all the different perspectives are there to to give you the best possible chance of understanding your own situation and getting clear on the right actions to move you forward.

In life and business, a broader perspective or viewpoint generally comes from receiving feedback. Asking for and listening to feedback is a central component to growing a heart centred business. When you're talking to your clients, try asking the simple questions, "Has this been useful for you?" or, "Does that make sense?". These are great ways of getting feedback and also making your clients feel heard. Sometimes feedback from your clients will lead you to adjust your behaviour. Sometimes it will reinforce it. Without feedback, however, you are flying blind and cannot improve the depth or quality of your customer service.

Whilst feedback is essential, it is also important to understand the level of experience that underpins the feedback. Everyone has an opinion. For example, when you are perhaps sharing ideas from this book, or talking about growing your business, someone will always be willing to share their opinion. Sometimes this is helpful, particularly if that person has first-hand experience of what you're discussing. However, there are also a lot of armchair experts who might sound as if they know what they are talking about, yet have never used their own advice, let alone created a successful business from it. Make sure to ask the follow up question when people proffer their opinion, "Thanks, is this what you used in your life/business/job etc?" If their opinion doesn't come from actually implementing what they're suggesting and getting results, then thank them for their opinion and move on.

Theory is great and some people share it with such conviction it is easy to think it must be gospel. Talking about the 'right way' or 'how to' in theoretical terms, compared to doing it in the messy world with real people, is a completely different experience. This is also why we'll share so much of our and our client's experiences. We want to make it real for you so you know this works and you'll have the confidence to use it. Of course, there are likely to be things you'll need to adapt to fit your particular circumstances and this is why having multiple points of view is so powerful.

2. Identify your blocks

Your body and emotions are much like the control panel on an aircraft, with lots of buttons and dials. In an aircraft, these buttons and dials give us the signals to know if things are or aren't ok. Your body isn't as straightforward as this though, as we rarely born with warning lights or altitude monitors on our skin. Instead, our body sends various messages through physical feelings and emotional reactions and we have to work out what is going on. It is our bodily reactions, our thoughts and emotions that tell us how we feel about what we're going through. The challenge though, is that what we are reacting to, is often something from our past rather than what is happening to us in the present day. Past trauma and experiences can be re-awakened by present events and our body and emotions respond as though it is happening all over again unless, we process the experience properly so we can move past it.

Most of us ignore the messages our body gives us until they become dramatic or negatively impact our everyday lives. If you get better at recognising and perhaps even recording these reactions as they come up, you can work out what is triggering the reaction and start that all important processing to put it to rest. In some instances, it might mean you need to do something different, or it could be that just pausing to work out what caused the reaction will help it to shift. Awareness is very powerful. Your feelings are feedback. Your body is sending you a signal to pay attention to. It is your choice as to whether you listen and take action.

At the back of the book we've provided you with a red Flag sheet with some key questions to help you decipher what your body is trying to tell you. We suggest you have one of these Red Flag sheets to hand whilst reading this book and perhaps as you go through your day so you can note what is coming up for you and start really listening to your body's signals.

The questions the Red Flag sheet asks are:

- Describe the thought that has come up, as best you can.
- What is the emotion associated with this thought? (e.g., sorrow, fear, anger, sadness, despair, hopelessness, etc.)
- What do you feel in your body? (hot, cold, pain, nausea, tiredness, a need to run screaming from the room etc)
- Where in the body do you feel this? (Legs, arms, chest, stomach, head, throat, neck, jaw, etc.)
- Summarise the thought in one sentence.

As you read this book, or in any situation in life, you might get angry, or sleepy, or feel sick. These are all signals from your body. You might get these when reading a particular sentence, paragraph or chapter. You may have already experienced some feelings in just picking up this book and flicking through it. Either way, get yourself a piece of paper or turn to the back of the book and start answering the questions and noting down your responses as they occur for you.

We use this exercise at our Events to provide an extra tool for our clients when they are struggling with an idea, exercise or action. It has allowed many of them to move through blocks much more quickly and provided a very powerful tool for them to better pilot their own lives.

3. Be Open

If you read this book passively, you will have one level of experience. However, if you engage, challenge your thinking, question your usual ways of working and take action; your experience will be very different. We speak at business and financial conferences around the world and getting our audience involved in any presentation we do is key to them retaining what we teach them so they can take action. We want the same for you here, so if it sounds like we're having a conversation, great, that was our intention. A conversation means you'll remember more, take more action and more fully engage. This is how you will create the results you want!

By using this book as a workbook for your life and your business, you may be able to tap into the undeniable success our clients have achieved. Information alone is not enough for people to transform, otherwise with all the content available on the internet about making money or losing weight, we would all be Billionaires with washboard abs! As this isn't the case for most of us, it is vital to take action and put the information you learn in this book into practice. Every chapter has a series of action steps to follow and will provide you with strategies and principles to implement right now in your business. Avoid the temptation to wait until the end of the book to start taking action. Just get started!

If you read this book and do nothing, your life will go on. However, things are not likely to change. If you read this book and follow the actions we suggest, your life and business have the chance to change beyond recognition.

What if....just whilst you are reading this book, you adopted a different approach to how you usually do things. Imagine what might be possible for you by the end of this book if you made a commitment to taking action. This is what we do in our own lives: we work out what actions we need to take to move something forward. This could be in our businesses, family life, relationship, charity work, fitness or any other area of life. Every day there are actions we could take and every day we choose whether to take action or not. Taking action is like a muscle: the more you use it, the stronger it gets. Get clear on what you want, take action every day and see what might be possible for you.

Perhaps if Karene shared some of her property experience it might give an example of how we've used this in our lives...

We read the book, *Rich Dad, Poor Dad,* by Robert Kiyosaki. If you haven't read it, you should. And you also need to do something with what you read so it can really change your life. We read it and put it into action and guess what, it has changed our lives. After reading *Rich Dad Poor Dad,* our action was to find and view properties so we could buy more houses/flats and make more money whilst helping people have accommodation. We did all that was suggested in the book: we found, we viewed, and we offered. One of our offers was accepted whilst I was in hospital being induced to give birth to Mya. Chris was on the phone with the Estate Agent and relaying what was being discussed to me while I was lying on a hospital bed waiting for the drugs to kick in. We looked at each other, shrugged and said "let's go for it". Chris confirmed the deal, hung up the phone and I then spent the next 24 hours in labour. Nothing quite like the right start, eh?

It was all rather an emotional experience and also not our best purchase. We had only scratched the surface of what was possible in property and as it turned out, whilst we had made some safe decisions that resulted in us making money, if we had really known what we were doing, we would have made much more.

Regardless, we had exercised the action muscle. Even better, we had a positive result. This encouraged us to keep exercising our action-taking muscles.

Now, several years later, we have a multi-million pound portfolio supporting asylum seekers and young professionals, as well as the elderly and families across the UK. It all started with growing our action-taking muscles.

What condition is your action-taking muscle in? This book will give you lots of opportunity to take action, so we're expecting buff and ripped action-taking muscles by the end of it because this is what's going to transform your life!

4. Do the right things in the right order

We can't afford to make assumptions about what you know and what you don't, so we will start simple and then build on that knowledge to get more complex. This way we make sure you have the foundations covered, so when you advance you will have a strong base to build on.

Recognise you may have heard some of what we share before. However, if you find yourself saying the most dangerous words in the English language, "I know that...", ask yourself whether you have done anything about it. If you haven't, then do you really know it?

When our brains say, "I know that...", they shut off and stop listening. For those of you with children, at some point you will have heard them say, "Yes, Mummy/Daddy, I know that...". After which, they will no longer take in anything you say and will be convinced that they know best. If you are nodding at this point, great. If you don't have children but can remember being a child yourself, we guarantee you had this same conversation yourself at some point.

If you find yourself saying "I know that...", you will stop yourself from learning. So perhaps fill out a red flag, work out what caused you to say it and then ask yourself, "...do I really?".

We would love for you to remain open to the possibility that you can always learn. Now might be the perfect time for you to hear something in a different way. Far better to be open to an opportunity that may transform your life and/or business even if you think you've seen it before, than be closed off to the chance to grow and stay stuck.

5. Complete the journey

Just keep going! Rather than giving up halfway or flicking through and skimming to the bits that look interesting, just read the entire book. We don't know when you're going to get your 'ah ha' moments; or learn a key insight that might save you from making costly mistakes; or hear a strategy that will make you hundreds of thousands of pounds. What if you skipped the page you really needed?

By all means, dip in and out and use the bits of this book you most need. After all, this book was designed as your personal business growth tool. However, also read the rest of it, because who knows what might 'speak' to you and when it might happen. An example of this, outside the world of reading, was when Chris attended his first Sales seminar when he was struggling in his Osteopathic Practice...

Karene is being polite here - when she says struggling, I was drowning! I was earning around £2,000 a month and we had about £8,000 a month going out. Why were our expenses so high? I was around £100,000 in debt from 15+ years trying to earn money from my expertise and not knowing how to do so effectively. Mya, our daughter was 18 months old and Karene had decided not to return to her highly paid corporate job so she could be a full-time mum. I was the sole breadwinner for our family and had no idea how to provide or earn more money from what I did.

After watching me struggle and flail around trying to make things work, Karene suggested perhaps I should attend a free Sales Training seminar and learn how to sell. Of course, being a health practitioner focused on customer service and ethics, I was caught up in the negative belief pattern that sales of any kind were wrong and icky. With this mindset, I was massively resistant to attending a sales seminar. However, I could also admit something was missing in what I was doing and our financial pain was big enough that I was willing to try something new in order to succeed.

Sitting in that seminar, listening to the American presenter teaching sales techniques, it completely reinforced my belief that sales are just wrong. I sat there with my arms crossed, judging him and making him wrong for everything he said. Until, towards the end of the day, he said one line that has quite literally changed my life. He asked, "If you don't start doing things differently, what happens to your life?"

This line stunned me and I went into my head and fast forwarded my likely future if nothing changed… Karene would be forced to give up being a full-time mum and go back to work; we would probably lose our house and have to move in with my parents; Karene would understandably resent me massively and I wasn't sure our relationship would survive the strain, meaning I would lose both her and my daughter.

I know this might all sound a bit dramatic, however, when you are over £100,000 in debt and sinking deeper to a tune of £6,000 a month, life is a bit dramatic! With this wake-up call, I started to see the presenter differently. I realised that although I might disagree with the ethics of how he did sales, what I couldn't disagree with was that he was a multimillionaire and a successful businessman, whereas I was not. If I could learn what he knew, I could apply it in my business, using my ethics rather than his and save my family. With that realisation, I went to the back of the room and said I was buying whatever he was selling. I didn't have spare money to buy anything, yet my conviction that I would do whatever it takes was enough that I went further into debt, spreading the cost of getting a mentor across several nearly maxed-out credit cards.

12 months later, having applied what I was taught, I had grown my income over 650% and was running my first six figure business. 5 years further on, I had built my first seven figure business and my family were set financially for life. If I had left that seminar early, I wouldn't have had the realisation that changed everything and none of this would have happened. We don't know when your life-changing moment will occur during this book, it could be early on, in the middle, or not until the last page. Just keep reading until you get your ah-ha and then take action!

However, if you're impatient and want the answers sooner, or just want to get direct answers specific to your situation, here's a link for a free business strategy call with one of our Coaching Team. These calls are valued at £1,000 and your Coach will work with you to identify the 3 top areas of growth in your business. If it's appropriate, they will also discuss how we might best work together to achieve results even quicker. To be clear, this call is our gift to you, and we want you to use it as a springboard to a new level of success. Only get on this call if you are serious about transforming your business and income this year!

Please now visit

www.heartcentredbusiness.com/book-offers

to book your call.

6. Respect

This is a good principle for life: respect yourself, respect your time and respect others. If you are reading, then read. Don't be on social media, don't try and do the dishes, sort out the dinner or anything else at the same time. Give yourself the gift of investing this time in yourself. If you learnt just one thing, it would be worth the time investment, right?

If you haven't realised it by now, this book is all about you growing your business so you can make a bigger difference in the world and help more people. Respect your clients and potential clients enough by taking the time to learn from this book how better to serve them, so you can have the impact you want.

If you struggle to find time to read and this book is just one of the many waiting for you on your 'to-read' list, perhaps consider the little and often principle. If you were to read just 2 pages a day, that's 60 pages a month and assuming an average of 150 pages a book, you will finish a book in 2.5 months. That's 5 or 6 books a year and who knows what new worlds and opportunities might open up for you with that amount of learning each year.

Also respect the fact that change requires effort and also time to embed and stick. To explain what we mean by this, here's how we explain the importance of sleep to our daughter Mya. As an aside, if you can't explain things you do to your children in ways they can understand, you are over complicating them.

Mya, our 7 year old daughter, is resistant to going to sleep. Like most of us, she thinks cool things are happening without her if she goes to bed earlier than we do. She also, like most of us, doesn't function well without sleep. At school all day she learns lots of new things. Learning these things creates a map in her brain. Her brain is then full of pathways (neural connections) to the treasure of knowing something new.

Who doesn't like treasure maps? To make sure her brain remembers these paths, she needs to sleep so they become part of her brain, rather than something that goes in one ear and out the other.

Sleep is a type of incubation or processing time. So is meditation, taking a walk in nature, or switching off the conscious brain in some way. It is the incubation time that allows the brain to sort and process what you have learnt so it becomes knowledge rather than just information. When you are learning anything new, remember you need incubation time for it to become a lasting change or transformation. In other words, for your brain to form treasure maps, you need incubation, respect this step in the process so that you can make the most of this book and life.

7. Dream Big

Throughout this book, we are going to challenge your thinking and also to get you to picture your future, to really see it. Why. Because your mind can't differentiate between real and imagined so if you visualise something your mind will think it has already happened and work with you to turn it into reality.

Right now, we want you to close your eyes and picture whatever you want in your mind's eye. Pick the biggest goal you can think of. With the exercise you're about to do, if you listen to what we're saying and focus in the right way, you will make this goal become real. However, if you truly get what we're saying throughout this book, this goal will be just the first step of you creating a life beyond your wildest dreams.

As you do this exercise, make sure you really engage all of your senses, to make it as real as possible. Ask yourself:

- What do you hear having accomplished this goal?
- What do you see when you picture having made this happen?

- What do you feel in your body physically once this goal becomes real?
- What do you feel emotionally having achieved this goal?
- What do you taste, what is the taste of success?
- What do you smell having achieved this goal?

Now you have embedded this goal in all your senses, repeat this exercise regularly to reinforce your neural pathways and build your treasure map.

This type of exercise is common practice with athletes. Tom, our best friend, is a great illustration of this. He was training for an Ironman Triathlon. This consists of a 2.4 mile (3.86 km) swim, a 112 mile (180.25 km) bicycle ride and a marathon 26.2 mile (42.20 km) run, raced in that order. It is a hardcore endeavour and not for the faint hearted!

Tom regularly imagined the entire race: the swim; the bike ride; and the marathon. He really felt like he had done it in his head already. When he did it in reality, he found it easier than expected and beat his predicted time significantly, finishing in under 11hrs. It was an amazing achievement and demonstrated the essential combination of doing the right things in the right order. Of course, Tom had to train hard and effectively to get his body ready for the event. However, that was only part of the equation. 10+ hours of intense physical activity is as much a head game as a physical endurance event. Business is the same, and visualising what you want will make attaining it much more likely to happen!

8. Start Small (and messy)

Remember, to transform anything, you have to take action. Chris and I are big action takers and we encourage all of our clients, and in fact anyone we meet, to take action. It is all well and good to talk about things, and occasionally we all want to complain about something. However, it is far better to take action and change things. Ever read a book you thought was great and yet you did nothing with what you'd learnt. We all have right. Of course, there is a risk you could repeat that same experience with this book. However, we are going to work with you so you take different actions and create a different outcome. After all, a definition of insanity is repeating the same actions and expecting a different result.

Taking action, for some of us, is easier said than done... we're talking to the perfectionists amongst you. Go on, hands up if you are a perfectionist. Karene and I know we were, and sometimes still are, perfectionists. However, we've discovered we're far more successful when we are progressionists. If you keep working to perfect something and never share it with anyone or take any action, you are guaranteed it won't be perfect as you won't have received any feedback from the people you're trying to serve. If it's pretty much ready and will get the job done, then share it, use it and take action, get feedback and transform. This is going to be far more successful than endlessly revising something that doesn't go anywhere.

In our business, we would never have got started and certainly wouldn't be where we are today if we'd carried on being perfectionists. When we first started our Mentorship Programme teaching practitioners and experts how to grow their businesses, we hadn't even finished building it before we took on our first 12 clients. Scary right? However, we had enough set up for people to get started and create good results whilst we finished the rest. Might that be the case for you? Is there something you have started and could already be serving your clients with even if it's not yet perfect?

For us, not only did we finish our first vision of our Mentorship Programme, we have continued to refine the content and consistently added more over the past 5 years. We got great results for our first clients even though what they had access to was a fraction of what we give our Mentorship clients today. One of the clients who joined that first group of clients was Amelia. Amelia worked 3 long days each week in a call centre. Part time she followed her passion as an outstanding practitioner working with her clients to decrease their stress. Unfortunately, Amelia couldn't afford to give up her £8 per hour call centre job because she didn't earn enough money from her passion. Using our initial programme, the one that wasn't even complete when we launched it, Amelia tripled her income within the first 3 months. Within 6 months she had increased her practitioner income more than 7 times and quit her call centre job.

If we had waited for it all to be 'perfect', we would still be waiting and still working on making everything right. Where would our clients like

Amelia be if we were still being perfectionists? They'd still be stuck where they were! So being perfectionists would have harmed the very people we want to help!

And what drives perfectionism? Our need for things to be perfect comes from our fear of not being enough, or being judged and found wanting. However, it is often seen as acceptable to label ourselves as a perfectionist. Like when you are at a job interview and asked what your weaknesses are. "Oh, yes, I would have to say my weakness is that I can be a perfectionist" If this is you, stop hiding. If you don't take action, nothing moves forward in life or business.

Dream big by all means and work your butt off to make it as good as possible. Start small and messy so at least you get something out there and start making a difference! After all, who might be suffering because you are not yet serving them?

9. Commit to what you want

If you are willing to focus for 5 years like most people won't, you get to live a life most people can't! And we say commit, we mean like the pig in this quote by one of the world's greatest tennis players, Martina Navratilova...

"The difference between involvement and commitment is like ham and eggs. The chicken is involved; the pig is committed."

With so many distractions and so much choice available today, it is possible to flit from one thing to another and not really commit to anything. You need to put in the effort consistently to make real change and transformation. So if growing your business is something that you really want, then commit to it. There will be bad days, and times when things don't work, when you have a difficult client etc. etc. It is therefore important to know why you are doing what you do.

We are 100% committed both to our goals and to those of our clients. When we first launched what is now Heart Centred Business Ltd, it was small and messy as we described above. Now it is a 7-figure business and growing ever more rapidly. What this really means is we have been able to help thousands of people get what they want and as a happy coincidence, we also get what we want.

Has it been easy? No!

And Heart Centred Business is only one of the businesses we have. Whilst building this Mentoring Company, we were still running Chris' clinic business, were also building a multi-million pound property business as well as privately mentoring a variety of different clients. Add to this our personal commitment to be present parents, supportive partners to each other, and Karene's commitment to be a full-time mum involved with Mya's school activities, we had a lot going on! We still do.

None of what we have achieved would have been possible without 100% commitment. We went all in and yes there were times when Karene threatened to give up and go get a real job because it seemed safer and easier. There were late nights and holidays where we would put Mya to bed and then work through the night. However, we chose everything we did. No one made us do any of what has brought us on this journey. Sure, there were things we 'had' to do to survive and thrive. Yet, it is worth repeating, it was all our choice.

I knew going back to work wasn't really going to solve things, however, when you are having a cash flow crisis as a result of buying 3 investment properties at the same time, you don't always make rational suggestions. And it was the mindset of, "I will do whatever it takes to keep us going" that meant we found and created other solutions so I never have to go back to work again. We now get to follow our passion and help more people and make more money precisely because we got clear on what we wanted and committed to it 100%. If you discover what you really want and commit to it, anything is possible!

10. Get a supportive community who share your values

Karene used to think that she had to do everything alone. As an only child, this is understandable, and being self-reliant will get you a certain level of success. However, she has since discovered you can achieve far more with others. With a supportive community who share your values, you'll also get to enjoy the journey a lot more. As she reluctantly admits, occasionally, she still gets it wrong and thinks she has to do things alone. The someone or something reminds us of what we have achieved together with a supportive community around us, compared to before we met when we were trying to do things alone.

To best illustrate this, perhaps if Karene shares her story of running the London Marathon…

I won my place in a ballot, so I wasn't running for a charity. I also didn't have my name on my chest. What a mistake both of those things were. I was committed and that is why I made it around in under 5 hours, however, it was some of the hardest 4ish hours of my life because I was running alone, despite being in a crowd. No one was calling my name and I wasn't running for a bigger purpose. Had I been clearer on why I was running and then had the added accountability of having raised money for charity as well as the support of people shouting my name, even if they had no idea who I was, it would all have been much easier.

Now, I am very clear that having a supportive community is key to doing things bigger, better and easier. With our property investment journey, I joined a mastermind as well as supporting other people on their property journey. I made sure I was surrounded by like minded people who were similarly committed to making a difference, so when tenants played up or a purchase was delayed it wasn't the end of the world, just some events that are now interesting stories.

In every area of life, you are the average of 5 people you spend the most time with. If you don't like the results you have in a certain area, consider who you're spending time with and how they're faring in this area. Get rid of the naysayers and underachievers, they will give you permission to quit. Hang around people who will lift you up, people who are even more committed to success than you. Create a team of the best people you can find, get them as obsessed as you are about getting you where you want to go. Make sure your team is working towards their targets, and don't let them off the hook.

We are excited to be part of your community driving you to the success you want in your life and business! The world needs your expertise and is waiting for you to grow your heart centred business so you can make a bigger difference!

Let's jump into the first Chapter, start working together and make it happen!

Chapter 1
There's business & there's Heart Centred Business

It is very easy to avoid criticism, say nothing, do nothing, be nothing. When you challenge the norms when you make your voice heard, you are guaranteed to receive criticism but, in the end, it is all worth it.
The alternative is to be invisible.
– Elbert Hubbard

Business is just about Making Money, Right?

How you make your money is much more important than the amount of money you make. By making money from a heart centred approach, you will make a lot more money in the long run. However, you might find you initially make less money. This is one of the reasons perhaps people don't think or work this way. However, if you focus on making money only in ways that are aligned with your values, the sometimes slower growth rapidly converts into far greater long term success.

So, what does this mean in reality? On a very simple level, it comes down to customer service. Is how you're making your money serving your clients or your company in the best possible way? If not, how come? And what could you do to improve how you serve them?

A lot of businesses and people make their money by doing a task or a role and never pause to think of the impact what they're doing might have on the people they are working for or with. If a business is just about making money and they forget their customers, it is unlikely to last. A lot of businesses fail because they simply look to take advantage of a gap in the market or an opportunity to make money. Whilst in principle this might seem like a good idea, it usually isn't sustainable. Why? Because to make money consistently over the long-term, you need to make a difference to your clients. To make a difference you have to serve them. When you're disconnected from your customer's experience, you're just pushing a product or service. Whilst this might work in the short term, it isn't going to create loyalty. Loyalty is where true business longevity exists.

We've found that heart centred businesses are most successful when their focus is on passionately solving problems and providing outstanding service for their clients. Consider your clients, how can you make their lives better, easier, productive, fun or perhaps pain free? This requires you to apply your expertise to solving not only people's symptoms but also the root causes of their complaint. By resolving this root cause, they can then go on to achieve success, whatever that might mean for them. Providing these types of solutions will create loyalty and have your customers coming back more often. This repeat business is vital to creating a sustainable business in today's marketplace when there is so much choice and so many options available. There is always another expert to try if you don't create loyalty.

When it comes to how to make money in your business, the strategy and calculations for how to do so are quite straightforward. If you want to make more money, there are two approaches:

- Help more people. This is a volume business.
- Help fewer people and make a bigger difference for them. This is a premium service business.

It really is that simple. This is best illustrated with the many ways you could make £1million.

You need 1,000,000 people to buy a £1 product
You need 5,000 people to buy a £200 product
You need 2,000 people to buy a £500 product
You need 1,000 people to buy a £1,000 product
You need 500 people to buy a £2,000 product
You need 300 people to buy a £3,333 product
You need 200 people to buy a £5,000 product

You need 100 people to buy a £10,000 product

You need 50 people to buy a £20,000 product

You need 25 people to buy a £40,000 product

You need 10 people to buy a £100,000 product

When you break it down like this it becomes far more achievable. However, I know already the little voice inside you is saying,
"But what about...".
Or, "But that would never work for me"
Or, "I'll never find that many people"
And if you are wondering what little voice I am talking about... that's the voice!

Already, a lack of knowledge or limited mindset is starting to ask questions that creates doubt and sends you into overwhelm or disbelief that this might be possible for you. This is exactly the reason why, so few people build a million pound business. The doubts, the disbelief and the lack of knowledge all get in the way and stop us taking action.

Something to consider is there is no timeframe mentioned in the calculations above. For many of us, if you extended the goal of £1 million over a lifetime, it becomes very possible. Now we understand it might still feel unreal with your background / your skills / your profession / your family / your financial history / your disadvantages etc.... (just circle the limiting belief most relevant to you.) The thing is, earning £1million could take much less time than you think. Let's perhaps tweak your thinking by turning this from theory into practice with an example...

Let's look at Belinda, one of our clients who is known as Brighton's answer for Stressed Out Mums. When we first started working with her, she had very few clients and the ones she did have, she was gifting her sessions rather than charging them because she was too afraid to ask for the money. Now, after using our Systems and working on her Money Mindset (we'll be covering Money Mindset in Chapter 5), the average investment of her clients is £1000. This works out to be roughly £170 per hour.

Let's say she spends the next ten years working on her business and she works 3 days a week and spends 5 hours seeing clients each of those days and she has 4 weeks holiday a year. What would she have earnt?

Let's do the calculation...
£170 per hour x 3 days x 5 hours x 48 weeks = £122,400 per year for 10 years = £1,244,000
Over £1.2million in ten years working just 3 days (15 hours) per week!

Now, you have seen how it works for Belinda, could this be possible for you? What would it look like if you were earning this sort of money? What would you hear or feel if you achieved this? Allow yourself to fully visualise using all of your senses so, it starts to become real in your mind.

Imagine the difference Belinda is making by supporting 170 families a year, to have a better family life because "mum" is happy and present and has better tools to handle stress. You can see and smell the fun mealtimes and hear the homework getting done. Of course, the usual frustrations around eating greens and going to bed still exist. It all just works better. A question to ask yourself is, would you be ok with making that kind of difference in 'mums' lives and over the next ten years earn more than £1 million?

We know some of you will have got stuck on Belinda's hourly rate of £170 per hour. The reality is that as long as your clients are getting the results they want, feel they are getting excellent service and are happy to pay what you ask, is there anything wrong with you making this sort of money? Of course not. However, we are aware that a lot of us have beliefs around what is 'allowed' in certain professions. We cover this more specifically in Chapter 5, Money Mindset. What if we shared the same calculations for another client?

Samantha is an Acupuncturist in South East England who works with women in their 40's struggling with stress. When we started working with her, Samantha had been in practice for two decades and had a waiting list of clients. However, her cashflow was not healthy, and she had to rely on credit cards to pay for extras such as holidays etc. Samantha's clients used to pay an average hourly rate of £50 per hour.

Samantha works 24 hours per week, spread across 5 days and takes approximately 8 weeks holiday a year.

So, the calculation for her would be:
£50 per hour x 24 hours per week x 44 weeks per year = £52,800
Earning £52,800 a year means it would take just under 19 years to earn £1million

Although we're pretty sure most people would still be happy with that outcome, things can be quite different in a properly run heart centred business. After working with Samantha for approximately 8 months in our Mentorship Programme and exploring how she could increase her service for her clients in order to get them even better results, she's increased her average hourly rate to £90. Initially, she lost a few clients. This caused a few minor panics, and then within 2 or 3 months, she was back to being fully booked with everyone paying her new rates.

Samantha's new calculation is now:
£90 per hour x 24 hours per week x 44 weeks per year = £95,040
At £95,040 a year, it will only take her 10.5 years to earn £1million!

Something to note is both Samantha and Belinda work with a similar group of clients yet charge different amounts. They have very different qualifications and skills sets and do very different work. They are both aiming to achieve a similar end result for their clients who are all getting great results and are happy to invest. If their clients are equally happy, getting the same results just through a different route, could they perhaps both be charging the higher amount?

So, when you look at business and earning money through the different lenses of how many people you are helping in the world and what difference you are making; business becomes quite different. This is why we're passionate about helping more heart centred business owners grow and step into their true potential! To make this happen, we have to do the right things in the right order...

Do the Right Things in the Right Order

There is a lot of advice out there on what people should do to build and grow a business. Whilst some of the advice is good, it can be really confusing and can lead to a lot of wasted time and money if you do the right things but in the wrong order. In our business we are focused on results and what works, rather than what's popular. This means doing the right things in the right order. If you go out of sequence, you will slow your growth, or worse, you could harm your business.

The thing is, to ensure you're doing the right things in the right order, you need to have clarity that "You" are a business. Many expert or service-based businesses are so connected with helping people, they forget they're running a business and it can therefore feel like it's a job or even worse yet, be seen as a hobby.

Businesses are a bit like buckets, they come in all shapes and sizes. However, no matter how big your bucket is, if you have holes in your bucket, you aren't going to be very effective. No matter what size business Karene and I get asked to consult on; whether it's a start-up solo practitioner, or an international multi-seven-figure company; we typically find they all have the same fundamental 'holes' in them. Without fixing these fundamental challenges, most businesses struggle to reach the next level of success, no matter what size they are.

One of the Core Principles in Heart Centred Business is clarity around what phase of business you are. Your Phase dictates your focus and what actions are most appropriate. However, if you have fundamental 'holes', your initial focus needs be plugging them so you can continue to grow.

The three Phases of Business for expert and service-based are:

- Phase 1 - £0-£100,000 Gross Annual Revenue
- Phase 2 - £100,000-£250,000
- Phase 3 - £250,000 +

Phase 1 - £0 - £100,000

This Phase goes from start up to £100,000, a reasonably decent income for an individual. In this Phase of business, you are typically a solo practitioner or self-employed person doing everything yourself. It can be hard work in this Phase if you aren't focused on the right things. You will need to ignore the wrong or inappropriate things. There is also a natural tendency toward overwhelm if you haven't established good working habits and systems.

If you have more than a single person working full-time in your business in Phase 1, such as an associate, employee or sub-contractor; something isn't working right income-wise. All experts working full time have the ability to bring in £100,000, so the more people there are in the business, the higher we would expect the overall business income to be.

Phase 1 is where most experts and practitioners reside. Typically struggling month to month, or earning enough to be 'comfortable' yet working many hours in what can feel like a conveyor belt style of job where they have to have a constant high flow of clients to maintain the income and lifestyle they enjoy.

As an expert, Chris spent years working both as an associate and trying to build his own practice. He was definitely not earning anywhere near £100,000 despite working 50-60 hours a week. In fact, he remained stuck at £20,000-£25,000 until he realised what was possible if he did things slightly differently. With this shift, he doubled his income within 2 weeks. Within 10 months he had earned over £100,000. Much like Roger Bannister and breaking the 4-minute mile barrier, once he knew what was possible, he opened his mind to achieving it himself. Until Roger Banister ran the mile in 3 minutes 59.4 seconds in 1954, everyone said it was impossible. Since then, more than 1400 athletes have achieved the previously 'impossible' feat of running a sub 4-minute mile. It's not that the human race had a sudden breakthrough in evolution and we're now fitter and stronger than we were before 1954, instead it's a simple mindset shift that once something is shown to be possible, we start to believe we will achieve it. Of course, it will require focus, hard work and a supportive community, however, once the mindset is in the right place, much more becomes possible.

For those of you who have a block around running a sub-4-minute mile, get a running book, or better yet, a running coach with a track record of achieving this with their clients, as this book won't help you with running. However, those of you with a block around earning £100,000 or more, or if you're wondering how this is possible, here's a simple calculation to show you how this would apply to you.

Let's keep the maths really simple and then we can play around with things to make it universally applicable. To do this we need to make some assumptions. Firstly, let's assume you are charging your clients £80 per hour. Now this would be cheap for most plumbers and tradespeople, yet might be considered a lot for some health practitioners or therapists. It might also be well below what some of you charge, however, it's a good average number to keep the math simple. Let's also assume you're working 5 hours a day and 5 days a week. We consider this full time for doing client facing work. More than 25 hours per week working with clients often leads to burn-out over time, whereas 25 hours per week seems sustainable long-term. We will also assume you take 2 weeks of holiday per year. So, the calculation is therefore...

£80 per hour x 5 hours per day x 5 days per week x 50 weeks per year = £100,000

The great thing is about this calculation, we can adjust it to fit whatever structure or way you want to work so you can clearly see what you have to do to earn £100,000 in your business.

For example, if you want to have more holidays each year, say 4 or 6 weeks, and still only want to work 25 hours per week, you will have to increase your hourly rate slightly:

4 weeks holiday per year increases your hourly rate to £83.33.
£83.33 per hour x 5 hours per day x 5 days per week x 48 weeks per year = £100,000

Or 6 weeks holiday per year would increase your hourly rate to £86.67.
£86.67 per hour x 5 hours per day x 5 days per week x 46 weeks per year = £100,000

If you wanted to charge less than £80 per hour, you simply have to work more hours per week or have less holiday to reach £100,000:

Charging £66.67 per hour, you would have to work 30 hours per week.
£66.67 per hour x 6 hours per day x 5 days per week x 50 weeks per year = £100,000

If you wanted to charge as little as £50 per hour you would have to work 40 hours per week. As an aside, £50 is massively undervaluing the difference you make for your clients and is harming both you and them, as we'll cover in Chapter 4, Heart Centred Sales.

£50 per hour x 8 hours per day x 5 days per week x 50 weeks per year = £100,000

Obviously, if you want to earn more or less than £100,000 per year, you simply have to increase or decrease what you charge, or the number of hours you work per week.

Something to consider if you have team members, employees or associates: these calculations are applicable for every person in your business. If they're working for you full time, this is what they should be generating for your business. Suddenly it becomes far easier to see how you could build not just a 6 but a 7 figure business without hundreds of employees.

ACTION STEP

Complete the calculation for your business to see how you (and your associates) could bring in £100,000 per year.

Use your existing pricing and numbers of hours worked

Then tweak the numbers to reveal what might need to change to reach £100,000 more easily

Once you've done this calculation for yourself you should have clarity on what needs to happen in your business for you to make £100,000 each year. If you want a different financial reality to what you currently have, you simply need to work out what you need to do to achieve the numbers shown in your calculation and work accordingly to put it into practice.

For example, you might need to be more consistent with client numbers each week to make this income sustainable. Or you might need to charge more? Or perhaps you need the confidence and a mindset shift to know that this is possible for you? You might need to get more organised so you get everything else done and still work 25 client facing hours consistently? Whatever the challenge you might have identified, there are some key questions to answer to work out what your next steps are.

First, you need to understand where you are. You next need to understand where you want to get to. We've used the example of £100,000, but you might want more or less than that so take the time to get clear on what you want to have.

ACTION STEP

What would you like to be earning each year?

How many hours at your current rate
would you need to work to do this?

If you fixed the number of hours you want to work each week,
what do you need to be charging per hour?

Now Chris had skills and experience when he grew his practice by over £100,000 in a single year. You might be thinking, whilst it was possible for him to grow beyond a Phase 1 business in a matter of months, it might not be the case for you. You might just be starting out. So, let's share Margret's experience. Whilst still completing her qualifications and having left her corporate job to set up as a Personal Trainer, Margret had no idea how she was going to grow a business from scratch. Yet following the same principles as Chris and using our Success System, 10 months later she is on target to earn £70,000 in her first year of working self-employed, more than she was previously earning in her corporate job. Perhaps - more importantly than that, Margret is thoroughly enjoying life, working on her own fitness and strength following back surgery and is very excited to be able to prove her parents wrong regarding her business success. Of course, this hasn't been easy, and she has worked hard to achieve these results, However, if you want something enough and have a system to follow, anything is possible.

Something we notice for many experts who never thought that 6 figures was possible is they plateau here in Phase 1. Whilst a good 5 or low 6 figure income might feel great, if you haven't been earning this for several years, you might not have adequate savings or a plan for retirement in case something happens, and you can no longer work. Please remember if you only set your targets for what will cover you today, who is going to sort out tomorrow?

Phase 2 - £100,000-£250,000

A Phase 2 business has gross revenue of between £100,000 to £250,000. You could still be a solo practitioner or self-employed person in this Phase. However, if this is you, you are probably feeling the strain and looking to take on extra support such as an associate, subcontractor or employee...or at the very least some admin support. Being able to expand your business with a part time or full-time associate provides resilience to your business through holiday/sick cover etc as well as being able to support more clients. Having support with admin means you free up more time to see clients or regain some balance and pursue other passions in life.

Speaking of balance and passions, let's take a look at one of our clients, James. James illustrates that it isn't always about earning more money. Quality of life and time are equally important once you've sorted out your finances and have some security both for now and retirement.

James is an Osteopath and clinic owner in Hertfordshire and was already a Phase 2 business when he joined our Mentorship Programme. With the number of practitioners and rooms James had, we helped him realise he could easily be a Phase 3 business. In working with us, he decided he didn't want to focus on income growth. He would rather free up his time and regain his mojo. Over the past couple of years, James has only increased his income by around £20,000-£30,000 a year, but now has a very different work/life balance. He works far fewer hours, has more time with friends and family and spends most afternoons in the gym, on the squash court or in the sauna. After more than 25 years in practice, he's fallen back in love with what he does and "found his mojo again".

Now you may be in a different phase of life and be wanting more. So what might that look like?

Phase 3 - £250,000 +

A Phase 3 business has a gross revenue of more than £250,000 and whilst rare, this can still be a solo practitioner/single person. For example, one of our clients is an experienced IT consultant who works as a contractor earning around £300,000 each year. It is, however, more typical that a Phase 3 business will have grown beyond a sole individual to at least a part time associate or small team and certainly additional support for admin functions such as accounting/appointment scheduling etc.

It is usually at this point you might consider replicating your business/ practice success in a new location so you can have a 2nd or 3rd site offering services to a broader geographic area. Or you might have diversified your offering, so you become an end-to-end service or solution for your clients rather than just a single step in their journey.

Marcus is a good example of this. He and his wife had a great clinic business in two locations in central London. He and his wife were both working full time in the business, and despite a high turnover, they were struggling with overheads, no work-life balance and paying themselves very little despite the amount of work they were having to put in. We've been working together for a couple of years and they've restructured and systemised their business to the extent that they now have 5 associates, have tripled their income and recently moved out of London. Marcus now goes into their business about once a month and his wife has been able to remove herself entirely to focus on their new family. They now have a portfolio of business interests alongside their clinics and apply the exact same systems and principles to their non-health based businesses.

There is really no limit to how big you can grow a service business. Just look at the large legal, accountancy, marketing or consulting businesses to understand multiple millions in annual revenue is very possible if you are helping enough people solve big enough problems.

With a clearer understanding of what is possible for an expert/service-based business and where you fit within the different Phases, you can now decide where you might want your business to be in the future.

ACTION STEP

Identify what Phase you are in currently?

Identify what Phase you want to be in?

Something to consider here is, if you are resistant to making more money, perhaps ask yourself who could else could benefit from you making more money? If you don't want more money for yourself that is totally fine but don't let that stop you making more money if you have the ability to do so. Not everyone has the ability to make money, so if you do earn more money, you'll have more to give to the people who need it.

Make more money in your business by using the heart centred principles of serving more people. Use that extra money to improve your own life and that of the people around you through heart centred giving. Making more money is a blessing for you and others when you view it this way so perhaps consider this anytime you hear that little voice in your head argue against your earning in your business.

Now you've identified your current Phase of Business and where you want to get to, the next step is to look at the three ingredients every business requires. Understanding these will allow you to identify where you need to focus to achieve the growth you want.

A Business is 3 Things...

You now understand what Phase of business you are in and where you might want to get to. To bridge the gap between these two points, you need to ensure you are doing the right things in the right order (you're going to hear us repeat this a lot...is it sinking in yet?). For every Phase of business there is a slightly different focus. Before we get into the specific focus of each Phase though let's go through the key 3 ingredients a business needs to survive.

1. **Marketing**
2. **Sales**
3. **Delivery**

Not recognising a business is three things, or merging these three things together, is usually where people get into difficulty. Mixing up the 3 things and associated behaviours will not create the outcome you might be aiming for.

For example, if you are trying to sell when you should be marketing, you will come across as pushy. We've all experienced those people out networking (a marketing activity) and all they can talk about is how you should buy whatever they are selling (clearly sales - although definitely not good sales). It doesn't feel good right?

At our Trainings, we even have a description for these types of people - they come across as if they have "Money Breath!" This means they are desperate to sell something and make money. This is not a great attribute! If you are networking, you should be marketing not selling. If you find yourself selling when you should be marketing, STOP IT! Selling whilst marketing will repel clients rather than attract them.

If you are marketing when you should be selling, you will never get around to asking for the money because you'll still be talking about how great your services are. This means you'll struggle to sell anything. For example, if someone has come to see you for a consultation, it means they want to change something in their life. This will usually require them to buy something, so you have to allow them the chance to pay you money. Learning how to sell effectively is a core business skill.

If you deliver your services when you should be selling, you will probably feel like you're doing a lot of work for free...because you probably are. If you are not selling, you are not getting paid. This can lead to resentment, or burn out, or just plain not earning money for all the effort that you are putting in.

When you understand each of these areas of business better and develop your skills in each of them, you will be far more powerful in growing your business. Learning to keep them separate and using them at the right time will also ensure you are as effective as possible in every situation. We're going to briefly describe each of the business areas here so you have a basic understanding before going into a lot more detail in subsequent chapters when we dive deeper into how to apply our 5 Step Success Formula and massively grow your business.

Marketing

Marketing is all about getting more clients through your door. Or, as we like to define marketing, it's how you attract more of your ideal clients. Your ideal clients are those ones you really want to work with. The ones who get good results from your services, you enjoy spending time with them, and who happily pay you whatever you ask. More of these types of clients is usually a good thing for any business!

Marketing can be online or offline and is where most business owners get confused wasting a lot of time and money. It is also one of the key areas of business to focus on because if you don't have any clients, you don't really have a business.

The confusion in marketing is usually as a result of merging marketing with sales and/or delivery. Marketing is a very discrete filtering process to help you stand out from your competition and to allow your potential clients to understand what solutions you might be able to offer them. At this point there should be no mention of price, or details of how you do what you do, as these are sales details and you don't have permission to do this yet as you are still marketing.

During marketing you need to establish whether someone is curious to find out more. If they are curious and want to understand more details, great. However, don't give them the details in this conversation. Instead, organise a longer conversation where you can really get to understand what is going on for them and they can get to understand how you work. This is when you move from marketing into sales.

Sales

Heart Centred Sales is all about service. How are you serving your clients and what problems are you solving for them to invest their money to work with you? Sales is key because in business, you make money when you sell something. Sales is also one area most people hate or will run a mile from, when in reality it needs to be central to any successful heart centred business.

Typically, people have a negative reaction to sales because far too often it's done badly or in the wrong order... remember we mentioned doing the right things in the right order? It is critical you have permission to sell. You get permission during marketing to allow you to transition to sales. But remember these are separate activities. Without having permission to sell, you will come across as pushy or negatively salesy, neither of which is a great experience for anyone.

Sales is all about finding out what your potential client wants/needs and then working out whether or not you are the best person to support them. We refer to Heart Centred Sales as the discovery of a match. If you are not a match, you don't work together. If you are, you do. The sales conversation is where you discover if you are a match or not. This could take place in an official consultation, or discovery session, or any form of more detailed conversation taking place with a potential client in person, on the phone or online where you have agreed to speak to explore working together.

Delivery

Delivery is all about fulfilling what you have sold. Whatever your expertise is, delivery is when you perform whatever it is you do for your clients. This can be client facing or could be activities required to support a person or business such as admin, compliance, or other professional services.

ACTION STEP

How are each of these areas covered in your business?

Do you recognise them as discrete things or are the lines more blurred?

Where do you think you could use the most help?

With a basic understanding of each of these areas, you will be able to use them more effectively in your client journey. Being more effective means adding more value to your clients. Adding more value will result in increased revenue. For example, perhaps you ask for referrals (marketing) from a client during their session (delivery). You follow up with the referral you are given (marketing) and perhaps offer some initial free advice (delivery). If they are curious to learn more, you schedule a consultation (sales) to explore working together. If you are a match (sales), you ask for and receive payment and schedule your first session in the diary (delivery).

Without understanding the distinction of these separate business areas, you are likely to end up in a muddle chasing your tail; being stuck trying to convince people to work with you and hating sales; giving away your time for free not growing your business; or even worse yet, having to give up your business and get a 'real job' because you can't make it work. So, let's read on to explore when and how you should focus on each of these areas to successfully grow your heart centred business...

Just Imagine...

Restructuring your business to make it a heart centred business may require some changes. Any change in life can be challenging, so before you take any action, we need to be clear on what outcome in your life and business you want to create from taking these actions.

One of Karene's first jobs after university was implementing large IT systems. This typically required large changes for lots of people. The impact of this change was usually ignored or taken for granted and this often led to failure of the systems. Without being clear on the outcome and how important the benefits were and what was in it for the people being asked to change, why would they change?

This will be the same for you. If you aren't clear on what you want and more importantly, why you are making a change or doing something uncomfortable, when you have a bad day or things don't quite work out, it will be easy to give up or go back to the safe old way. This, however, will not give you the life of your dreams. Which, let's face it, is probably why you're reading this book... you want to create something different in your life!

When Chris went to Singapore a few years ago, he had the honour of meeting and speaking with Sir Richard Branson. One of Richard's key messages, and something he personally lives by, is to design the life you want and then build the income and business to support it. Have you ever taken the time to identify what you really want in your life? If you have - great, this will be really easy for you. If you haven't, then this might be more challenging, however, it should also be fun. After all, this is your chance to wave a magic wand and dream up anything you like!

So, if you could materialise anything you like, what would life look like?
Where do you want to live?
What do you say to yourself when you wake up?
Who do you spend time with?
What do you do?
What do you earn?
How much do you have in the bank, or in investments?

All of these questions will help shape your dream life and get you connected with the benefits for you, your family, friends, or perhaps more importantly your community, industry or the world. It really depends on where you want to focus your attention and the difference you want to make in the world. There is obviously no right or wrong to any of these, just your personal preference. Whatever you choose, it just indicates what level of income and business you need to have to provide these goals.

For example, you might want to support your clients, ensure your family has financial choices and perhaps leave a small legacy. This might require you to build a Phase 1 or 2 business.

Alternatively, you might have larger philanthropic goals. One of our clients Katherine, is a Physiotherapist and Osteopath based in the Netherlands. She is actively involved in improving health in Africa by building hospitals and organising doctors and other medical professionals to visit and lend their support. For this, she needs to create her own financial success, so she has more to donate; as well as connect with others to leverage their capabilities - both financial and professional. The life she's now living and the difference she's making wouldn't be possible if she hadn't got clear on what she wanted by doing a similar exercise as you've just done.

ACTION STEP

What does your dream life look like?

What difference do you want to make in the world?

No one else is going to see what you answer here so make it resonate for you. Putting something down because you think it is what you should write isn't going to help you or anyone else for that matter.

Perhaps a question to consider is, do you believe success is possible for you?

"Whether you think you can or whether you think you can't, you are absolutely right"
– Henry Ford

Now we've established where you want to be and what having those changes will mean in terms of what your life will look like and who you will help, we can start to look at what changes you will need to make. At this point you have a choice. You can work through what will probably be some short-term discomfort in order to create the long term gain you want. Or you can delay things and keep going as you are, hoping things will change.

Many of our clients come to us having spent years, either dabbling, tweaking or just ignoring any problems they have. Often because they haven't resonated with other advice and/or they have tried many other things and are ready for something different that works. They all have something in common, they have made a commitment to pay now and stop paying later.

Applying this to your situation, you too have the choice to pay now or pay later. We all do. For everything we do. We all have to pay, it is just a choice of when. As a simple example, you choose to pay later in life when you choose to eat the cake now and do more exercise later or tomorrow.

Or perhaps applying this to your business, you choose to pay now, and do the actions you've been avoiding, such as making those extra phone calls and working later than usual. Or you can pay later by experiencing the consequences of not having enough clients.

At our events, we get people to think about where they have perhaps paid later for things. The most common examples are shoes, cars and other material goods that don't last, or you have to buy again at a higher cost. Ever heard that phrase, "Buy cheap, buy twice", pay now or pay later is a similar concept.

A great example to illustrate this is education. We have adopted a Pay Now approach for our daughter Mya's education, after we both recognised that perhaps we experienced more of a Pay Later approach in our own education.

Like all parents, we want our daughter to have a great start in life. Part of that is developing positive beliefs and thought patterns rather than the self-sabotaging patterns that most of us have that need to be unpicked later. We therefore chose to pay now for a school that has 'Growth Mindset' as one of its core values.

If you haven't heard of the concept of Growth Mindset, search for Carol Dweck. The basic premise is we can be anything until we label ourselves. As soon as we apply a label, such as smart or stupid, we limit ourselves. This is a principle we reinforce at home and Mya's school is similar. They are committed to rewarding effort rather than ability. There are no smart or dumb children, just those that do and those that don't yet know how to do some things. This is exemplified in Carol's book by the study they did when they gave a teacher the top performing class and told her they were the 'dumb' class, and conversely gave a different teacher the 'dumb class' and told her they were the top performers. By the end of the year, the classes had lived into the labels their teachers had been given.

Now aside from the damage done to these children, just imagine what we do to ourselves every day when we say things like,
"I couldn't possibly do that",
Or, "I am shy"
Or, "I don't do networking because I don't do crowds."
Or any other similarly limiting belief or label that will keep us small. Chris and I both had flavours of this and lots of other things we were subconsciously limiting ourselves with. This led to all manner of self-sabotaging behaviour in both our professional and personal lives. As adults, we made the decision in our 30's to invest significantly in ourselves to undo the negative or unhelpful patterns and thought processes that were keeping us stuck or limited. Over the past 6

years, we have invested more than £300,000 to ensure our education and mindset supports our ambitions.

Has it worked?

In more ways than we can adequately describe! Our life is different, better and richer in every way now compared to what it used to be. Looking at it from a financial perspective, we've made more than 12 times return from every pound we've invested. Would you do an investment that gave you back £12 for every £1 you invested?

Our investment in Mya's education will be no less significant. However, she is learning this now rather than waiting until her 30's like we did. Rather than having to pay whatever the inflation adjusted amount might be in the future, along with the years of struggle and learning things the hard way like we did. The thing about pay now is that it might not be less in financial terms, however, it will always be far less in wasted time and unfulfilled potential. So, are you going to pay now and transform your life, your business and your finances; or keep wasting time and pay later instead?

In choosing to read this book, you have probably already subconsciously decided to pay now. However, let's make it a conscious decision as you move through this book, so you continue to take action and transform your life and business.

ACTION STEP

Where in your life or business have you made the decision to pay later?

What has this really cost you?

Where in your life or business have you made the decision to pay now?

What have you achieved that is different?

Chapter Highlights

- ✓ Doing the right things in the right order is key to success.
- ✓ To know where you need to focus you need to understand what Phase of business you are in
- ✓ Separating the 3 key ingredients in a business (Marketing, Sales, Delivery) will allow you to upskill and consciously decide how to combine these for best effect.
- ✓ Design Your Life. Unless you know what you want, then how can you know what size of business or income to build?
- ✓ Pay Now or Pay Later. We never get out of paying in life, it's just a question of when we pay and therefore when we get the results.

Chapter 2
The 5 Biggest Challenges
How Everything You Want is on the Other Side of Fear

"Success consists of going from failure to failure without loss of enthusiasm"
– Winston Churchill

What's Your Challenge?

Having personally trained thousands of service-based business owners, we've discovered there are 5 key challenges that hamper their business growth, regardless of size or the modality. Whether you're a hands-on manual therapist, coach, architect, lighting designer, interior designer, talking therapy, accountant, IT consultant or any other expert selling your knowledge, skills and expertise, the challenges are the same.

As an additional point of clarity, you will see that we talk about service businesses and practitioners and experts and knowledge-based businesses throughout this book. These to us are all the same, so although we use these terms interchangeably, we prefer the term practitioners.

What keeps us practitioners experiencing these same challenges over and over again is fear. The fear of rejection, fear of judgement, fear of money, fear of missing out and fear of not being enough. We're going to go through these challenges and fears in depth in a moment because it's unlikely you're fully aware of how the fears are influencing your behaviour and stopping you from solving your challenges.

Now you might be really lucky like Chris used to be and be an overachiever with all of these challenges. Or it may be that you're only struggling with one of two of them. Identifying the challenge(s) you're dealing with is obviously the first step in being able to solve them. Even if you haven't yet started a business, sorry to tell you this but it's likely you already have at least one of these challenges going on. It may also be that because you're stuck with one of the challenges, you haven't felt the effect of the others yet. For example, if you have an issue with a lack of clients, you may not have connected this to any of the other challenges such as lack of time, confidence or money.

There are a lot of solutions in the marketplace that only focus on one or two challenges. This can be great to help people feel they are making progress with these challenges. However, generally, if you don't look at the entire system, you only shift a problem which is why most smaller 'fixes' don't work long term. Think of the air in those long balloons that clowns make balloon animals with. If you push on one area, the air shifts to another part of a balloon. It is the same with business, if you only focus on improving one area, it is like you are gripping the balloon in one place and you will discover new challenges in another area as the air shifts.

For example, if you only focused on getting more clients, you might end up really busy. However, you might not be earning much money! Depending on how you market your services and what incentives you offer, you might be working crazy hours at a massively discounted rate. By focusing on just one area, you are squeezing just one part of the balloon and pushing the air around.

Rather than look at any one of these challenges, our 5 Step Success Formula that gets such great results for our clients, covers all the key areas you will need to tweak and change to grow your business regardless of what Phase you are in. This ensures your business transformation is more rapid and sustainable as you aren't just shifting the problems around, you are solving them. So, what are these challenges exactly?

Lack of Clients

The biggest challenge most practitioners face is getting enough clients walking through their door. If you don't have enough clients, all other aspects of the business will struggle because there's simply not enough people or money flowing into your practice. Having spoken from the stage at business and financial conferences around the world, whenever we ask people if they would like a long line of new clients waiting for them when they get back to work, the response is always overwhelmingly, "Yes!"

However, to challenge that belief slightly, most businesses couldn't handle a long line of new clients waiting to work with them. They simply don't have the capacity or the business systems to handle a massive influx of new clients. We cover this later on in the book, because rather than just blindly wanting more clients, it's important to get clear on how many you really want and need, and more importantly, how you're going to serve them when they arrive.

The thing is though, there is an underlying fear of rejection that maintains the challenge of not having enough clients. This fear leads us to think we need huge numbers of clients because if we have lots of clients, clearly we are not being rejected. Unfortunately, this fear is often perpetuated by a lot of educators irresponsibly embedding the belief that "If you are good enough, people will come". Rest assured this is not the case! Being good at what you do is of course part of any successful business. But your potential clients have no idea if you're good or not and won't find out until they start working with you. It's all down to your marketing skills and not your professional skills that will determine whether or not you have enough clients. This is why the belief of "If you're good enough, people will come" is so damaging, because it means most practitioners and experts go out and keep getting more education and skills in their expertise, rather than just learning how to effectively market themselves.

Conventional wisdom in marketing and getting more clients is that to reach more people, you have to go online. Put your message in front of thousands of people online and some are bound to want to work with you right? However, if you can't get clients in your local area through person-to-person interaction, as in, talking to people, it's highly unlikely that your marketing message is going to be effective when put online in front of thousands.

Yet the online world is more alluring than going out and speaking to people, because real life people could say "No". Being told 'no' in person will trigger fear of rejection. Far safer to go online instead and hide behind a computer screen. However, the reality is, if you don't get clients from your online marketing, you are being rejected by thousands of people at a time - you just don't notice it because it's not as if everyone posts a "No thank you" message. Also, the competition online is far greater than in your local area. Suddenly, you are competing on a global scale with other experts who are more qualified, willing to work for less money and who are probably younger and better looking as well!

Now this is not to say that the online world doesn't work. Remember it is about doing the right things in the right order. Until you have perfected your message and know how to market effectively in person, going online will just create a more expensive challenge. For that reason, we don't think that going online is effective until you move into Phase 2 or Phase 3 and we'll go into this in a lot more detail in Chapter 3 Attraction Marketing.

Simone from Brighton is a great example of how this might show up. With a lifetime of accumulated skills and qualifications, she had no business, no direction and no paying clients. However, she had created a great website to hide behind that she spent hours tweaking and refining and she still had no paying clients. A great website is one thing, however, if there's no traffic (people) going to your website, tweaking the content on the website to make it prettier is like cutting the grass in a ghost town. This is the point Simone joined our Mentorship Programme and unfortunately admits she spent the first 6 months of it ignoring what we taught her and continuing to hide behind her website, hoping it would all work out. When she finally started implementing our system and doing the right things in the right order which, for her, was offline marketing, the results started to come in. 18 months later Simone has as many clients as she wants, all paying her over £1,000 to work with her. She works only during school hours, so she can spend time being a mum and she has been able to leave her part-time job as a teacher. As she puts it, she has "bundles of self-worth and loves living life full out!"

Lack of Income

The second challenge most practitioners face is simply not having enough money coming in. Too many well-trained experts struggle to earn enough money despite their expertise or even despite having lots of clients. If your income is low, it often reflects an issue with not charging enough for your services. This is a sales challenge. Having lots of clients won't help if you are working for free or very little.

There is an underlying fear of judgement that comes with this challenge. This fear is why too many practitioners end up working for free or heavily discounted prices. The fear of being judged by your clients, if you ask them for more money; or the judgement you might receive from your peers if they hear you are charging more; or even the judgement from your friends or family if you earn more per hour than they do. This fear of judgement is what makes us avoid sales entirely and for some practitioners, even avoiding talking about money at all with their clients...making it somewhat difficult for people to pay them!

Often, the issue with sales and the fear of judgement is simply that the experts haven't yet connected to the value they provide. As long as they are focused on serving their clients and creating an outstanding result for them, their clients actually want to pay them to say thank you. This then becomes the win:win of Heart Centred Sales: great results for the client and higher income for the practitioner business.

Sebastian was a great example of this challenge. A massage therapist, yoga teacher, visceral practitioner and much more - Sebastian was outstanding at helping his clients get out of pain and get moving again. However, when we first met him, he was flat out working in a fully booked clinic, totally exhausted and only earning around £32,000 a year. We showed him a different way of doing things and got him connected with the value of what he was doing for his clients. After 12 months, he had earned £97,000. The following year he made £134,000. He has now been able to fulfil his dream of buying a house by the sea and has moved out of London, whilst still continuing to help more people with his amazing talents. As a bonus, he also has far more time off to do more courses and have those holidays he had been putting off.

Lack of Money

Challenge number 3 is definitely not limited to just experts and practitioners. However, struggling to save money, issues with cash flow, or drowning in debt are unfortunately all too common in an expert business. For example, how many sole traders do you know who are financially secure enough to have a solid financial plan for retirement?

Lack of income is about bringing in money. Alternatively, lack of money is about not being able to keep enough of the money you make. This is a mindset challenge as well as a knowledge issue around money and how to manage it. The underlying fear of money that comes with this challenge means we typically hamper our efforts to keep money regardless of what we earn. So, you often end up with more month than money regardless of how much you might have earned.

Now we know that a lot of you might be wondering why anyone would be afraid of money. After all, wouldn't everyone like to have a bit more money? The thing is, consciously we might all want to have more money. However, subconsciously, if you are afraid of money, even if you have it, your brain will self-sabotage you until you get rid of it. Think of lottery winners... we've all heard tales of people who win millions on the lottery and then lose it within a short amount of time. It's a lot more common than you think and more often than not, lottery winners end up back where they were before they won or worse within a few years. Why would they do this? It's because they don't want to stand out from everyone else they know. This fear of being different leads to a fear of money and they self-sabotage and get rid of it all.

Of course, we're sure a lot of you are thinking, "I wouldn't be like that." And hopefully you wouldn't, however, it's not just lottery winners. Perhaps a less extreme example is to imagine you grew up in a family where money was scarce. Everyone was always struggling financially. You grow up, start working and doing well for yourself. Do you think everyone in your family is going to be happy for you if you start earning much more than they do? In order to fit in with our family, we sometimes subconsciously limit what we earn, or get rid of any extras without realising it, in order fit in.

Chris did this for years with his family without realising...

Working hard for money and not having much to go around was a large part of my family's unconscious mindset around money. The beliefs and mindsets we grow up with, we often adopt as our own and even when I had grown up and left home, I continued this pattern. I worked hard and put in the hours, yet always seemed to be struggling financially. This continued even when I started working as an Osteopath and earning what felt like a good income. Over time, things kept 'happening' to my money and whether I had a good month or a bad month, somehow, the money would disappear from my account. It wasn't that anyone else was spending it, but my own unconscious habits and actions meant my money was used up and I ended up scrabbling around financially most months. Although this was not what I consciously wanted to happen, and I knuckled down and worked even more hours to try and solve the problem; having this financial reality allowed me to continue to connect and relate with my family in the same way about times being hard and not earning much money. All unconscious and unspoken, yet my fear of money developed from a fear of being different to my family. This resulted in a pattern of behaviour that ended up with me being over £100,000 in debt before I finally changed the pattern and my mindset to create a different reality for my family and myself.

Lack of Confidence

Have you ever done course after course in advanced techniques or skills or extra qualifications so you can justify what you charge? How many practitioners and experts feel inadequate and that they don't have enough experience yet? As we discussed earlier, not feeling good enough is almost endemic in our industry and doing more professional qualifications is our typical coping mechanism.

Not feeling good enough drives us to do more courses in skills that won't help us grow our business. Feeling unworthy also stops us from connecting with the difference we could make for people with the skills we have currently. By all means, get more qualifications and more experience. However, assuming you have some experience and/or qualifications and are able to make a real difference for your clients already, do more courses only because you want to, rather than feeling you have to. Most clients will not pay you more just because you have more qualifications. You might be surprised at how few of your clients know what your qualifications mean. Unless you can translate your skills into a service that benefits them, why should they?

Confidence in yourself and your expertise is a key attribute to being successful in many different areas of business. For example, if you don't feel you're good enough, do you think you will come across as a confident expert when meeting people for the first time? Is this likely to attract many new clients? Probably not! Which, unfortunately will further reinforce the belief of not being good enough.

If you're lacking confidence that you're good enough, will your clients have confidence in you when you describe working together to get the results they want. If you don't explain it clearly and confidently, are they going to want to work with you? Probably not, and so it will affect your sales. Having confidence in your expertise and the results you produce for your clients is one of the quickest ways to create success. This doesn't mean arrogance. Instead it is an awareness of your skills and the difference you can make in your client's lives. Confidence in yourself will allow you to focus on serving your clients rather than focusing on yourself and what you need to improve in.

Felicity is a great example of lack of confidence. A massage practitioner, she has a PhD amongst a plethora of other qualifications and was still concerned that she wasn't qualified enough. After a lot of work together working on her mindset and business systems, she realised she really was an expert, yet wasn't charging expert prices or communicating with people as an authority. Now, she has created a thriving practice, earning a lot more money and is far more confident in the difference she can make for her clients. Yes, she still does courses - after all, continual learning is an addiction for many of us. However, she does extra courses because of her passion for learning, not because she feels she needs yet more letters after her name.

Lack of Time

Once you get busy with clients and have a waiting list, how much time do you have left to focus on growing your income, on having a life outside of work, or on training your team of associates so they can start replacing you?

Time is our most precious resource and we all get the same amount. However, some people just seem to be able to fit in more to their days. How come?

The simple answer to that is that they have sorted out their priorities. They are hyper focused on what will move them forward and what is perhaps a nice thing to do, but doesn't move them forward. What this gives them is the power to say no. This is the real secret to having more time, the ability to powerfully say no to people and things that aren't aligned to what is important to you. You will see this single-minded focus in many successful people like Arnold Schwarzenegger whose single-minded focus turned him into Mr Universe, then a movie star and the Governor of California. Now we are not suggesting that you need this level of focus, as taken to the extreme it can impact the relationships around you in ways you don't like. However, focus will allow you to achieve more in the time you have.

The underlying fear that keeps us stuck in not having enough time, is the fear of missing out. FOMO, it's called nowadays. None of us want to miss out on anything. When it comes to business, typically what we fear missing out on, is money. The mental script goes something like this, "If I change something, maybe my clients will leave, and I won't earn enough money to support my family. Therefore, I'll keep doing things the same old way, even if it's killing me."

Fortunately, with focus, it is possible to work out what does and doesn't move you forward in your business. You can assess what tasks and activities could be performed by someone else, therefore freeing up your time to focus on the things that only you can do, such as working with your clients. This means you can earn more money yet still enjoy more free time. Who wouldn't want to earn as much if not more money, working the same or less hours?

A great example of lack of time is one of our clients, Rebecca. She specialises in working with children and had a very busy Phase 2 business, yet was weighed down by admin, meaning there was a cap on the number of clients she could work with. Just the other week, she was telling Karene how her life has changed. By freeing up her time through outsourcing certain admin tasks, she is able to fit in more clients each week. In just a few months, she's significantly increased her income. Even though she is seeing more clients each week, she now has more free time to do the things that she loves and add extra value for her clients, rather than writing endless reports and filing.

It makes sense doesn't it? We can't imagine anyone getting into their profession thinking they want to do admin. Even Bookkeepers and Accountants who focus on admin, want to be doing this for their clients, rather than themselves. Jody is an Accountant and one of our clients. In the past 6 months, she has increased her billable time and is enjoying what she does even more because she has better boundaries with her clients protecting her time.

ACTION STEP

What is your biggest Challenge?

What is the fear that is keeping you stuck?

How does this show up for you?

These challenges are the problems nearly all experts and practitioners face at some point in their careers. These challenges are exactly what we solve with our clients. In the following chapters we cover the 5 solutions to these challenges and give you the blueprint and action steps to grow your heart centred business. That is what our 5 Step Success Formula is; solving the 5 key challenges all practitioners face. Now you know what challenges you currently face; you will know where to focus your attention.

Something to note is your challenges might change as you and your business grow. Whatever Phase of business you are in these changes are equally applicable. We find most businesses cycle through the challenges at least once in order to progress to the next Phase. They then cycle through the challenges at a different level in order to keep growing at their new level. We therefore encourage you to read all of the other chapters as well as the key ones you need right now. This way you keep increasing your knowledge and taking action, so you keep transforming as far as you want to go.

Chapter Highlights

- ✓ There are Five key challenges every expert businesses faces.
- ✓ These challenges are a result of fear. Fear of rejection, judgement, money, being enough, and missing out.
- ✓ Once you understand your fears, you will be better able to address your challenges.
- ✓ Address all the challenges rather than just the main one, otherwise it's like squeezing air around a balloon and nothing changes long term.
- ✓ The challenges show up in every Phase of Business, just in different guises. Keep cycling through them to continue growing.

Chapter 3
Attraction Marketing
How to Get More of Your Ideal Clients Walking Through Your Door.

"Good marketing makes the company look smart. Great marketing makes the customer feel smart."
– Joe Chernov

Marketing is a Filter not a Net

Marketing and more specifically, Attraction Marketing is about having more of your ideal clients walking through your door. This is how we solve the challenge of Lack of Clients. If you don't have enough clients, this is where you need to focus your efforts.

If you are lacking clients, you may, like most people, be trying to market to anyone and everyone in the hope that it delivers clients. Most people think of marketing as a net to catch customers. This is not a very collaborative, nor a useful metaphor for either the business or the customer. As a business casting a net, it appears that they are indiscriminately trying to snare anyone who comes their way. From a customer's perspective, the net analogy does not feel great because it implies that they are merely fish or unimportant individuals who have no choice other than to be parted from their money.

Heart Centred Business turns this typical net view of marketing on its head. Instead of marketing being a net that takes in anyone it can catch, we view marketing as a filter. As there are over 7 billion people living on this Earth, marketing is the filter a business uses to find the perfect customers who will most appreciate and benefit from its services. This is why it's called Attraction Marketing.

Attraction Marketing does exactly what is says on the tin and attracts ideal clients, actively filtering out everyone else who might not be appropriate. This means being very specific about who you want to work with, something that many business owners are resistant to doing. We admit, we were also very resistant when we first learnt this approach.

Most businesses think by marketing to everyone, they will generate a high demand for their products and services. Yet, in reality, it's the complete opposite. It might seem counter-intuitive but the more specific you are in your marketing, the more clients you will attract. Market to everyone, you'll end up attracting no one! This is because the more general the marketing message, the less specialised your services appear, and people can't see themselves in your solution.

In business, you can either be seen as a specialist or a generalist. Both have their place and we would always recommend your business be positioned and seen as an expert or specialised service. How come? Very simply, specialists make more money and help more people.

Think of it this way... if you had a severe headache that had lasted for several weeks, would you rather visit your local GP (Doctor) or a Brain Surgeon? It's the Brain Surgeon every time isn't it, even if you desperately hope you don't need brain surgery?! Why is this? A GP is a generalist, whereas a brain surgeon is a specialist. When we have big enough issues or challenges, we want a specialist because they will be better positioned to be able to help us.

Now who would you pay more money to see, the GP or the brain surgeon? Again, it's the brain surgeon every time isn't it?! We all naturally expect to pay more to see a specialist and if we have a big enough problem, we'll happily pay whatever is needed to get a solution. This is why any business will be more successful if it positions itself as a specialist rather than a generalist in its marketing. Of course, a specialist service is not going to be for everyone, so marketing in this way acts as a filter and actively turns off people who do not have the problems that your business solves. Simultaneously it will also attract people who need and want your specialised services.

In order to be seen as a specialist rather than a generalist, we have to communicate effectively who we are best suited to work with and what particular problem we specialise in solving. A lot of businesses try to be everything to everyone. This is why they struggle. And even if this type of marketing did work and they could appeal to every person on this planet, remember there are over 7 billion of us. Most businesses would collapse if all 7 billion people suddenly appeared asking to buy their services. Let's face it, even one hundred new clients turning up on the same day, or even within the same week, would be a challenge for most businesses because they simply do not have the capacity to handle that number of new clients.

As we've mentioned before, we are big fans of doing the right things in the right order and being as efficient as possible with our time. We're sure that you, like us, have many other things you could be doing with your time. Getting a consistent flow of new clients into your business from a minimal outlay of time and effort would make things a lot easier, right?

In this chapter on Attraction Marketing, we are going to get clear on what you need for an effective marketing filter. To do that we need to understand 4 things:

1. What is needed for marketing to be effective?
2. Your message to market using Person Problem Solution.
3. What level of results you need in your business, e.g. how many new clients do you need, or how much more money do you need to make?
4. Where and how to get your message to market by sharing it effectively with as many people as possible, matched to the Phase of business that you are in?

We're going to cover these progressively in the following sections.

Marketing is 2 Things

To create an effective marketing filter, we firstly need to know what is needed for marketing to be effective. Very simply, marketing needs two components. Achieve these two components and your marketing has been successful and you can now progress into sales. Fail to get either of these two components and your marketing just won't work and you won't have anyone to move into sales conversations. These two components are:

1. Attention
2. Curiosity

The first component of any successful marketing is getting attention. If you don't break through the everyday noise that surrounds us nowadays and get someone's attention, then how will they know your business exists?

Attention can be gained in both positive and negative ways and we've all experienced both.

For example, if you're standing on a crowded platform and someone stands on a box and starts shouting, "Listen to me!" They probably have got your attention. What they say next though determines whether it is a positive or a negative experience for you.

If they say, "Look out, there's a fire over there. Come this way!" You'd probably be pretty glad they got your attention. If they instead started swearing or shouting abuse, you'd probably just dismiss them, thinking they're a waste of your time.

A business needs to break through the noise in the marketplace to get people's attention, but it doesn't always have to shout. The more specific the message you have, the more your marketing will stand out to certain people. This means if you are an early stage business and have a low budget, it's ok as you don't need to produce an all-singing, all-dancing, slick marketing campaign. And if you are already a well-established business with an online presence, using a more specific message will mean your marketing budget will be spent more wisely. The most effective way of getting attention is to connect with your local community as this will get the attention of people who need your services. So, become part of your local community and serve them. By being ultra-specific, you get the reputation of being an expert. This reputation, then further spreads the word about what you do, so you will reach more people.

Will this specificity get everyone's attention? Of course not, and that's a good thing! Remember, most businesses do not have the capacity to work with hundreds of people, so we need to filter out a LOT of people to find the ones we can help.

Once we have people's attention, we now need to generate curiosity.

Curiosity is essential to move from Attraction Marketing into Heart Centred Sales. Without curiosity, people are not ready for a sales conversation because they have no interest in buying. Think of the situation in a shop when you are just looking and the salesperson tries to convince you to buy whatever you glance at. It's irritating and a complete turn off because you're not at that stage yet. This is the mistake many people make around sales. They get people's attention and without waiting for curiosity, they move straight into sales. This means they end up trying to force or convince people to buy their services. This is not Heart Centred Sales!

If curiosity is generated, it means the other person is ready to explore whether or not the product or service is right for them. This means marketing has been successful. It is now appropriate to move into a sales conversation.

How do we gauge curiosity?

If you get people's attention in the right way, it will generate curiosity in people who your services are relevant for. Of course, if your services are not relevant to someone, it is unlikely to elicit curiosity, so the filter works. There are many clues to look for that will indicate whether someone is curious to explore more about your services. The most obvious being, they ask for more information. If they haven't asked, they might still be curious however, you will need to assure yourself in a different way. It might be that you ask them, "Would you be curious to know more?" It is very important you use the word 'curious' here, as you can be curious without making a commitment so it is safe. The minute you use the word 'interested' there is an implied commitment and we aren't there yet. I know this might not seem like a big deal, however, it really is. The subtlety of the words that you use can be the difference between you making a connection or not so always pay attention to both your language and the other person's.

If you're speaking to someone in person, other indicators of curiosity could be more subtle, such as an altered body position like leaning in or stepping forward. Paying attention to someone's response will allow you to determine if you have achieved attention and curiosity and is critical to understanding if your marketing has been successful.

In order to effectively get people's attention and generate curiosity, we need to go right back to basics and determine what your business does, so we can start communicating effectively with the people who need your services. Once we have created the right message to get the attention and curiosity of your clients, we can then determine how many new clients you need per week to make your business successful, and what marketing modality will be best suited to generating you those clients.

ACTION STEP

Does your marketing currently have both components of marketing covered?

What do you currently do to attract attention? What else could you do?

What do you currently do to gauge curiosity? What else could you do?

If you can't yet answer these questions read on.

Person, Problem, Solution

Most businesses struggle to articulate what they do. This might seem strange but just think about it for a moment. How many businesses do you know that can succinctly articulate the exact type of person they work with and the perfect problem that they are able to provide a solution for? And do it in less than 20 seconds? Not many, right? And often when the problem or solution is described, it uses technical jargon only familiar to people trained in that area.

To give you an example, Chris trained and worked as an Osteopath for nearly 20 years. Many Osteopaths (as well as Chiropractors, Physiotherapists and all manner of other practitioners) could describe what they do by saying something along the lines of…" We manipulate the vertebrae to realign the spine and restore the correct neurological and vascular balance to the body"

Now how many of you understood that?! Whilst technically correct, a statement like this completely alienates a lot of people because it uses technical jargon and doesn't tell us what problems these Osteopaths or any other practitioner solve or who they work with. If a business description cannot be understood by a 7-year-old it doesn't work and is too complex.

If we re-wrote the exact same statement above in a different way, it could say… "We help people in pain to stand up straight, so they get out of pain and look and feel better." This is saying the same thing but in terms anyone can understand. The more people understand what you do, the better chance you have of getting more clients walking through your door.

Now, the simplified description we gave of what an Osteopath could say is an improvement on the first statement. Yet it is still positioning the business as a generalist rather than a specialist service. Yes, it's slightly specific because it mentions that they work with people in pain, yet it is still in GP territory rather than Brain Surgeon levels of perceived specialism and expertise.

Something to note, the simplified description doesn't include anything about the practitioner's expertise or how they get clients results. There is nothing about 'how' Osteopaths get their clients better. This is a good thing. Discussion about manipulation, mobilisation, soft tissue massage or any other technique is completely irrelevant to potential clients. Of course, most business owners are very proud of their skills and techniques and may have spent many years building up their expertise, so of course they want to show them off and they assume everyone is as interested in their skills as they are.

The reality is somewhat different. We're going to be direct here… "No one cares what you do, until they know what you can do for them!" Until we know what's in it for us, we just don't pay attention. This sounds harsh, yet it's the simple reality that as humans, we filter out most of the things around us to allow us to focus on what we perceive as important. If something doesn't appear immediately relevant to us, it gets lost in the background noise. No matter how proud we are of them, our titles, qualifications, techniques, skills etc all fall under the category of irrelevant to most people because they don't understand how it relates to them. Therefore, there is no benefit to saying any of it in your marketing if you want to be effective!

One further thing to consider is your clients really don't care 'how' you get them the results. They just want the results. In Chris' clinic he specialised in working with women with over 10 years of unresolved low back pain. He was known by his clients as the go-to guy in London to 'fix' long term back pain. The thing is though, none of his clients cared he was an Osteopath, they didn't care what techniques he used - they just wanted to get out of pain. He could have waved feathers around or done a rain dance and they wouldn't have batted an eyelid - as long as they got results.

So, if we don't say our titles or how we do what we do, then what do we say?!!!

Think about what your potential clients need to hear in order to decide whether or not to work with you. Primarily, they just want the headline information about what outcome you get for your clients. For example, when we are asked what we do, we simply say, "We Grow Heart Centred Businesses from Passion to Profit." This obviously will appeal to some people and not to others, so it acts as a filter.

However, sometimes it's better to give a bit more detail in order to help people get a greater understanding. Again, focus on what will cut through the noise and give your potential clients the information they need. We need to focus on saying who you work with and what problems you solve for these people. Distilling this down to basics, it comes down to:

Person – Problem – Solution

First describe your ideal client, then the problem they come to you with, and finally the outcome or solution they get from working with you.

To give you some examples of what we've personally used in some of our businesses…

Our Heart Centred Business Mentoring Company…
"We typically work with women aged 35-45 who own a 6-figure business and are frustrated they're still working too many hours for too little money. We grow their business from 6 to 7 figures, so they can start taking home more money and enjoy the lifestyle they sacrificed whilst building their business."

In Chris's clinic, he used to say…
"I typically work with women aged 45-55 who own their own business and have struggled with over 10 years of unresolved low back pain. I get them out of pain and create a long term solution whilst helping them step up in their life and business in ways they haven't been able to for years."

In our Property Investment Company, we say…
"We help families who can't afford to buy their own home by providing high-quality rented accommodation in commutable locations across the country."

Now in each of these businesses we are describing our ideal clients. Why is this so important.? Well, if marketing is a filter, let's filter for the clients you want, rather than just any old client!

The challenge most business owners face though is deciding who is their ideal client.
"I can help everybody" is the classic resistance we hear when we suggest becoming this specific and Chris was no different when he started with this. Remember, there are 7 billion+ humans out there. Yes, you might have the ability to help everyone, but you most definitely do not have the capacity to help everyone.

Similarly, you might be thinking you need multiple versions depending on who you are talking to. No, you don't. Roy, for example, a client of ours who typically works with women in the corporate world to help them break through the glass ceiling, would still say this to a room of men. Why, because although he markets to women, it doesn't mean he only works with women. He would also work with men if they were a match to work together. However, because his ideal clients are women, that is who he markets for. If he changes his marketing message depending on his audience, he is no longer a specialist and is just a generalist trying to appeal to everyone. Some men hearing Roy's marketing message want the outcome he describes for themselves and so ask for a further conversation. Other men, hearing that he works with women will be completely turned off and are therefore not a match to work with him. This is the benefit of using marketing as a filter. Roy ends up being seen as a specialist, having sales conversations with people who are already predisposed to working with him, rather than trying to convince everyone and ending up being a generalist working with no-one.

We know that you will be tempted to do things differently and to try it your way. Chris certainly did this for a while, and guess what, it works best when you just follow the system of what works rather than trying to reinvent the wheel. We also know you probably are having a "Yes, but..." moment so by all means go ahead and try if you must, however, know that you will get the best results when you follow the system.

If you're having a blank on who your ideal clients are, here are 3 questions to help you define them. Once you know your ideal client, you can create your own Person, Problem, Solution marketing statement and start attracting more of them into your business.

Question 1.

Out of all the clients you've ever worked with, who had gotten the best results?

This would be someone who thinks you can walk on water because you have made such a difference to them.

Question 2.

Out of all the clients you've ever worked with, who have you most enjoyed working with?

This person or group of people are so fun to work with, you actively look forward to them showing up and would happily work with them for free.

Question 3.

Out of all the clients you've ever worked with, who paid the best? Now we know this is deliberately clunky English, however, it refers to several different components:

- Which client has paid you the most in one transaction?
- Which client has paid you the most over time?
- Which client has told you that you're too cheap and should be charging more?

Try answering these questions with a specific person in mind, if possible; or at the very least, a small number of people. Once you have an answer to each question, go through the answers and look for similarities that appear in all 3 answers. This will then help you create a picture of your ideal client: someone who gets good results from what you do, is fun to work with, and who happily pays you a lot of money!

For example, it could be that the answers to these 3 questions are all women; or all men; or they're all in their 20's; or 40's; or all play tennis; or all come from a particular networking group; or all suffer from headaches; or all need confidence coaching etc etc.

Once you know the characteristics you can create a marketing statement that lists Person, Problem, Solution for your ideal client. Having this clarity and being able to say this in response to the question, "What do you do?" will dramatically increase the chances of having more of your ideal clients walk through your door.

Now, let me just check... are you thinking,

"Surely getting more clients can't be this simple?! I just stop telling people my title or qualification, stop talking about skills and techniques and simply describe my ideal client, the problems they have and the solution I provide, and I will get lot's more clients?"

Yes, it really is that simple. When we learnt Person Problem Solution in Chris' clinic business, Chris had already been in the Practitioner world for nearly 15 years. He was very good at what he did, yet only earning around £2,000 a month and struggling to get new clients. Two weeks after starting to use Person, Problem, Solution as a marketing message, he had earned £4,000. He had doubled his client numbers and therefore his income in just two weeks!

ACTION STEP

Answer the 3 questions to determine your ideal client.

Create your Person, Problem, Solution marketing message.

Get on the phone and share it with at least 10 people this week and ask for their opinion. This will allow you to test it out and therefore refine it through experience and feedback, as well as spreading the word to your friends and family about what you do in your business so they can start making referrals to you.

Now you might be a Phase 2 or Phase 3 business and you can see how you apply this to yourself however, how does this apply to your clinic/practice/other services you offer?

The simple answer is, it applies in much the same way. However, you do it at a practice/business level and your employees all have their own individual marketing messages that fit within the company message. Whether, as the business owner, you describe what your practice does, or what you do personally, will depend on what outcome you are after. If you want to grow the practice, describe the practice. If you want clients for a particular person or area within the business, then describe that.

If you have a group of different therapists as a business, you might be more focused on your values or approach rather than the individual professions. As an example, Marcus, our Phase 3 business client we mentioned earlier, is focused on 3 areas of wellness: Body, Mind, Nutrition to cover the various different things his business covers.

Karene used to work for a very successful multinational consultancy.

To describe what they did, she would say, "We typically worked with FTSE 100 companies struggling with profitability. We supported them in delivering increased shareholder value with an engaged workforce." There is a clear person or in this case organisation. A clear problem: their struggle with profitability. And a solution: increased shareholder value whilst caring for their people. The how is irrelevant as it either attracts attention and creates curiosity or it doesn't.

How Many Clients Do You Need?

Now we know that for many people the mere mention of numbers and calculations will create a reaction. Perhaps get your Red Flag Sheet ready for this section. We need to do some math to understand how many clients you need. When you know this, you can work out how and where to focus your efforts in sharing the message you have just created. Many businesses don't take the time to clarify their numbers so they don't know how important marketing is to their business or what they can afford to spend.

How many new clients could you handle in your business this week? No matter what size your business is, it's probably less than you think. Of course, if you have a team of people working for you, you can handle more clients. However, something to consider is do you really want more clients? Or would you rather have the same number of clients you currently have and they pay you a lot more money?

There are two routes you can go in business:

1. Large numbers of clients paying low prices
2. Small numbers of clients paying premium prices

Whilst both these models of business can be effective, the key difference between them comes down to the level of service you give your clients. To have clients happily paying premium prices, they will obviously expect more, meaning higher levels of service and a higher level of result. Personally, we're in favour of the higher service premium price model. If you have fewer clients, you have more time to serve them and create better results. If you are just starting out, this model allows you to work out what your clients want and need in order to best serve them. This in turn leads to a better reputation and a steady in-flow of new clients.

Alternately, the low-price mass number of client's model generally leads to a race to the bottom on price as businesses try to undercut each other. At some point it will no longer be viable for you to deliver your services and it rarely leads to a decent result for the clients as it's a low quality high volume model.

Is the premium, high service model for all client?! No. To be direct, some people won't be able to afford it and some people don't want a long-term fix, they are happy with just a quick fix or a patch up. You can choose whether you offer this quick fix service, or whether you refer to someone else to deliver this. The good thing is, with a premium service model, you will earn more. Once your business is established, if you are earning more, it means that you have more choices. If you want to help people who can't afford you, you have more options as to how you can do this and still help everyone. You might offer pro-bono or charity days; you might have scholarship clients. There are lots of options of how to positively support people who might not otherwise afford you once you have started earning enough so you are no longer the charity yourself.

ACTION STEP

What kind of business do you run?

What kind of business do you want to run?

A premium service or high volume?

Perhaps you would like both. This is possible however, you will need a team to do this effectively.

The business model you choose to adopt will determine how many clients you need. If we asked you now how many new clients per week you want, some of you who understand the metrics of your business might be able to answer. We suspect that for many of you, how many clients you need will be guess work. So how do you work out how many clients you need? The easiest way is to start with the end in mind. Remember we did the calculations Chapter 1 to work out how much you can earn, well to work out clients numbers we need to build on this calculation and introduce the concept of Client Lifetime Value.

Recapping on the calculation of how much you want to earn. Whilst you may now be ready to leap to 6 figures, let's be conservative. Let's say you'd like to earn £60,000 and you want 4 weeks holiday and you are prepared to work 25 hours a week charging £50 per hour.

£50 per hour x 5 hours per day x 5 days per week x 48 weeks per year = £60,000

So many clients would you need to achieve this? This is where Client LIfetime Value comes in. Client Lifetime Value refers to the average amount that each client spends in your business. When you know this, you can work out how many clients you need to achieve the revenue you want.

To work out Client Lifetime Value we need to understand a little more about the nature of the work you do with your clients. Before we get into math, if we understand the concepts, you may be better able to follow along. At a very basic level, if you are a high volume business, your Client Lifetime Value is going to be low. Whereas if you are a premium service, this is going to be high. From our experience of mentoring thousands of businesses, as well as building our own multiple businesses, we've found the tipping point from low to high is approximately £1,000.

For example, if you were a hairdresser in a barber shop, you are likely to see lots of clients infrequently for a low amount of money per client. This is typically a volume business. Whereas a hairdresser who works with extensions or colour is more likely to see fewer clients and charge more. They might also see those clients for blow dries and other maintenance in between their larger sessions meaning they will be more of a premium service with a high Client Lifetime Value.

If we worked through this for the example above with a Client Lifetime Value of £1,000.

Annual Gross Revenue divided by Client Lifetime Value
= Number of Clients per year.

£60,000 Annual Gross Revenue / £1,000 Client Lifetime Value
= 60 clients per year.

To work out how many new clients per week this is, because we are working 48 weeks in this example, it will be an average of 1.25 new clients a week, or 5 new clients per month.

Number of clients divided by the number of weeks worked
= number of clients per week.

60 clients per year / 48 weeks = 1.25 clients per week.

1.25 clients per week x 4 = 5 new clients per month.

If we go more towards a high volume business, the number of clients needed increases. With a more premium service it will decrease.

For example, if we drop the Client Lifetime Value to £500, we will need 120 clients a year or 2.5 new clients per week, 10 per month.

£60,000 gross revenue / £500 Client Lifetime Value = 120 per year.

120 clients /48 weeks = 2.5 clients per week.

2.5 clients per week x 4 = 10 new clients per month.

If we increase the Client Lifetime Value to £2,000 for example, we only need 30 new clients a year, or an average of 0.625 new clients per week, or an average of 2.5 new clients per month.

£60,000 gross revenue / £2,000 Client Lifetime Value = 30 per year.

30 clients /48 weeks = 0.625 clients per week.

0.625 new clients per week x 4 = 2.5 new clients per month.

Hopefully, you will have now realised that the numbers of new clients is less than what you had probably guessed. Obviously, to get started you will need more clients however once you are fully booked, the numbers that you then need to add are much less. If you have a team, you will need to work this out for each individual.

So how do you work out what your Client Lifetime Value is?

Here's the calculation we use in all of our businesses and what we teach to all of our clients.

- Pick a period of time such as 3, 6 or 12 months (the longer the time period the more accurate the result but the more time consuming the activity)
- Count up all the client sessions completed in this time period.
- Divide this total number of sessions by the individual number of clients seen during that period.

This tells you the average number of sessions per client. When multiplied by what you charge per session gives you your Client Lifetime Value.

Put a different way:

$$\text{Lifetime Value} = \frac{\text{Total Number of Sessions}}{\text{Number of Individual Clients}} \times \text{£ per Session}$$

Let's work through this with a client example before we get you to work this out for your business. Let's take Janet, a coach, who has in the last 6 months completed 288 sessions (as we mentioned above a longer period is more accurate). On average, for 3 days a week she is seeing 4 people. During that time, she has had 30 individual clients and she charges £70 per session.

288 sessions / 30 individual clients x £70 = £672

Janet's Lifetime Value is therefore £672

If Janet wanted to earn £100,000, she would need to have 148 clients a year or 3 new clients each week, assuming she is also having 4 weeks holiday so working 48 weeks a year. At this current Lifetime Value, we would consider Janet to be more of a commodity service and therefore more heavily reliant on marketing. If Janet however, moved toward a premium service and solved bigger problems for her clients then marketing whilst always necessary would be about quantity and more about quality.

ACTION STEP

Work out your Client Lifetime Value.

Work out 5 ways you could increase your service for your clients and therefore solve more problems for them, so they would happily pay you more money and you turn your business into more of a premium service.

The business model you adopt is up to you, each has its own challenges and successes. However, by being clear on what route you're taking allows you to determine the correct marketing strategy to make your business a success. And that marketing strategy, where and how you share your message, will vary depending on what Phase of Business you are in. Something we will now discuss in the next section.

Matching Your Marketing to the Phase of Business You're In

We have now worked out what marketing is and your message using person, problem, solution. You will also have an idea of how many new clients you need each week, month and year in your business to achieve your goals. Knowing all of this however, is only useful if you let your market know about it. This means getting out there and sharing it. If you don't share your message, no one knows what you do. If no one knows what you do, you won't get any clients.

The Phase of Business you're in determines what the best route is for you to get your message out there. As always, we focus on what works, by doing the right things in the right order. This doesn't mean doing what's popular or fashionable, so our suggestions might be a little different to the usual advice floating around. Here are the best routes to market depending on the Phase of Business you're in:

Phase 1 - Offline
Phase 2 - Online
Phase 3 - Offline

Phase 1 Business £0 - £100,000 Gross Annual Turnover

The quickest route to getting more clients in Phase 1 is offline marketing. What is offline marketing? This is good old-fashioned human to human interaction. It can be in-person, on the phone or via video calls, such as Skype. Nothing beats the growth potential in Phase 1 of connecting with real human beings.

Now we know what you might be thinking...."That sounds like a lot of work!", or, "I don't have time to go out and meet people", or maybe, "That sounds scary, I would much rather just post on social media (and hide behind my computer)."

This is exactly why the online world is so appealing to many business owners. Yet in Phase 1, the online world is mostly a distraction and a time drain, rather than a quick route to getting more clients. The reason for this is because when you are online, you are competing against millions of other people in order to be heard. There are so many people online trying to sell their products and services, what is going to make yours stand out? Remember, successful marketing requires attention. You can have the best product or service in the world, yet if you can't get attention, it might as well be the worst.

We understand a big part of the appeal of the online world is being removed from the interaction, which makes it feel less real. This may make it less scary. And we talked earlier that for most of us, a lack of clients is rooted in a fear of rejection. However, if you can't control who or how people see or interact with your message, you have no control in your business over whether it grows or not. For us, that is a lot more scary!

For example, showing up at a business networking event and talking to a room of strangers about your business might be pretty daunting for some people. The fear of being rejected, laughed at, no one listening, or of stumbling over your words. All these thoughts go through our brain and we retreat thinking it's easier and safer to just market online. Yet, if we write a post on Facebook offering our services and no one likes it, no one comments or shares; we're being rejected in just the same way. However, it hurts less and feels less personal as we don't see or hear the people rejecting us. Something to consider is if your posts and articles don't get interest online, you're being rejected by millions of people not just one or two. What feels better now?

Why is offline person-to-person marketing so effective in Phase 1? Very simply, people buy people. The more people get to know you, the more they trust you and will be willing to buy from you. The more removed you are, such as them getting to know you through an article or a social media post, the less connection they have with you. With decreased connection comes increased reliance on other reasons to make a purchasing decision. Reasons such as price! If you are compared with other professionals based on price, it becomes a race to the bottom with the cheapest person winning the race that everybody loses.

If people connect with you as an individual and know, like and trust you, price is far less impactful on their decision to buy from you. This turns your business from a commodity (something like gas and electricity where there is no loyalty to a particular company, people just go with the cheapest option) into a value business, where price is not the reason for people choosing to work with you. In fact, when you are serving your clients as a premium service, your offering is often a lot more expensive than your competitors. Yet you can still have a waiting list of people wanting to work with you because they want the results you get for your clients and you are known to be the best.

The other reason why offline marketing is more effective for a Phase 1 Business is because it's cheap! Offline marketing really comes down to asking for referrals and networking. These are both very cost effective because the only investment that they require is your time. When you don't have many clients, you have plenty of time. Anytime you don't have clients is time you can spend marketing to get clients.

Now we appreciate this is counter to most of the advice out there. However, having personally used offline marketing to grow our many 5,

6 and 7 figure businesses, and thousands of our client businesses we go with what works, rather than what's popular.

Whilst you are earning under £100,000, you don't have the budget for online marketing. Even if you are tech savvy and can do it all yourself, you probably haven't yet perfected your message to market, even if you follow all the advice above, because it takes feedback to make it perfect. This means you have to test your message out and see how actual people respond.

If you seek this feedback online, it is called split testing and it costs money. When you are talking to real people directly, such as when you do your shopping, or by phoning your friends and family, they can give you feedback. You also get to ask follow up questions and really understand their response. This feedback is more in-depth than what you can get online and is free. The online alternative is split testing where you compare what people respond most favourably to online. Whilst effective, it can be time consuming and expensive especially if you don't already have a degree of clarity on what works before you start the split testing.

For Chris, when he was in clinic, he was earning around £20,000 a year. He was a Phase 1 Business. The quickest way to grow a Phase 1 Business is through offline marketing. This meant getting on the phone and working through contact lists speaking to everyone. If you are a Phase 2 or Phase 3 Business, you still need to make the most of offline marketing. However, it might be that your associates are getting on the phone and calling past clients instead of you; or you might be using flyers, signs or the plethora of other options available. In this book, we have focused on the most effective options and included the many other options in a Bonus Chapter: 100 Ways to Get More Clients Now at the end of the book.

Was getting on the phone challenging Chris? Yes! Perhaps if he shares the unvarnished reality...

Did I hate getting on the phone and sharing my message?
Yes!

Did I like the results created two weeks later?

You bet! And the results continued from there because within 6 weeks, I had tripled my income and earned over £6,000. I know for some of you, this sounds too good to be true. I learnt a simple marketing formula, made a few phone calls and 6 weeks later had tripled my monthly income.

Let's break it down a little more because we are never going to promise you that building a business is easy. Having the right system can make it straight-forward, however, we have never found it to be easy.

I made more than a few phone calls. I phoned around 100 people in that initial two weeks. Some of these were past clients, some of them were friends and family, others were people I'd met through networking. I worked my way through the contact list on my phone and progressively called everyone I knew.

For some people making phone calls is easy. For me, speaking on the phone was something I dreaded and would avoid at all costs. I was upstairs in the temporary office we had created in our attic space. I could hear Karene and our one-year-old daughter Mya playing downstairs below me and I would find excuses to come downstairs and see them. I would take on 'busy' tasks, such as tidying my desk, or re-organising the CD collection (yes, I am that old). I would check my LinkedIn profile and scroll through Facebook, telling myself I was looking for connections to help build my business; I would spend hours writing blog posts and articles for my website that no-one visited. Anything to avoid talking to people on the phone.

And then my business mentor, who I engaged in desperation during that sales training I mentioned earlier, gave me a simple instruction to help me climb out of the financial hole I had got myself in. He told me to get a picture of Karene and Mya and put it on the desk beside my computer. Every time I avoided picking up the phone, he wanted me to look at the picture of my family and imagine going downstairs, holding them in my arms and telling them I didn't love them enough to be a little uncomfortable making phone calls to earn enough money to support them.

Bam! Like a shot to the heart, that stopped me! It forced me to realise what was at stake and how my avoidance was actually affecting the people I loved most in this world. I hated it! I hated my mentor for suggesting the exercise! I hated the thought of picking up that phone! And even more, I hated myself for putting my family in this financial position!

And it worked! My fear of what would happen if I didn't make the phone calls, was greater than my fear of picking up the phone and feeling like I was touting for business. So, I made the phone calls and I got the results. And it did become easier over time. If you repeat an activity and pay attention to how you do it, you progressively get more skilled at it and get better results. This meant the calls got easier, but I didn't lose my dislike of using the phone until a couple of years and thousands of phone calls later. The thing that finally made phoning people for my business the fun and enjoyable activity it is now, was falling in love with the concept that by speaking with people, I got to make a difference in their life. We'll explore this in much greater depth in Chapter 4, Heart Centred Sales.

When you connect with the concept that your business is serving people, make this the focus of every single business activity. The more people you get to speak with, the bigger difference you get to make in the world around you, and the bigger returns for you and your business. It is the perfect win:win! Living and acting from this position, along with constant daily practice of picking up the phone is what finally turned this essential yet hated business activity into the fun and profitable action it is today.

Do I still have a picture of Karene and Mya in my office? Of course I do and it drives me just as much today as it did then, however, for very different reasons. Back then, when I was avoiding making phone calls, the photo was there to hold me accountable to be the husband, the father, the man I wanted to be. It was to connect me with the pain of not taking action. Now Karene and Mya's photo is there to keep me appreciative of everything my actions have created and the joy of sharing this journey with the people I love. Ok, and a little bit of motivation if I am having a particularly bad day.

So, when it comes to marketing and putting yourself out there, sometimes it's going to be uncomfortable. You might have some challenges or internal demons you need to face and overcome to ensure you get in action and then stay in action. Something we can guarantee is if you carry on doing what you've been doing, you're going to get the same result. And we assume you're reading this book because you'd like a different outcome, yes? So maybe it's time to hold yourself accountable to living a different way, of taking different actions and becoming a different person. It doesn't mean there is anything wrong with who you are or who you have been. It just comes down to the simple facts of, if you want a different reality, show up differently and create it.

ACTION STEP

What excuses immediately come to mind when talking about making phone calls and talking to people?

What will motivate you to take action?

What is your equivalent of my photo of Karene & Mya for you? If you don't have something like this, then chances are when things are difficult you will quit, not because you want to but because "what is easy to do is easy not to do".

No matter what, pick up the phone and make those calls!

An example of how this might work as a Phase 2 business is probably best explained by looking at James' experience. He was fully booked with a waiting list, so it wasn't about new clients for him, however, he needed to get his new associate busy. He tasked them with calling past clients to re-engage them. Think of it like a customer service call. You first check in with the client and make sure that they are ok, then in James' example, the associate was offering a free health check-up. This could be similarly applied to accounting, content or whatever expertise you offer. This way, for those clients that were curious, they would come in and have their check up and if there was anything that needed further follow up, the associate was able to provide that service and went from having no list to 60% full in the first 2 weeks.

ACTION STEP

What could you offer to re-engage past clients?

Might be that you have expanded your services, or you have a new person, or you are just looking for feedback on a new marketing message. All of these things provide options to call clients and re-engage

How many calls do you need to make to create the success you want? Well that depends…

Here's a simple calculation we teach to all our clients so they can work this out for themselves:

On average, it takes 10 Curiosity Conversations to get 1 new client.

A Curiosity Conversation is a conversation with someone where they know what you do and therefore have the opportunity to be curious about working with you or not. Now, we believe someone only knows what you do if they have heard your Person, Problem, Solution marketing message. If they know your title or qualifications, this doesn't mean they know what you do.

So, to get 2 new clients per week, you need to have 20 Curiosity Conversations per week.
To get 10 new clients per week, you need to have 100 Curiosity Conversations per week.

Now, keep in mind, these are average figures - they will vary with your skill level, the product or service you sell, and your price point and client lifetime value. However, from working with thousands of different businesses, we've found 10:1 to be the average across the board.

Something that tends to freak a lot of people out is how many people they need to speak to. Attraction Marketing is a numbers game. The more people you speak to effectively, the better results you get. Put in the time and you'll get the results you want. This is also why people try to shortcut the process and go online to reach more people. However, if you haven't done the work in person first, then you don't have the feedback on your message to know what works so you're more likely to waste a lot of money. We know, we've done it!

Also remember as we worked through in the last section on Client Lifetime Value, that most expert and practitioner businesses cannot handle large numbers of new clients each week, so you may need less new clients than you initially think. A business that can handle more than 10 new clients every single week is either a mass number, low lifetime value business, or it is a premium service business with several team members working for you.

ACTION STEP

On a 10:1 ratio, how many Curiosity Conversations do you need to have a week?

How many calls are you going to make per day?

Go through your contact list and make your chosen number of calls each day no matter what!

Regardless of the Phase of business you are in, asking for referrals from your existing clients is the best way of getting more clients. Make sure that you and your team are doing this consistently. If your clients are getting great results, why wouldn't they want to share this experience? Always follow up on any referrals given and ensure where possible you're given the person's details so that you can control this process. Remember when asking for referrals, you are offering service. This means the request is to have a chat with the person and see what's going on for them. It might conclude in setting up a consultation with you, or you might make a recommendation for them to see someone else. Keep in mind that this is marketing and not sales. There is no guarantee that you will work with this person and it is key that you remind whomever you are asking of this so there is no pressure or weirdness.

To highlight this, perhaps if we looked at Chris' clinic business where some of his best referees were people who he had never worked with. What? You might be asking. Well when Chris had a call or consultation with someone, if he wasn't right to work with them, he referred them to someone or something else that would help them. This way they got the solution they needed without wasting any time or money on something that wasn't appropriate for them. This level of integrity, of not taking people's money and just selling them something regardless, meant that many of these people he referred elsewhere started referring a lot of people to him, even if it was clear they would not be suitable for his services and he would have to refer them elsewhere. When he asked them why they referred people to him, he got the same answer every time: They knew that he would tell people what they needed, rather than what he wanted to sell them. This meant they could trust the advice they were given.

You can also ask your friends and family for referrals and we suggest getting on the phone to as many of them as possible and testing out your new Person, Problem, Solution marketing message on them. You'll be amazed at how many people in your life will be genuinely surprised to learn what you actually do. They typically only know your title or qualifications and often have no real idea of what that means or who you work with. Once they know what you do, they will be able to make referrals to you.

In a Phase 2 or Phase 3 business, all of the members of the team need to be asking for referrals. However, they might be resistant to this as some associates just turn up and expect to be given clients. It's often worth introducing a competition or incentive scheme to get them to do these simple activities. As a referral is a cost-effective way of getting a client, the savings marketing budget could in part be diverted for such incentives. Also remember that recognition is a great motivator. It might be that you can incentivise your team in non-financial ways. Talk to them to find out what their blocks are and what would get them in action.

The other main way to get more clients is through networking. Networking is simply meeting other human beings and can be done formally, such as Business Networking Events; or informally just by striking up conversations wherever you go. the more people you can speak to person-to-person and share your Person, Problem, Solution message, the more likely you are to get more clients. And if you're thinking you can't possibly speak to strangers, or it would never work just randomly chatting to people you meet in the supermarket or on the train, here's an example from one of our clients called Roy.

Roy is a Voice and Body Language Coach and as we mentioned earlier, he specialises in helping women find their voice in the corporate world and break through the glass ceiling. He attended one of our Training sessions where we recommended people have a conversation with the person sitting next to them on the train or bus on their way home after the Training. Now, most people at the Training didn't do this because of that crazy unspoken rule of, "Don't talk to anyone on public transport!" Roy broke that rule and struck up a conversation with the lady sitting opposite him on the train. They spoke for 15 minutes before she reached her stop and exited the train. Before she left, they exchanged numbers and set a time in the diary to continue their conversation. 10 days later she had become his newest client and paid him £5,000 to work with him. Worth taking the risk of speaking to a stranger on the train?

Networking is one of the key offline marketing activities and is especially important if you don't know many people or don't have a big network. There are many different forms of networking and really it is just about talking to people wherever you go. For example, we have a client who is a massage therapist who also does some cross fit and yoga himself. He has found that talking to people who also do cross fit and yoga has been a great way for him to 'network' and get more clients. Similarly, we have another client who has found all of her clients at school pick up and drop off just by letting the other parents know what she does. Remember it is about creating curiosity as, by talking to people you have their attention.

ACTION STEP

List all of the places that you could network.

Where might your ideal clients be found - sporting clubs, school, offices etc?

When we mention networking, the most effective in Phase I are the more structured or organised business networking meetings. The biggest advantage of business networking is that everyone present has the same goal as you - they are there to expand their network so they can grow their businesses. This means it is much easier to get to know people as they actively want to talk to you. The best networking organisations also include training on how to become better at networking if you're concerned you've never done it before.

When it comes to business networking events, we generally recommend most experts and practitioners attend one or two networking events per week, depending on their business needs. More than this is generally not necessary otherwise you end up becoming a professional networker and don't have enough time to work in your own business.

How to choose the right business networking meeting for you?
Here's the Top 7 Networking Criteria we personally use and recommend to our clients for selecting networking groups:

- The meeting has to have more than 20 regular members: If the group is smaller than this, it often struggles to have the critical mass needed to be effective in passing enough referrals.
- The group has to meet regularly: Our preference is groups that meet weekly, although some very effective networking groups we've attended meet monthly. Regular and frequent contact time is key to making a group successful.
- There needs to be an enrolment fee or a meeting fee: If the group is free, it often attracts people who are not serious about their business. By making people pay to attend, it ensures everyone who shows up is there for the right reasons.
- There needs to be evidence of good networking habits as well as business referrals: A critical component of good networking is the desire to help someone. If you go to a business networking event and no one asks what you do or how they could help you, they are not good networkers, so it probably isn't worth going back. You also want to see evidence it is not just a social club - there needs to be business referrals being passed between members.

- You need to be able to fit the meeting into your diary: If you can't attend the meetings regularly or don't make space for them, there is no point in going as you won't be present frequently enough to build proper relationships with the other members.
- There needs to be some form of accountability: Whilst none of us like being told what to do, without a structure to follow and set tasks that have to be completed, a lot of networking meetings turn into social clubs. Having key networking activities that are part of the requirements of membership ensures everyone there is more likely to benefit from being part of the group.
- You need to enjoy it: If it's not fun, you won't want to go, so what's the point?!

To find a local business networking meeting in your area simply use Google and type in your postcode followed by Business networking. You'll be amazed at how many different groups are running in your area, no matter where you live. When it comes to which specific network to choose, after you've been through our criteria above, everyone has their personal favourite.

Our personal preference, based on what we and many of our clients have found the most useful, is BNI - Business Network International. It is a very structured meeting with a set agenda that happens every meeting. This means no matter where in the world you attend (and they're in a lot of different countries), you will follow the same meeting agenda. Some people like this, some people find it too rigid.

However, the main thing we love about BNI is the philosophy that governs it: 'Givers Gain'. This is the same principle Karene and I practice and teach our clients: Give first when you go networking and try to help the other person, before thinking about yourself. You are going to benefit far more in the long run and build better relationships and a better reputation. You'll get many more referrals and build a much more successful business compared with networking to see what you can get. For this reason, and because they provide excellent low cost training to improve your networking skills, we recommend every practitioner and expert attend a BNI meeting to see if it could work for them.

Now, it is very straightforward to network when there is just one of you. How does this work for Phase 2 and 3 businesses?

It is a very similar process; however, you need to be clear on what outcome you're looking for. It may be you want more clients for your business overall; you might be looking to build potential collaborations; or it might be that particular team members need additional support in building their client lists.

Overall, you can simply treat each team member within your business as their own Phase 1 business if they are generating less than £100,000 in revenue. From a marketing perspective, you and they would then work together to apply the principles listed in this book in order to grow their client list. For example, one of our clients Julia, runs a multidisciplinary clinic in Southend-on-Sea. She has a team of associates working for her with their own client lists on a revenue share basis. She's talked to all of her team as to how they want to focus on growing their businesses. For at least 2 of her team members, they wanted to use networking, so as a collaborative venture, she pays their networking fees and they go out and network to build their client list. This creates a win:win for both of them.

Alternatively, you might network to get the business busier. Using Roy, the smasher of glass ceilings for corporate women as an example again, he is a Phase 2 business owner who still personally networks for his business, as his associates work for him as part of his overall solution to clients rather than having clients of their own. This means potential clients meet Roy and have a conversation about working together. He creates a prescription for what they need. This will include some time with him and a lot more time with his associates. The sessions with Roy are more of an overview of the clients' progress and he is positioned as the leader who is guiding the client and his associates on the journey together. If Roy had his associates network for him, his business model wouldn't work as well, as his clients wouldn't know, like and trust him in the same way compared to if they personally met him through networking. Something to note is that Roy has freed up around 8 hours per week by structuring his business this way and added around £30,000 in revenue in the last 6 months alone. If you're curious about setting up a structure like this in your business, always make sure you are set up as the leader. This means that you need to be the one having the first consultation, doing the checkpoints along the journey; and wrapping up the client's journey in the final session. If your associates do these sessions and take on this role, the client will inadvertently become theirs and not yours.

For more information on how to network effectively, we have a free downloadable guide called 10X Your Networking Success. This covers the Top 10 tips we teach to our clients so they can make networking both fun and very profitable!

Please now visit

www.heartcentredbusiness.com/book-offers

to download your free guide.

ACTION STEP

Download the Networking Guide and improve your networking skills.

Type your business postcode and the words 'business networking' into Google and see how many business networking groups you could attend in your area.

Contact the organisers and book visits so you can explore which ones might work best for your business. Equally importantly, which ones do you enjoy?

Phase 2 Business £100,000 - £250,000 Gross Annual Turnover

The best route to market in Phase 2 is a combination of offline and online marketing.

What is online marketing?

This is anything that is computer to person interaction. It could be email or social media or paid or free advertising.

Having grown your business beyond £100,000 indicates you must be effective at attracting clients. This means you must have a clear message to market as well as an effective way of meeting and communicating with your potential clients. This will ideally be because your message has been tweaked and refined through Phase 1 by testing it out and getting feedback from real people. If you have made it to Phase 2 and you haven't really focused on marketing, you will need to go back to basics and ensure you are clear as to what your marketing message is using all the principles in the previous sections.

One of our clients, Adele, has a large Phase 3 business employing more than 20 staff. Yet she reached this point with many of the same 'holes in her business bucket' as most Phase 1 businesses. Without perfecting her marketing message, her business was fortunate to have attracted some large contracts in the early days. This provided momentum, a big revenue boost and a constant flow of new clients. Unfortunately, though, some of these contracts had come to an end and she had a large team she was paying every month who needed more clients. This meant going back to the basics and 'fixing the holes' to ensure she could keep building the business without the same level of reliance on a couple of large contracts. One of the key 'holes' to work on is her marketing message in order to know what to put online.

Phase 1 as you will now realise is all about getting clients through the door. Phase 2 is about scaling your services and building a team. Yes, you can still be a solo practitioner in Phase 2 however, typically, most business owners start to build a team here in order to leverage their time.

To be able to support a growing team, you need enough clients coming through the door and a wider reach than can usually be reached through in-person and word of mouth marketing. This is where the online world comes into play.

Please note, this doesn't mean that a Phase 2 business can stop offline marketing. Offline marketing is still a massively important part of the business continuing to grow as we explained above. However, the offline marketing processes should be pretty systemised by now so you can focus on developing an effective online presence.

The mistake most businesses make when going online is forgetting the basics of marketing: who are you marketing to and how many clients do you want? There is no point to marketing worldwide if your business is an in-person business where clients need to visit you physically to get your services. There's also no point in marketing to millions if you need less than 20 new people per week.

ACTION STEP

Go back and revisit the calculations around Client Lifetime Value and how many clients you need in the section above if you are still unsure about client numbers.

Online marketing could be an entire book in itself. However, so you can get started or perhaps grow what you have, we have focused on the key steps we believe will build a credible online presence and most importantly deliver paying clients. The principles around person, problem, solution in offline marketing still apply for online marketing, so if you ignored this for whatever reason go back and read it now.

When it comes to online marketing, something we get asked all around the world, no matter what stage we're presenting from, are the two questions,
"What social media platform should I use?"
"What should I put on my website?"
Unfortunately, the answer to both of these questions is one that most people don't like, "It depends..."

What social media platform you use and what will work best on your website depends on many different factors and could be different for each person and business. The advice we give our clients is a more simplistic approach based on the philosophy of what's the quickest route to cash. By this we mean how can you spend the least whilst increasing the likelihood of getting paid from your actions. To understand what this might look like for you, we will be covering off 4 steps to get you started including:

- Reviewing what you already have and making sure it is consistent
- Cost effective options that will get you noticed
- Building a following/community
- Converting people into clients

What do you already have online and is it best serving you?

How are you currently represented online? What shows up online when people Google you or your business? Whatever comes up when you put your name or your business name into Google, is what your potential clients will see, so you want to make sure there are no unpleasant surprises.

Make sure that you know what you have and ensure it is consistent and supports your brand. Just like with offline marketing, whatever you have online needs to be Person, Problem, Solution oriented. You might want to use it to support themes for your website, referencing the type of symptoms or problems that you clients might have. Your "Person" might dictate the social media platforms you focus on. "Problem" or "Solution" might drive how you set up paid advertising etc.

For example, our client Marcus who we mentioned earlier, runs a Phase 3 Wellness Business with a number of different specialties including Chiropractors, Massage Therapists, Podiatrists, Counsellors and Private Doctors. He is on his 4th iteration of his website. After much resistance, it now provides very clear sections on 'Help me with..." so that visitors can understand the potential solutions to their specific problems. He also sorts his practitioners by title, as some people are looking for this specifically, however, many more people search for symptoms such as back pain. His clinics see around 60 new clients per month and he spends approximately £5,000 per month on ads to drive traffic to his website. Remember earlier we mentioned if you have a website you also need people to visit it. Buying advertising is one such option. Just like most business owners who are aware of the realities, Marcus readily admits that half of his ad buying is wasted, he just doesn't know which half. However, he can afford this because he has built a profitable Phase 3 business and has sorted out his marketing message. He is clear who his clinic's ideal clients are, as well as having a clear understanding of his numbers, including Lifetime Value per member of staff. He is, therefore, very clear as to what is 'affordable' when it comes to online marketing to generate the volume of clients that the clinic needs.

One other learning to glean from Marcus's growing business, is that his new website also offers free advice for people who aren't yet ready to take action, or don't have a big enough problem to pay for support. By giving support and advice without expectation of anything in return, it reinforces the idea that you are an expert. It also builds a reputation and connection that could mean if these people have a problem in the future, they are more likely to come and see you because they already feel they have a relationship with you.

To help determine what you say about your business or services online (other than your person, problem, solution message), put words relating to your problem/solution into Google. At the bottom of the page under that search result, there will be a section that also provides 'searches related to..." This will let you know what other keywords you might want to include on your site or profiles.

It might be that you need to simplify what you have online until you are clear how to make the most of online marketing. It might be your website is a great place holder, however, social media might get you more attention more quickly and be more cost effective. Remember, you can have the best profiles and websites in the world and if no one knows they exist then they are of little value. Online marketing is still about getting attention and curiosity so just having a website and profile isn't enough, you need people to see them.

To that end, a vital component for your website and social media profiles are clear contact details. Make it easy for people to contact you ideally by phone and email so that they can take action if they connect with your message, or solution. If there are no action steps for people who visit you online then you are better off with nothing.

ACTION STEP

Review what you have online.
Is it Person, Problem, Solution oriented?

What easy changes could you make to ensure that it is?

Can people easily contact you online? If not, ensure they can.

Have you got all your keywords covered?

When you type your name into Google, the first results are always Facebook, LinkedIn and Twitter. Why? Because they spend the most in SEO (Search Engine Optimisation) and advertising. This means even if you have a website that is yourname.com, Facebook and the others will always rank higher than you or your website for any search of your name.

And what comes up on Facebook for you? Quite often it's the photos and information we wouldn't want our clients to see. Those tagged holiday pictures of you drunkenly enjoying yourself with friends might be a great memory, yet not demonstrate the professional image you want to portray to our clients. Of course, there are privacy settings and your profile might not be publicly available. However, we've all watched too many movies where data is readily hacked by teenage computer wizards. Whilst these might be just fictional movies, we personally don't believe anything online is truly safe or private. Have a simple rule, if you wouldn't want your mum or your clients to see it, don't put it online!

Whenever we say this at the events and conferences we attend around the world, there is always someone who argues with us saying their personal life is separate to their business, so it doesn't matter what they post on Facebook. Our reply is always the same, "Is there really any separation between business and personal any longer?"

For example, will your potential clients differentiate between business and personal photos? Will they look at those Friday night party pictures and maintain an unbiased view of your professionalism and ability to solve their problems? It's unlikely, so why take the risk? Take the time to make sure what shows up online is what you want people to see.

ACTION STEP

Google your name and review what comes up. If you're not happy with it, or it doesn't reflect the image you want your clients to see, change it.

Go through your social media accounts and sanitise them. Untag yourself from images you don't want your clients to see. Review your profile, your posts, your photos and videos and edit or remove them so your online presence reflects the image and message you want publicly available.

What cost effective options do you have that will still get you noticed?

Before you invest in a website, it is pertinent to check whether you have made use of all of the free options to build an online presence. Remember, social media platforms, Google Business pages, review sites, and other aggregators as well as Yelp etc all spend millions on ensuring they are noticed when you do a search on the internet. Ensure you are covered on all of these platforms and get more visibility for very little investment.

Most people seem to have a compulsion to check people out online as this is now a form of social proof. We recently saw some advertising saying, "if it isn't online, it isn't real" The irony of this statement doesn't make it any less true for some people, so even if you are still in Phase 1, being searchable by name or business name can be done very cost effectively with free resources.

The social media platform that is right for you depends on your ideal client and where they might spend their time. Social media continues to evolve and there will always be a new option. However, always remember, if none of your potential clients are likely to use it, then you shouldn't either.

For example: If you sell professional services such as accountancy, career coaching, management consulting etc. LinkedIn would be your best platform as it is tailored to the professional market.

If you offer a health service such as osteopathy, massage, nutritionist etc, then Facebook would probably be your best platform due to its social nature and sharing of people's experiences.

If you offer a visual or aesthetic service such as hair stylist, makeup artist, painter or personal trainer, etc then Instagram might be your best platform due to the highly visual nature of its content.

ACTION STEP

What social media platform do your clients use?

If you don't know what they use, ask.

Are you represented on that platform? If not, this might be a good place to start?

It doesn't have to take a lot of time to ensure that you have a profile and remember that people still buy from people. This means you need to personalise your online business profile as much as possible with photos of you so people can connect with the human at the end of the brand. You need to be seen as approachable yet professional.

Make sure that any images, photos or videos show you looking professional in both dress and manner yet still connected with your target market. This doesn't necessarily mean you're booted and suited, unless this is the type of client you work with. Aim to dress one or two degrees smarter than your clients. For example, if you work with builders, they might show up in dirty ripped jeans and a t-shirt. If you did the same, you wouldn't be taken seriously as a professional. However, if you dressed in a suit and tie, then you wouldn't be approachable to them. Somewhere in the middle such as smart trousers and a button-down shirt, no tie could be a good compromise.

Also ensure that you write your profile with Person Problem Solution in mind. Who are you talking to? What language might they use? How would they describe their problems? Are there particular symptoms that you need to cover off? When it comes to a solution, by all means explain how it might feel and what results people get from working with you and remember that you need to be compliant with the Advertising Standards. If you have no idea what these might be for your profession, check in with your professional/governing bodies or where you received training, to see whether they have any specific advice.

The best strategy for effective online marketing for most businesses is to focus locally so can people find you locally. It is very easy to add yourself as a location on Google Maps. If you put in a search for your business name and it doesn't show up there is an option to add a missing place. You enter your details and if someone searches for your business locally, they will find you. The best bit about this is that it is free.

As an aside, this is a great reason to ensure that your business name is also problem solution oriented and if your business name is something to do with back pain then you will automatically come up in a local search for "Back Pain".

ACTION STEP

Is your profile on your chosen social platform professional and problem solution oriented?

What might you need to change?

Make sure that you have a profile set up as well as a Google Business page or Yelp entry and be locally searchable

You are now online, how do you make the most of it?

You have now reviewed what you have online and cleaned it up. The next question is how do you make the most of being online? The best option is by giving content that your local community can benefit from and engage with. Online marketing has many similarities to offline marketing in that you want to build a community or network of people who know, like and trust you. Without this, you are merely pushing your product or service onto a group of uninterested people and you quickly get lost in the noise of the online world.

To do this, you don't even need to be adding content to your profile or building your own group, you might find some local community groups that are already set up and you can start to answer questions in those groups to demonstrate your expertise. You might find other local people's profiles with complementary services to support. So, for example, as a nutritionist, you might comment on the uses of various products that might be on offer at your local health food shop on their profile. Once you start being seen as a local expert, then it might be with some of your advice you point people in the direction of your website or profile for more information. This will then build your following.

Something to note if you are setting yourself up online, is to be consistent. Once you start online, you need to ensure that you can maintain your presence, or you will do more harm than good. For example, if you create a Facebook page and start posting daily and then get busy and this drops to perhaps once a week and then once a month and before you know it, you haven't updated anything for ages. Then, when you need more clients you ramp up your activity again, leading to a boom and bust presence. This isn't helpful. Far better that you start at a more manageable level so that you can be consistent.

To build your own following of people online, remember that whilst this is marketing, we are trying to get clients. Most people providing advice about online marketing focus on getting you likes, clicks and follows - not new clients. Whilst this is useful and builds an audience and credibility, it is not the quickest route to cash as you can't spend 'likes' to pay your bills. Yes, we know some people make a lot of money from simply building up massive followings and becoming an influencer. However, until the audience numbers reach the hundreds of thousands, it is typically quite challenging to make money from this without being a celebrity.

If we focus on getting clients when building a presence, then we need to give, and we also need to ask. The best way to build your online community is by giving. Sharing advice, useful content and engaging people in conversation is as useful online as it is offline. However, like offline, when you have established that people are curious, you need to give them a next step or an action so whether using social media or on your website make sure you include an action. We generally find that a ratio of 5:1 is the ideal balance between giving and asking.

What do we mean by asking?
Asking is when you make an offer or ask your audience to take action and do something. An ask could be an offer of a half price session, only available for the first 3 people who apply, and the offer expires in 24 hours. An offer or ask should be the opportunity for people to get something cool but if you do it too often, people lose interest and get turned off as they know you are trying to get them to buy something.

By working on the 5:1 ratio (5 gives to 1 ask), you build up a reputation of being of service so that when you make an offer, people respond positively to it and take action as they understand the value of the services that you are offering.

What sort of things could you provide when you are giving online?
It could be as simple as giving advice and sharing your knowledge. What for you might seem self-evident and basic could be mind-blowing for someone who doesn't have your expertise. Giving small and pertinent snippets of useful advice is a great way to build a following, such as a health practitioner posting about the importance of staying hydrated and drinking water; or giving posture advice to help decrease back pain. Just be careful not to go too in-depth! A full article is not needed here and will turn people off rather than engage them as it'll be too daunting.

Other ways of giving could be some short videos of you giving advice. Or a link to a useful or interesting TED Talk or YouTube video. Just make sure to avoid using professional language or jargon that the general public might not understand. Remember the key rule that if a 7-year-old can't understand it, it doesn't work! Simple suggestions, advice, knowledge or things of interest will all support your community. 5 Days of giving in this way allows you to make one ask or offer per week.

ACTION STEP

Who could you connect with or add your expertise to locally?

How can you get noticed by complementary business services in your area?

What local businesses have a large following online already how can you contribute our expertise?

Turning people into clients

We have talked about giving and asking however, how might you practically do this? With a focus on getting more clients, we suggest you create an online funnel. This will include social media and potentially a specialised website and will be focused on giving, as we discussed above. Now we know some of you are wondering what an online funnel is. Simply put, your funnel is how people get to know about your business and the journey they take in the process of deciding to work with you or not.

Your marketing can follow this principle by first appealing to a wide audience. This audience may all be the demographic of your ideal client or just everyone connected to you on social media. Not all of them will be curious or ready to take action so progressively you filter that audience to a smaller and smaller number until actual clients come out of the other end.

You can use this funnel concept in many different ways, our preference is to keep it as simple as possible. Here's an example of a funnel that we and many of our clients have used successfully:

Step 1. Market your services on a social media platform.

You don't need to have a business page for this or a group, you can purely do this as yourself. We talk about personal branding in Chapter 6, Confidence. Build your community and followers by following the principle of 5 gives to one ask.

Step 2. Give a Gift.

Create a free gift that people can download or that you can email them such as an eBook, an article, a video series or something else that is useful and interesting and allows them to gain an understanding of what it might be life to work with you. You may even have the gift as some of your time for free. Make sure that the gift is as high value as possible because there are a lot of businesses out there who just share rubbish. Another reason to give away good content is that your free gift will impact the perception people will have of your business and you want this to be favourable. People can access the gift by clicking a link you put in your social media or by sending you their details.

Step 3. The Opt-In

You need permission to share your gift with people and make sure you are using their data responsibly. The most straightforward method of doing this, is to get people to send you their contact details via a direct message and you then email them the gift. If you are offering your time then again, they can send you a message with their details and you would then call them to perhaps provide them with some free coaching or an assessment of their tax position or similar. There is no need to have technical skills or to pay for a website to be able to do this. This is the most cost-effective way that you are able to deliver high value content to potential clients in exchange for their details. This then allows you to market to them in different ways whether via phone, text, email etc.

The next step up from totally free would be that you would provide a link that takes them to a website to provide some more information about the gift and captures their details. This is typically referred to as a landing page. This is a one-page website that only has a single call to action - as in there is only one thing people can do when they get there. This action is to fill out the opt-in form. This is a form that takes their name and contact details in return for sending them their gift. It's a two-way exchange - you get their details and consent to market to them; they get something cool that they want. There are many different ways to then provide the gift and also tools out there that can help you with this. Perhaps Google "Click Funnels"

Step 4. Nurture your database

People who have given you their details, received your free gift and permission to remain in contact, are more likely to be interested in what you have to offer. Look after them and gain their trust by nurturing them through interesting content and articles via social media and also email. Making use of email is more personal than via the public social media platform. Use email responsibly and don't want to fill up people's inbox unnecessarily. There is value in email marketing if you are following the principles of 5 emails/posts that give something to every one that asks for something.

Step 5. Make an offer

Make an offer for your services, such as a free consultation to the first 5 people who respond; or, discounted tickets to your next event; or whatever you'd like to offer. Because this group of people have already proven they are interested in what you do and say, because they downloaded your free gift, your offer is more likely to have people take advantage of it and so you get new clients.

The benefit of this simple online funnel is that as long as you work to provide useful information and support to your contacts, you'll build a community of people who want to hear more from you, and who are happy to buy your services.

Phase 3 Business £250,000+ Gross Annual Turnover

Whilst online marketing is still very important in a Phase 3 Business, the focus shifts back to offline marketing as your priority.

By this stage of growth, your online marketing should be systemised and working well. Of course, there will always be areas to improve and updates and changes to keep up with in the online world. However, as the business owner, in Phase 3, we need to spend increasingly more time offline marketing and build up a network of referral partners.

This is higher level networking where the focus isn't on getting more clients through the door, like it was in Phase 1. Instead in Phase 3, the focus is on networking for collaboration. This might mean getting to know local businesses to explore setting up a corporate contract to support their employees. It could be setting up collaborative relationships with other professionals or businesses to cross-refer or jointly work together with your clients.

One of our clients David, has been going through this experience recently. When we started working with David, he had already built a Phase 3 multi-six figure Physiotherapy practice. However, he had 3 associates who were not fully booked, he was working 60-70 hours a week himself seeing his clients and running the business and approaching physical and emotional burnout. We focused primarily on the clinic marketing message, how David structured his time, and his sales process (see Heart Centred Sales in the next chapter). One year later, he has reduced his clinical hours by 25%, increased his team to 5 full-time fully booked associates and increased his business turnover by more than £50,000. Having more time, along with more emotional and mental capacity to focus on growing the business, David, just recently, managed to secure a £200,000 contract from the NHS. This contract would not have happened without him being able to dedicate the time needed to build the relevant relationships.

There are many different routes and formats collaborations and partnerships can take, the key is expanding the business reach and network in different channels. Failing to do this effectively is one of the reasons why many seemingly successful businesses plateau around the £300,000 turnover mark. From outward appearance the business appears to be doing well, but there is usually not a huge degree of profit left in the business after everyone has been paid and the business owners are typically stressed out, overworked and under-paid while they look after everyone else. Fundamentally, the tactics that got the business to this point, are not the same tactics that will get it to grow to the next level. This is why higher-level offline marketing becomes a key focus in Phase 3.

Again, the focus is best kept local for this type of marketing. Trust at this level takes longer to build and collaborative arrangements usually take a long time to put in place. Making it a regular part of the weekly business activities will ensure that the relationships and partnerships grow progressively alongside the business.

The mistake that many business owners make when trying to build these collaborative relationships is the same one that people make in Phase I when they are networking just to get more clients through their door. Networking, just like sales, is all about service. By focusing first on serving others, you then get what you want. Unfortunately, most people tend to act according to a specific soundtrack: "What's in it for me?"

Turning this round and always looking to create win:win interactions and collaborations is how you build an outstanding reputation as well as joint venture partners where both of you make a lot of money. Here's our suggestions for how to adopt this mindset when looking for higher level partnerships:

1. Have a clear outcome

As always, we suggest starting with the end in mind. Get clear on what you are looking to achieve or get out of the actions you're taking. This will save you and the people you talk to a lot of time because you know exactly what you want and also what you can offer the other party.

2. Do your research

Be clear on who or what you are looking for. Understand who's out there that fits the profile of professional or business you want to collaborate with. Take the time to research them specifically and understand as much as you can about them before you approach them. See if you can uncover what their vision is, what key challenges they have and what might be the best solution for them.

3. Speak to the Decision Maker

This is a key concept in sales - always speak to the decision maker otherwise you are just wasting your time. Approach the conversation with what's in it for them first - this will get their attention and help you to stand out from everyone else. Only when you have discussed what they want and what's good for them, do you move onto what's in it for you.

4. Date before you marry

Build the relationship slowly and get to know each other. Start off with smaller projects and steadily progress as your relationship improves and the successes start to roll in. If you jump in too soon with partnerships, it can be a nightmare to get yourself out if things go wrong and can irreparably damage your reputation. Build slowly and always check in that it truly is a win:win rather than just assuming everything is ok.

5. Communicate

Stay in frequent contact and always check to make sure that the relationship is still the win:win you both intended. It is easy for one side of a partnership to progressively feel undervalued or under-rewarded without anyone particularly being at fault and heading this off before it develops is the key to longevity. Set the tone of open and frequent communication and your partnerships have much more chance of being both profitable and durable meaning you can grow far beyond the typical plateaus of your industry.

Chapter Highlights

- ✓ Attraction Marketing is a Filter not a Net. Be a specialist rather than a generalist.
- ✓ Marketing is two things: Attention and Curiosity. Without these you cannot progress into Sales
- ✓ Develop your message to market: Person, Problem Solution. Always market for your ideal client rather than any client
- ✓ Know Your Numbers. What's your Client Lifetime Value and how many new clients do you need per week to hit your goal
- ✓ Use the right marketing strategy for your Phase of Business

!!!!!!EXTRA BONUS!!!!!

Because getting more clients is such a key challenge for most businesses, we have included an exclusive bonus at the end of this book:

100 Ways to Get More Clients

This straightforward, no nonsense Marketing Guide includes 100 methods for getting more clients through your door based on what we have tried and tested in our own businesses as well as with the thousands of clients we've worked with.

The Guide is divided up into online and offline sections. They may require trialling to find out what your clients respond to and therefore how best to use it in your business.

Resist the temptation to try everything at once otherwise you will become too distracted from the key task of running your business. Perhaps pick one action per week and test it out in your business. Let us know how you get on at hello@heartcentredbusiness.com

Chapter 4
Heart Centred Sales
How to Earn More from Your Expertise

"Pretend that every single person you meet has a sign around his or her neck that says, 'Make me feel important.' Not only will you succeed in sales, you will succeed in life."
– Mary Kay Ash

You Make Money When You Sell Something

Businesses are all about solving problems. They do this through products or services and in return for solving these problems people pay the business money.

A business, and therefore you, only make money when something is sold and yet for many expert businesses this is the key area that they've never trained in and do not focus on. In fact, for a lot of experts and practitioners, sales are something that is actively avoided. Sales has a very bad reputation and we're pretty confident that unless you're familiar with Heart Centred Sales, you might already be having some kind of resistance to this chapter and topic already, either consciously or unconsciously. Remember the Red Flag Sheets at the back of the book.

The thing is, if you don't sell anything, you don't make any money. And if you are resistant to sales and avoid talking about money or payment with your clients, the message it sends them is that you don't want them to pay you. Or to see that from your client's perspective: "If you don't want me to pay you, it must be because you don't believe you're good enough to be paid."

Often our fear around sales stems from two things:

Fear of judgement and fear of money itself. Fear of judgement is relevant to sales as we concern ourselves with what people will think about us if we sell something. This can be a concern over what our clients might think, our colleagues, family and friends, anyone really. The real concern with judgement is that we are being rejected.

Let's explore the fear of rejection first...
As humans we are a tribal species. This means we have learnt over thousands of years that survival depends on being part of a community. Now, in today's world, this might seem strange. However, if you think about humans back in the cave-man times, we were a vulnerable species. Our nails and teeth are of limited use in a fight and we were slower and weaker than many of the other animals out there. We had few advantages, yet fortunately they were profound enough for us to survive and thrive into the existence we enjoy today. Those few advantages were:

Our ability to think. This meant we could predict and adapt to circumstances as well as problem solve so we were no longer limited to animalistic reactions to stimuli.

Our ability to make and use tools. Giving us the ability to defend, by building shelters, walls etc; and the ability to attack through use of weapons.

Our ability to communicate. Communication was the glue that bound everything together and exponentially magnified the other key advantages. It allowed us to exist in co-ordinated groups and through the ability to think and the ability to make tools, the human tribe became far greater than an individual human and something no other animal could replicate nor destroy.

The strength of the tribe was in numbers. If you were part of the tribe, you enjoyed relative safety. If you were outside of the tribe, you were vulnerable and at great risk from other more powerful animals and predators. This meant the desire to belong to a tribe became part of our DNA and what makes us human. Not having a tribe was feared in the same way as death because they were essentially the same. If you were rejected by the tribe and cast out, this was a death sentence and so societal rules evolved around this concept of fit in and support the tribe or be cast out and die. Quite a powerful motivator towards acceptable behaviour and avoiding judgement and rejection!

Now whilst our humanity and society has evolved massively since this distant time, our fundamental make-up as humans has not changed a great deal. Species evolution happens over many thousands of years and in this context, cave-man days are still relatively recent, so we haven't had a chance to change much. This means we are still hard-wired to want to belong to a tribe for our own safety and will often do anything to avoid being rejected or cast out. It doesn't matter that sabre tooth tigers no longer prowl the Earth and we can quite happily survive alone in today's world. Our unconscious minds still act as though we lived thousands of years ago and we have to avoid rejection at all costs.

Now how is this relevant to sales, we hear you ask!

In sales, we are making an offer to somebody to buy something. They may choose to do so or not. If they say no to us what they are really doing is saying no to the service or outcome you provide to people and not you. However, our unconscious brain can take this as a personal rejection and remember, rejection = imminent death from a dangerous animal. Survival is any creature's primary drive so our unconscious, and sometimes, the conscious brain goes into overdrive and makes us act in all manner of unhelpful ways in order to avoid being rejected.

This is often why people avoid asking for money in a sales situation. Or they avoid getting them to make a decision. Anything to avoid being rejected! It shows up in other areas of life too…
It's why we hesitate when we should go in for the kiss
It's why we hang out with friends or groups we know are bad for us
It's why we stay in unhealthy relationships
It's why we gravitate to joining clubs or groups or creating a community
It's why we dress, speak, act, eat a certain way
It's why far too many experts don't ask for the money!

Most of the things we do are all unconscious acts designed to keep us in whatever tribe we have become associated with. Stepping out from this feels scary and is why many people never leave the communities or grow beyond the groups of friends they had in school.

Now this doesn't mean that this desire to be part of a tribe is always bad. Tribes can often be hugely beneficial and pretty much everything we take for granted in this world has been created by a tribe or team of people. The key thing is to recognise where in your life and business, this desire to belong and avoid rejection could be damaging your prospects. By becoming aware of what's driving our actions unconsciously, we can then consciously train ourselves to take different actions in order to create a different result.

If you notice the fear of rejection coming up for you in sales conversations, or indeed in life in general, this would be a great time to start using the Red Flag Sheets at the back of the book to begin reducing the impact this fear is having on your life.

So, with fear of rejection dictating many of the actions in most sales conversations, fear of money is the second area that creates challenges for experts and practitioners. Now we're going to explore this topic in much greater depth in Chapter 5, Money Mindset. Money is such an emotionally charged self-sabotage area for most of us that it needs a whole chapter to itself. However, with regards to sales, a surprising amount of people are afraid of handling money, so no matter how much they may want or need money, by being afraid of it, they actively avoid the situations where they might end up receiving it!

This might seem strange, especially if they are running their own business but it is surprisingly common. To give you an example...

Karene's parents live in Sydney, Australia and we visit once or twice every year. Living on the other side of the world while Karene's parents get older is challenging and although modern technology such as Skype, does wonders to bridge the distance, it's not the same as being there in person to support them. Every time we visit, we try and make their lives easier by doing things for them that they struggle to do themselves. This has involved chopping down trees, gardening/landscaping projects, cleaning out cupboards and garages, taking stuff to the scrap merchant/charity shop/rubbish tip and organising council clean-ups.

Of course, being parents, they always try and take care of us instead and pretend they don't need the support. And the reality is that they spent a lot of time in the past worrying about us, supporting us and lending us money as we went through various failures and financial challenges on our journey to success.

One of the things that we have wanted them to change for years is their car. They'd had the car for around 20 years, it wasn't new when they got it and unsurprisingly it was starting to fall apart and felt less and less safe to have them driving around in it. Despite our reservations, they always maintained that the car was fine, and they had no need to waste their money on a new vehicle. We suspect partly because they were always trying to hold back some reserves in case we needed something.

When we visited them last Easter (2019) and the car locks got jammed meaning we had to crawl through the boot of the car (this is the trunk for any American readers), we decided enough was enough and drove straight to a car dealership to look at options. Many discussions, negotiations and viewings later, Karene and I came to the conclusion that a new car was the best option for them in terms of safety, reliability etc so we simply said, "Let's make it happen, we're paying!"

By the way, being in a financial position to support the people you love in this sort of way is one of the greatest gifts Karene and I have ever received. Her parents had gone without for so many years and had watched and supported us while we worked to build our businesses, so being able to reward them and say thank you by buying them something they needed but would never dream of buying for themselves felt incredible.

If for no other reason than being able to do this for the people you love, please please please build a successful heart centred business so you have the financial means to make a bigger difference!

Once the decision to purchase a new car was made, we helped negotiate the price down and ended up in the dealership signing the paperwork. Not allowing us to pay for all of it, Karene's parents arrived with the $2,000 deposit in cash and this is when the fear of money revealed itself in a very amusing way. Up until this point, the car salesman had been confident, smooth talking and a little cocky. He had handled himself reasonably well in the negotiations - well up until the point that he gave us a far bigger discount than he was supposed to, with lots of extras thrown in because he (perhaps foolishly) revealed he needed to sell this car to us in order to hit his monthly quota. Even with this mistake and the fact that we ended up negotiating the same price for a brand-new car as they were asking for the second-hand versions, he came across as self-assured and confident talking about relatively large sums of money.

That confidence lasted until $2,000 cash was put on the desk in front of him. From his reaction you would have thought Karene's mum had placed a poisonous snake in his lap! He jumped out of his chair and backed away with his hands raised before him. He went pale and mumbled that he wasn't allowed to handle cash and would have to go and get his manager to deal with this. He almost ran across the dealership and into his manager's office where we could see through the window some frantic conversations taking place. He and his manager then walked to the other end of the dealership where we watched them consult with someone else before all three of them returned to where we sat. Watched by the other two, the manager then proceeded to very carefully count the notes before putting them in a bag held by the third gentleman. Our salesman then returned to his seat, mumbling many explanations about how he wasn't allowed to handle cash and frantically tapping away at his keyboard trying to distract us from what had just happened.

Karene and I could barely stop ourselves from laughing out loud at such a demonstration of the fear of money, yet it's potentially very serious in a business context. How do you think that a customer is made to feel in a situation like this? Karene's parents were making a very large purchase and the salesman reacted to their money as though it was dangerous! They were made to feel like criminals for paying the deposit in cash and it totally soured the purchasing experience for them. They admitted to us afterwards, if we hadn't been with them, laughing at how the salesman and his team were reacting, and explaining that it was a fear of money rather than something they had done wrong, they would have left without buying the car - it felt that uncomfortable.

One salesman and his managers demonstrating a bad reaction to cash could have cost that dealership tens of thousands of dollars. Make sure this doesn't happen in your business or your sales conversations by clearing any blocks or self-sabotage patterns you might have around money! Time spent doing this will be one of the most profitable actions you ever take so pay close attention to Chapter 5, Money Mindset.

What is Heart Centred Sales?

When it comes to sales, most people have only ever experienced the negative aspects of this essential business and life skill. The icky feeling people have around sales comes from the pushy, don't take no for an answer, get the money at any cost, used-car salesman type of sales that unfortunately is all too common.

Yes, this type of sales can be effective and can make you and your business money. However, at what cost? Unfortunately, sales done in this way rarely leaves the other person feeling good so rarely leads to repeat business. With no referrals or customer loyalty, there always needs to be new punters or victims to take advantage of. In a world of more than 7 billion people, of course, there's always someone new to sell to, however, this form of business doesn't leave you happy with what you see in the mirror each day and it has a limited shelf life!

Sometimes, unfortunately, it's possible to replicate a used car sales experience even when your heart is in the right place. If you want the sales to work more than the other person does, this is a negative experience for them. Clients often break our hearts because we know what a difference working with us will make for them, yet they still say no. However, as the old saying goes, you can only lead a horse to water, you can't make it drink.

It is very easy to take this type of rejection personally and adopt the attitude of "I can't believe you don't want this", or "You're crazy not to do this!" Let's be clear, this isn't heart centred. This is bordering on used-car salesman territory. Your heart might absolutely be in the right place and you want only the best for your client. However, if you aren't listening to what they are saying, or asking them what they want, you are always at risk of convincing/manipulating or being pushy.

Sure, be passionate and an advocate for change. However, not at the expense of making decisions for your client's and cutting off any other possibility but your solution.

What's the alternative?

This is where Heart Centred Sales comes in. It's a fundamentally different approach to selling that focuses on creating a win:win for all parties involved. Karene and I want more people to become aware that sales can and should be done this way, so it becomes the 'norm' rather than the exception.

Without a win:win for both parties, someone is being taken advantage of. Heart Centred Sales, being based on service, is the complete opposite. To explain this difference more clearly, here are the 5 Key Principles that govern Heart Centred Sales.

Principle 1. Heart Centred Sales is the Discovery of a Match

We don't mean the kind of match you use to light a fire. This discovery of a match is working out if you are suited to work together or not. Can you offer a solution for the challenge someone is struggling with. If you're a match, you sort out the finances and start working together. If you're not a match, you don't. It's that straightforward.

Imagine approaching your next sales conversation in this way. It feels very different doesn't it?! Or imagine you're a potential customer and the person you're speaking to says, "Let's explore what's going on (the problem you're having) so we can work out if we're a match to work together or not. If we are a match, we'll set up a plan of action and get started. If we're not a match to work together, I'll give you some recommendations of who else might be able to solve this problem with you."

How do you think your customers would respond to this type of approach? Far less 'salesy' right? Approaching sales in this way makes it an enjoyable experience for both parties with much more chance of finding a mutually agreeable outcome because either you work together and solve your client's problem, or you don't. If you don't work together, you refer them to someone else who could help them.

This takes all the pressure out of the sale process and it reinforces the concept we discussed in Attraction Marketing where you are filtering out the people you are not best suited to work with. Again, we're aware that there might be some resistance to this concept initially, because if you need the money, it can be very challenging to turn down money and refer people to someone else! Remember, although it sounds counter-intuitive, the more selective you are with who you work with, the more clients you will attract.

Something else to consider is that by focusing on whether you are a match or not, you are naturally going to end up with clients that you are much happier working with and who get better results. Because they get good results and enjoy working with you, they'll happily pay more for your services and make referrals, so you get even more clients like this. It really is a win:win and it is only possible by stepping back from the money and making sure the person you are speaking with is going to get the best possible result, whether that is from you or someone else.

One last component of determining if you are a match to work together or not is to consider whether you want to fix symptoms or the root cause of your client's problems. Just working on the immediate problem is typically what clients present with and what they want fixing. Yet, often, the problem they present with is indicative of something much bigger or deeper under the surface. The problem had to come from somewhere right, things rarely just appear out of nowhere. If we only focus on solving the immediate problem, we are doing the client a dis-service because we know that their problem is likely to reoccur.

Now we are aware that a lot of businesses think that not permanently solving a client's problem is a good thing as it means repeat business. However, from the perspective of building a massively successful heart centred businesses, let us reassure you that having a client come back repeatedly with the same problem is not a good business strategy. Instead it is a recipe for dissatisfied clients who ask for refunds and creates a bad reputation.

Far better to spend the sales conversation exploring what is causing the challenges the client is presenting with and working out how to resolve that. This way both you and the client have full clarity on what's going on and what their options are. Then if you decide you're a match to work together, the results you get with this client will be far more impactful and more satisfying for both of you.

Of course, a profitable business can be made just working on the symptoms or the presenting problem. This business model is a high turnover, mass client business with a low Client Lifetime Value. As we discussed earlier in Attraction marketing, our suggested business model is the premium service, high Lifetime Value model. This is achieved by solving bigger problems for your clients rather than just patching them up.

Chris used to experience this a lot in his clinic with people asking for just a quick 'click or crack' to get their neck or lower back in the right position and get them out of pain. They would justify this by saying their back or neck goes 'out' all the time and every other practitioner gets them sorted in just one session by 'clicking' them back into place. Chris would usually ask if they would be curious to explore getting it fixed properly so they didn't have the same problem and therefore wouldn't need to keep getting 'clicked'?

Sometimes people said yes and that they didn't realise that there was another option. Other people said no thanks, just 'click' me back into shape. Those that were curious to explore another option, Chris went on to have a sales conversation to explore what was going on and whether they were a match to work together or not. The people who insisted they only wanted to work on the symptoms, Chris told them to save their money and not work with him as he specialised in the longer-term solutions of fixing things, so they don't come back. He then referred them to experts who would work in the way the client wanted.

We come across this same thing in our Mentoring Company as well, with business owners asking us if they can just buy one or two sessions with us to help them through something. And this isn't just small businesses - sometimes it's the multi-seven-figure businesses offering to pay us large sums of money to do a one-off Training or Strategy day. We respond in the exact same way as Chris did in the clinic. If they are not interested in the bigger picture and the bigger potential outcome, then we already know we are not a match to work together and so we politely refer them to other options and wish them every success.

ACTION STEP

Let clients know at the start of every sales conversation that you will help them find a solution to their problem, even if it's not with you. Have the courage to follow that through and refer people to someone else if you think that's better for them, even if you desperately need the money from that sale yourself.

Solving bigger problems for your clients rather than settling on the surface problem has myriad of different benefits for both you and your clients. This is why the second Key Principle of Heart Centred Sales is Service!

Principle 2. Sales is Service.

Imagine you are selling something door to door. In the old days it was things like encyclopaedias. Nowadays, it's more likely to be iPhone cases or cleaning cloths. Either way, imagine walking onto a new street and looking at the long row of doors stretching out in front of you. What thoughts and feelings do you have about knocking on those doors one by one and asking people if they want to buy your products?

Probably doesn't feel great right? Perhaps feelings of nervousness that people won't like you, a fear of being rejected, a concern of wasting people's time, that no one will want what you're selling, worry that people will slam the door in your face, or set their dogs on you?

Thoughts and feelings like this probably aren't the best way to start having sales conversations. And yes, we know that it is probably not as dramatic as this in your own business; yet there is probably an undercurrent of many of these fears running through most people when they have to discuss their prices or ask a new client to pay. The fear of having dogs set on you or doors slammed in your face might be unique to door to door sales, but the other fears are all too familiar for most people!

What if you adopted an attitude that sales is service? What if you imagined you were dressed in a Santa suit and whatever you're selling is gift wrapped and stuffed in the large present sack that you are carrying over your shoulder. You are knocking on doors today to give people a present that will improve their lives. They can choose to accept the present or not, but either way, you're giving them a gift. If they don't want it, that's fine as it means you can give it to someone else who will appreciate it. And as you're Santa, everyone is going to be happy to see you because everyone loves getting presents and everyone knows that giving out presents is what you do. So, you put your sack of presents over your shoulder, adjust your red hat and walk up to the first door…

Do you think this would make a difference to how you felt about sales? Sales is giving people a gift - this is how you serve them. However, this doesn't necessarily mean that they buy your product or service. Now we know what you're thinking, "How do we serve people if they don't work with us?"

A Heart Centred Sales conversation is part of how you serve someone. This conversation should help someone get clarity around what is causing the problem they are experiencing and what options they have to resolve it. This clarity is valuable for the person regardless of whether they end up working with you or not, because with proper understanding of their problem they can make a true choice of what they want to do about it.

Many people don't have clarity about their challenge to be able to make an informed choice and this is what often keeps them putting up with something or indulging in destructive behaviour for far longer than they should.

To give you a couple of examples of this…

- In health: Smoking

If people who smoked were physically shown diseased lungs that were dissected from people who smoked and died of lung cancer; and also had the percentage likelihood of that happening to them along with an estimated time frame based on their daily smoking habits; as well as all the options of how to successfully quit; we're pretty certain that a lot less people would be smoking today.

Without enough connection with the likely consequences as well as clarity on the best ways of quitting, people just brush the concerns aside thinking, "It won't happen to me, I'll quit before it affects me" and they just carry on. In this situation, a Hypnotherapist with a proven method for stopping people smoking in just one session, would be doing people a dis-service if they didn't help the smoker understand their options and encourage them to find a solution, even if they chose not to use Hypnotherapy. There are a surprisingly large number of Hypnotherapists who have a great track record of getting these results so if you smoke, or have any other destructive health addiction, please consider having a chat with one of them!

- In Business: Experts who are struggling to make enough money to survive

Chris struggled to make money for around 15 years....
The reality was I didn't know I had any other option. It wasn't until I had a conversation with someone who helped me realise the truth about what was happening and face up to the consequences of what would happen if I carried on down this path.

What was the truth?
I simply didn't know how to run or build a successful business because I had never had any training in finances, marketing, sales or any of the other essential business skills.

What were the consequences?
At the time of that conversation, I was bringing in around £2,000 a month, yet we had £8,000 of expenses each month. I was over £100,000 in debt and hadn't told Karene how much debt I had because I just kept putting my head in the sand and hoping it would be ok. We had a young daughter and Karene didn't want to go back to her well-paid corporate job because she wanted the opportunity to be a full-time mum. If I didn't bring in more money fast, either, Karene would have been forced to go back to work; or, we would have lost everything and had to move out of London and back in with my parents. I'm not sure our relationship would have withstood either option.

Once I had clarity on these points, I was given options: carry on as I was or get a Mentor. Now the right choice may seem obvious, however, the catch was that a Mentor was going to cost a lot of money. Money I most definitely didn't have, being so deeply in debt! However, the service I received of walking me through this process, allowed me to see things in a way I never had before. I took a deep breath and faced the uncomfortable reality. I paid for the mentoring using multiple credit cards with no idea how I would ever pay it back. And it is the best (and the scariest) decision I have ever made. I am so grateful that someone served me enough to give me clarity. In the following 12 months, with the right support and a lot of hard work, I grew my income from around £20,000 a year to over £130,000. As a result of this growth, I was honoured with the Elite Legacy Business Award for Profit.

In short, focus on serving your clients and giving them clarity during your sales conversations and recognise the gift you're giving them in both that initial conversation and the subsequent work you might do together. The difference this attitude will make in their lives, and in your own is more profound than you might realise!

ACTION STEP

Write down all the ways your product or service is a gift for your clients. This list needs to be all about them rather than including what's in it for you.

Practice having sales conversations that serve people by focusing on giving them clarity around their current situation, the repercussions of inaction and their options to make a change.

Once you're clear on the benefits of your sales conversation, as well as those of your actual product or service, imagine putting on your Santa suit before every sales conversation and start giving out gifts!

Principle 3. We have 2 Ears and 1 Mouth - use them in this ratio!
Typical sales people usually talk a lot as they are trying to convince the other person to buy their services. This is bad sales!

In Heart Centred Sales, we want to speak as little as possible and have the other person speak. How else can you find out how best to serve them or determine whether we are a match to work together or not? Asking questions and then staying quiet enough to hear the answer is key. Now what do we mean by, 'staying quiet enough to hear the answer'?

Listening is a skill like any other and is something that fewer and fewer people do in today's fast paced world of technological distractions. Have you ever had a frustrating phone call with someone where you knew they were doing something else such as watching TV? It's just hard work and irritating isn't it because you know they're not engaged in the conversation and not listening to what you're saying? Or those dinner conversations where someone keeps checking their phone or responding to messages. It doesn't create a good conversation does it?

Really listening to someone requires giving them your full attention. This means no distractions and also shutting off your thoughts so you can hear what they are saying. If you are thinking while someone is talking to you, the main voice you will hear is your own and it will drown theirs out. We've all been in that situation where someone says something, and it triggers a thought in our minds. It can be something as trivial such as wondering about what to have for dinner, yet all of a sudden you realise the other person has stopped talking and is waiting for you to say something. Then it hits you that you have no idea what they just said. If we are thinking or having an inner dialogue during a conversation, we are not present for the other person.

In sales conversations, this is when the you as the salesperson is thinking about what to say next. Or formulating a response to what someone has said whilst the other person is still talking. Unfortunately, all the inner dialogue and planning does is disconnect you from the other person, so you'll miss key information and fail to build rapport. We'll explore rapport further in the next sales principle.

The need to focus and listen, is one of the reasons why we teach our clients principles rather than giving them scripts to follow in Heart Centred Sales. Scripts mean you're following a set process and will be thinking ahead for your next lines. By its very nature, following a script means you cannot be present for the other person and it becomes a one-size fits all approach rather than exploring what someone needs. We've all experienced the frustration of this type of conversation when dealing with call centres. You have a complaint or concern but no matter what you say the person on the end of the line responds in a formulaic and non-specific way that doesn't move the conversation forward or make you feel heard.

When it comes to sales, how heart centred is it to read from a script that convinces people to buy things?! We know it works for some people and some sales trainers offer scripts as a key part of their offering. Using this method does result in more sales, but the long-term cost of this business model is not something we're prepared to pay.

Far better to act from a set of principles, have a real and flexible conversation that results in what they want and need to create win:win outcomes. This is where listening and being fully present comes into play. Because you're not operating from a script, you don't need to plan what to say next, so you can stay out of your own head! Giving someone your full attention in this way will be far more effective at helping them open up and share the information you and they need to determine what's going on and what their options are for getting a solution.

Listening is something we men are typically pretty bad at doing, as Karene sometimes reminds me. We usually want to swoop in and fix a situation rather than just listen. For a lot of men, listening can feel too passive and we can feel useless and non-helpful, especially when we're speaking with someone we really want to help, such as a loved one, or a client in distress. As I'm sure the ladies reading this would agree, sometimes we just need someone to listen to us - we need to be heard. Listening itself is a big part of the solution. So, when it comes to sales, if we consider that we can't create a solution until we have properly listened to the other person, this takes the immediate pressure off having to say something clever, or to come up with an immediate answer. Just be present, listen, ask questions if necessary, to get more information, and recognise that listening rather than speaking is how you are already serving this person.

ACTION STEP

Practice listening.

Simply give someone your full attention and explore how easy, or not, this is for you to do. How quickly do you lose focus or find your mind wandering?

Does time pass more quickly or more slowly?

How do people respond when you give them 100% of your attention?

Does the quality of your conversations go up or down?

Do you find people more interesting the more you focus on them?

The more you practice being present with people, the more it becomes a habit and the better conversations you will end up having. When put in sales terms, this means more happy clients!

Principle 4. Connect and Build Rapport.

Rapport officially means the creation of a close and harmonious relationship in which the people or groups concerned understand each other's feelings or ideas and communicate well.

So what does this mean and why is it relevant in Heart Centred Sales?

Rapport is how well we connect with other people. When we are in rapport with someone, we usually have a shared viewpoint and have an enjoyable connection and interaction. This is something that is talked a lot about in typical sales training, although the reasons for suggesting rapport are perhaps slightly less clear and sometimes a little murky ethically speaking.

When you have good rapport with someone, they are more likely to trust you and therefore, are more likely to purchase from you as we buy from people we know, like and trust. This is fundamentally why most sales training focuses on how to build rapport - it is a deliberate tactic to improve success rates. However, this totally misses the real point of rapport and why we should work to build it as quickly as possible in Heart Centred Sales.

Rapport is simply human to human connection and it allows us to understand the person we are speaking to at a much deeper level because we start to understand the world from their perspective. Whilst the steps to build rapport might be the same in 'normal' sales as they are in Heart Centred Sales, the principle behind the actions is very different. In Heart Centred Sales, it is the understanding created by rapport that we are primarily after. With that understanding we can better determine if we are a match and therefore better serve the other person. This does not mean a sale has to take place. There are times that building great rapport with someone will save you from months of frustration and stress because you uncover the information you need to not proceed with working together!

Rapport and connection take place on many levels. Like anything, becoming conscious of it and practicing it, we can all naturally connect with people more easily and quickly. One of the exercises we do with our clients is to challenge them how quickly they can move from a superficial conversation into a deep emotional conversation with a total stranger. We ask them to strike up a conversation with a random person and see where it goes.

Now whilst this might seem scary, it is just having a conversation with another human being. Rapport just makes it easier and one of the key principles is that of matching and mirroring. This is where you match someone's movements and habits and present them a mirror image of themselves. Whilst this might sound strange, people will not consciously notice you doing this, unless you are particularly obvious. Instead, they will feel that you are just like them and therefore trustworthy. The real benefit comes from your deepened understanding of what the other person is thinking and feeling because you temporarily experience the world in the same way they do.

Whilst there are many different areas and levels of rapport, the key areas to focus on are:
Physical
Verbal - language and voice
And Breathing

Physical rapport refers to the body, movements/gestures and touch. How someone sits, stands and moves is an external reflection of their internal world.

For example, if someone is slumped over, head down, shoulders drooping, eyes on the floor and making small lethargic gestures when they speak; we could all confidently predict that this person is feeling somewhat depressed.

By contrast, someone sitting upright on the edge of their seat, looking you in the eye and making direct and high energy gestures with their hands to emphasise what they are saying is someone excited and engaged with life and the conversation they are having.

Matching and mirroring whatever the other person is doing will allow you to experience the world from their perspective. If they are sitting with one leg crossed over the other, you do the same. If they uncross their legs and stretch their legs out in front of them, you do the same. Of course, do it naturally, rather than moving immediately as soon as the other person does, or it will seem weird. We find it easiest to pay attention to when someone has moved position, yet we wait until it is your turn to speak and use the shift in conversation to coincide with changing position to mirror the other person, so it comes across more naturally.

The same goes for posture and how someone is sitting or standing. If they are bolt upright, do the same as long as it is comfortable for you to do so. If they are slumped over, do the same within reason unless it would be inappropriate such as when someone has a back issue and mirroring their body position would be odd. Generally speaking, as long as you do an approximation of what the other person is doing, it will help to build rapport and connection. If it is uncomfortable to cross your legs when sitting, cross your ankles instead.

With movement and gestures, we can match and mirror both the actual physical movement as well as the pace of the movement. Some people gesture a lot, some don't. Some people have very fast movements, often accompanied by fast speech. Others gesture slowly. Again, it's not about being something or someone you're not. Instead just be observant and explore what it is like to be the other person so you can better understand their world.

When it comes to touch, some people will welcome touch and it'll connect you more quickly than any other way. Whilst others have a very clearly defined personal space and dislike any touch. Whatever your preference is, respect the other person's habits and try out the same. If they use two hands when they shake your hand, do the same. If they touch you on the arm when they make a point, do the same when you speak and see how it feels and what insights you get into their experience of the world. If, however, they keep their gestures within a clearly defined space and do not touch or engage physically at all, mirror this and see how it feels for you.

Verbal rapport refers to language and the words people say as well as the way they say them such as volume, pace, tonality etc

Some people speak fast, some people slow. Some are loud, some are quiet. Just notice their style and within reason do the same. One area to be careful of here is accents. Everyone has an accent and when you are practicing building rapport, it is easy to get so caught up in the practice that you end up adopting the other person's accent as well as their other mannerisms. This is going too far and will be odd for the other person if your accent changes entirely!

When it comes to the language and words people use, we tend to use this to repeat back to someone what they said. This both builds rapport as well as allows the other person the chance to reflect on whether that is what they mean or not, so they gain a deeper insight into themselves. The key is to use the exact words someone uses, not your version - this is called backtracking and is a lot more important than many people realise.

For example, if you ask someone what outcome they would like from working together and they say, "I want to look great, feel amazing and wake up every day raring to go!"

If you backtrack their words to them and say, "So if you could look great, feel amazing and wake up every day raring to go, what would that be worth to you?" This is a closing sales question that would build rapport as they would know you had really heard them and are connected with what they want.

If you said, "So if you could look good, feel good and get up in the morning excited, what would that be worth to you?" Whilst the concept of what you said might be similar, the actual words are quite different and will not connect you in the same way meaning, they will have less engagement with your question.

Breathing is one of the more challenging areas of rapport as it is sometimes difficult to tell how someone is breathing, especially if they are a shallow breather. This is not going to build rapport in the way you want!

If you can connect with and experience how the other person is breathing, you will learn so much about how they are feeling. This insight will go a long way to understanding what they need to move forward because our breathing patterns are mostly unconscious and reflect exactly what is going internally.

Now, although we have kept this at a very simple level, we're aware that some of you reading this are now freaking out with how many things you need to pay attention to. And of course, if you focus on all these things at once in a sales conversation, you won't be present and listening to what the other person is saying or doing and so won't build rapport anyway. Remember that rapport is just like any other skill - it requires practice and you need to walk before you can run.

ACTION STEP

Pay attention during your conversations in everyday life and practice building rapport.

Start with physical rapport and pick just one aspect such as gestures, or body position and focus on that first. Once this feels natural, move onto a different area of physical rapport. The more you practice, the more it will become second nature.

Once you feel comfortable with physical rapport, move onto one aspect of verbal rapport and slowly add in new areas as you master the previous one and it becomes habit.

The last area we'd suggest tackling is breathing as it's more subtle and challenging than the others. The good thing is, by building up slowly and practicing the other areas first, by the time you get to breathing, you will already be able to quickly create a connection and rapport with someone so breathing is just the icing on the cake!

Always remember... if you are building rapport in order to increase the chances of closing a sale, STOP IT as this is a form of manipulation.

Heart Centred Sales uses rapport to deepen your understanding of the other person, so you can better serve them and determine if you are a match. Ironically, by focusing on better understanding your clients, rather than on closing the sale, you will make many more successful sales.

Principle 5. You Sell Your Way to Your Dreams.

As we've said before, you make money when you sell something. We'll go into this in more detail in Chapter 5, Money Mindset, however, in the late great Zig Ziglar's words, *"Money is not the most important thing in life. However, it is right up there just under oxygen."* We all need money to survive in today's world and virtually every dream you have will require money to make it happen. Even if the dream itself is free, more often than not, money is required to create the time and freedom needed to enjoy the dream.

If we avoid sales, then we are avoiding making money. If we avoid making money we can create a huge challenge. Chris knows this from personal experience of spending 15 years avoiding the reality that he was in sales and ending up over £100,000 in debt as a consequence. Many of our clients have done the same thing, fortunately without incurring quite the same level of debt.

Everything you have in your life, you achieved through sales. You might not just be aware of it.

"I have always said that everyone is in sales.
Maybe you don't hold the title of salesperson,
but if the business you are in requires you to deal
with people, you, my friend, are in sales."
– Zig Ziglar

You had to sell yourself to your friends when you were just strangers meeting for the first time.
You had to sell yourself to your partner, to fall in love and to build a relationship together.
You had to sell yourself through an interview to get a job.
You had to sell yourself and your expertise to get clients to work with you.
You have to sell your children on why they should go to bed when they're told.
You have to sell yourself on the reason to get up early and do exercise.
You have to sell yourself on wanting to have anything different, or better or more because it will always require effort and change to create something different to what you already have.

The thing is, most of us never acknowledge that sales is part of our lives and instead we've noticed that a lot of experts and practitioners feel in some way that they're 'selling out' if they actively engage in sales (no pun intended). Perhaps consider this from a different perspective, by not being conscious of sales, how can you ensure you are doing it ethically and in a heart centred way? Without practicing it, how can you ensure you are doing it well to the best advantage of all parties involved?

We really do sell our way to our dreams, along with everything else in life. The life you have today is based on how successfully you sold in the past. If you want a better quality of life or different opportunities in the future, you need to become better at selling.

Underpinning this is the concept that how you sell is perhaps even more important than what you sell. If your sales technique in life and business is about winning at the expense of others, how much good feeling is there really going to be in the results you create and how long will it last? Do you think other people will be happy for your success?

If you sell in life and business from the perspective of always creating a win:win, this is the secret to happiness, lasting results and having the people around you celebrate your success!

ACTION STEP

Create a Goals List - write down what you want and put a date beside when you want to achieve that goal.

Put a financial figure beside each goal for how much money you need to make that goal a reality.

Work out how many new clients you need to achieve each goal based on your Average Client Lifetime Value.

How many new clients is this per week based on the goal time frame you chose?

Based on an average 10:1 conversion ratio, how many Curiosity Conversations do you need to have each week to make this happen?

Now get on the phone, have the conversations and start serving the people you speak to so you can sell your way to your dreams!

The 5 Step Heart Centred Sales System

Sales is a skill and to become good at it requires practice. How do you practice sales? Well, role-play is always a good start. This combined with following a system that has been tried and tested in tens if not hundreds of thousands of conversations will supercharge your sales skills and experience.

We originally learnt the concept of Heart Centred Sales from other heart centred professionals and we refined it further into the step by step process we're explaining in this book through the experience of having thousands of successful (and also many many unsuccessful) sales conversations in our own businesses. We teach our clients the exact same 15 Step Heart Centred Sales System we personally use and continue to refine in our own businesses. However, this advanced approach is only accessible once the Fundamentals of a Heart Centred Sales System have been mastered.

Master the Fundamentals we cover here in this book and your business will dramatically improve as many more of your ideal clients say "YES" to working with you. Progress from the Fundamentals and work with us to master our entire 15 Step Heart Centred Sales System and your skills growth and financial results will be exponential and unstoppable.

Brad, an Alexander Technique practitioner from London, with 20 years of experience, who was busy yet not earning enough, had a massive sales challenge when we met him. In his words, he thinks that the investment he made to learn heart centred sales was the best he has made for his ongoing personal professional and business development. The realisation that he is selling a result, has a system to walk clients through and also his own unique system of how he will get clients the results has changed his life. He now works less and has doubled his income. This has freed up time to start another business and spend more time with his loved ones.

The 5 Fundamental Steps of a Heart Centred Sales conversation are:

1. Set the Context
2. Discovery
3. Your System

4. Offer
5. CARE

1. Set the Context

This is the easiest step to do, yet the one that is most missed out. If you fail to effectively set the context, the chances of having a mutually beneficial outcome, a win:win, are significantly reduced.

The context is a summary of what to expect and the possible outcomes of the conversation. Without it, the other person doesn't have clarity on what's going to happen or how long it's going to take. This unknown component will create a low level of anxiety for most people because as humans we automatically feel less safe if we don't know what to expect. And if someone doesn't feel safe, they are much less likely to be open to thinking differently about their life or the way they do things to consider what you are offering. Put another way, the chances of having a successful sales conversation are significantly reduced.

Setting the context needn't take long - in fact it shouldn't take more than 30 seconds and it needs to include these key pieces of information:

1. How long the conversation is going to take.
2. What will happen during the conversation.
3. What is expected of the other person.
4. What the possible outcomes of the conversation are.
5. Check that the other person understands or has any questions.

To give you an example, here's what we say to Practitioners and Experts when we have a sales conversation in our Mentoring Company…

"We've got just 45 minutes together and to use that time effectively we're going to explore what's going on in your business, what your goals are and where you'd like to get to financially, and what's stopped you achieving those results up till now. From there, we'll work out what are your options for making those results happen. If it's best we work together to make the results you want happen, we'll create a step by step plan together and get started straight away. However, if we are not a match to work together, we'll explore who we can introduce you to so you can still get the results you want. Does that make sense?"

This statement takes us around 20 seconds to say and clearly lays out what's going to happen during the conversation along with the possible outcomes. Notice that we say upfront that we might not work together. This way the person we're talking to knows we are focusing on what is best for them, rather than just trying to make a sale.

It also clearly explains that we will be leading them on this journey rather than it being a random or haphazard experience. Being the leader with your clients is a key part of helping them feel safe so they can take the sometimes scary step of creating change in their life. Remember the tribal nature of humans that we discussed earlier? Tribes always have a leader and as humans we always unconsciously look for who's in charge. It is the basic survival concept of who's going to keep us safe from danger. Being the leader with your clients doesn't mean being pushy or taking away their freedom of choice - that's called being a dictator. Instead, it's about giving them clarity of the boundaries as well as what's possible and letting them know you are able to guide them on the journey if they want to take it. All this can be established in the first few seconds by effectively setting the context. This is why it's such a key step to add to your sales system.

If you're still struggling with the concept of saying something like this at the start of your consultation or discovery session, consider a different example... you wouldn't get into a taxi without understanding your destination and telling the driver where you are going so why would you expect someone to enter a sales conversation without giving them this? This one step of setting the context will provide more clarity in all your conversations even the ones you have with your loved ones or children. By setting out your expectations of any conversation, you let the other participants know how long you have together and what the expected outcomes look like.

ACTION STEP

Write out your context setting intro statement.

Practice it until it comes out naturally and doesn't sound like you're reading it.

Use it at the start of every sales conversation.

2. Discovery

This step is all about Heart Centred Sales Principle 3....we have 2 ears and one mouth so use them in that order. It is also where you will get the chance to practice your rapport building skills from Principle 4 because the Discovery step is all about understanding your client.

During the Discovery step, your main focus is for you and your potential client to get clarity around what is going on, what is keeping them stuck, where they want to get to and what happens if they don't make any changes. This information is vital for you to determine if your skill set is able to provide them with a solution or whether you need to refer them elsewhere in order to serve them better. It's also vital for your potential client so they can properly understand what's going on, how severe (or not) it is and what level of urgency there is around needing to change.

Ask questions and then actively listen to the answers you're given. Listen and consciously work to build rapport to better understand the person, how they think and their perspective of the world.

Consider: how they think, what type of words and language do they use, what does their map of the world look/sound/feel like?

Ask questions to explore their desires and needs. By helping people clearly see the 'gap' between where they are now and where they want to be, you are doing them a huge favour. Until your potential client is aware of an urgent need or problem, they'll never take action to change and you can't then help them any further.

If you're finding the person you're talking to is not very forthcoming with information, try asking in other ways...

- Use effective question words to start your questions with: Who, What, When, Where, How? Avoid using the word 'why' as it can sound accusatory or confronting.
- Bring movement into the conversation. Try doing your consultations standing so people are not static in their chairs. Our physical body and movements will reflect and be influenced by how we think or feel and vice versa. If you want to help

someone get unstuck emotionally or mentally, get them unstuck physically so they are moving.

- Build deeper rapport. The better connection you have, the more people will feel safe to open up as they will feel you are more 'like them'.
- Recognise that sometimes there isn't more information to get. Occasionally, the problem really is very simple and there isn't a deeper level or causative factor. Avoid the temptation to create problems when none exist just because you want to help somebody.
- Have your typical questions planned out before the consultation so you have a process to follow and also fall back on when you need it. Having a pre-planned system that you can dip in and out of allows you to be fully present with your potential client rather than worrying about what to ask next. This is where a Consultation Form is particularly useful for you to follow and write notes on, although make sure it contains the info you need and follows your thought process rather than being a general one that might be provided by your profession/governing body etc.

The Discovery section of your sales conversation is the longest component by far and you need to make sure you allow enough time to do it properly. Cutting this section short is doing you and the person you're talking to a dis-service. If your consultations are one-hour duration, we would suggest planning on 30-35 minutes for the Discovery section. If your consultation is 30 minutes duration, then take 15-20 minutes for Discovery.

ACTION STEP

Write out the types of questions you could ask.

Create a consultation form so you capture all the information you need and can focus on the answers rather than having to remember what to ask.

3. Your System

Once you and your potential client have the information you need from Discovery, you will be clear on whether you are a match to work together or not. If you are not a match, then instead of doing Steps 3 and 4 (Your System and Offer), focus on making sure they get the support they need elsewhere and explaining this process fully, so they understand why you are not going to work with them.

If you feel you are a match to work together, this needs to be explained to your potential client and the best way to do this is by explaining your unique System of working and how this will get them from where they are to where they want to get to. Now, you might be thinking you don't have a unique system for working with your clients. And we can guarantee that you absolutely do.

You are qualified in a certain set of skills, such as Osteopathy, Architecture, Dentistry, Photography, etc etc. Every qualification has taught you a System of working. This is something you can explain to your potential client as they might not understand how it all works. However, every other person with the same qualifications as you, probably has the same basic skills. What makes you special is that you are the only one of you that there is. This means how you use your skills and training is unique because it's based on your personality, your experience, your mindset and the million other things that make you a unique individual different to every other one of the 7 billion humans inhabiting this planet. This means no one else on this planet, (even if they have the same qualifications) does what you do. Because no one else is you.

With this in mind, we now need to explain what you do and how you are going to help the person in front of you in a way that ensures they understand. Typically, most of your clients will not have the same technical knowledge and training that you do so you can't use technical language or jargon. You also can't go into too much detail because, to be blunt, people just don't care. They simply want to know that you have a duplicatable process that will get them the results they want. The best way to get this across is to explain what you do in 3, 5 or 7 steps.

Why the odd numbers? Odd numbers seem to stick in the brain better than even ones for some reason. Look at movies - trilogies have been around for years but we rarely see quadrilogies. Even if there are four movies in a series, think Lord of the Rings, it's still sold as three movies with one movie presented in two parts.

Your System needs to explain the principles of what you do and how you will get this person the results they want. It doesn't mean explaining the techniques, the timescales or any actual detail at this level. Think of it like the governing philosophy that will dictate how you apply the skill and knowledge you have to the clients benefit. Clarity, simplicity and being succinct are all vitally important for a well-understood and appealing system.

To give you a couple of examples...

The simplest and perhaps the best System we have ever heard was by an excellent Personal Trainer in San Francisco. His promise was that he made people look good naked. When asked how he did this, his 3-step system for success was as follows:
Step 1. Move More
Step 2. Eat Less
Step 3. Repeat

Pretty simple right? Yet is it clear what people can expect by working with him?

Chris used this system to explain what he did in his clinic...

Step 1. Identify the root cause of your problem
Step 2. Resolve it permanently so it doesn't come back
Step 3. Enhance how the body works in its new alignment so you start to feel great.

One way to make your system even easier to understand and to help your potential client connect with you on a different level is to draw it out for them on a piece of paper while you explain it. Here's an example of how we use this in our mentoring company. Feel free to use this in your business as it can be applied successfully to almost any service-based business and will make a massive difference to your sales. When Chris added the following system to how he explained his System (Identify, Resolve and Enhance) in clinic, his closing rate and Client Lifetime Value significantly increased!

N.B. This usually takes us around 30-60 seconds to explain. Explaining it in this book without being able to talk to you is a lot more challenging and time consuming.

First, we draw a cliff sticking out of the water…

Then we draw 3 people...as Chris is not good at drawing, these are always only stick figures, so rest assured you'll be able to do this!
One person is in the water looking unhappy.
One person is out of the water and standing on the edge of the cliff looking neither happy nor unhappy.
One person is far from the edge of the cliff, looking happy with arms in the air.

Once we've drawn the picture, we then simply say, our System is:
Knowledge
Mindset
And Community
We write these words on the top of the picture.

We explain that when experts and practitioners approach us, they are usually in some sort of pain or danger. This is Person one who is unhappy swimming around in the water.

Perhaps they are struggling financially; or they're overwhelmed in admin and paperwork; or maybe they want to exit their business and don't know how to structure it; or maybe it's all just become a job and they have lost their mojo.

Relate the person in the water to whatever your potential client told you in the Discovery section.

If you want you could add a shark fin or two in the water to make your point, but it's not really necessary.

We then say that what we do first is get people out of danger. This means getting them out of the water and on top of the cliff - Person 2. This is done by giving people effective strategies and knowledge, so they create quick results. Knowledge is what most other business coaches start and finish with. The trouble with knowledge alone is that people don't continue progressing, they self-sabotage and they don't have a supportive community to keep them on-track.

So, they fall back in the water - back to Person one.
Most business owners and business coaches operate in this cycle. Getting out of danger and then falling back into it over and over again.

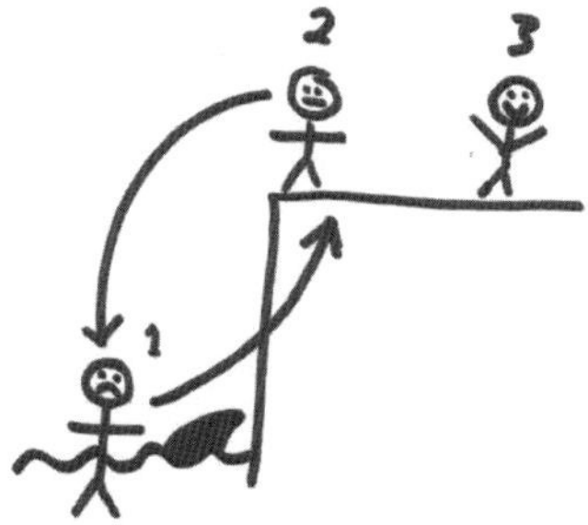

How we differ with our clients is that knowledge and strategy is just Step 1. Once someone is out of danger and on top of the cliff (Person 2), now the real work begins to move them away from the edge, so they don't fall back in the water: Person 3.

Look how happy Person 3 is. This is because along with the right knowledge, and the right strategies, they also have the right mindset and the right community to keep them progressing in the direction they want to go.

The best strategy in the world is useless if you don't use it. Think of going out for a walk, getting lost and then refusing to look at your map. Yet this is what so many business owners do until they work on their mindset and remove the self-sabotage patterns.

What holds everything together is our community of heart centred business owners. Surrounding yourself with other like-minded people who will celebrate your success is vital to long term growth and is something that most practitioners don't have. This is why they often struggle to do it alone.

At this point we often draw lots of extra people all smiling with arms in the air surrounding Person 3

This System gives a descriptive overview of how we work with our clients and would be personalised to whatever we found out in the Discovery Session. After explaining our System (which is so much quicker in person than when written in a book), we'd check if it makes sense and then ask if they want to explore their options for how this could work for them.

Asking this question is very important as we need permission to move to the next step otherwise, we are just pitching at someone. If they don't like the sound of what you do from your system, this allows them the chance to say so and save you both time.

If they are excited by your system, having them give you permission to go to the next step reinforces their connection with being able to make their own choice whilst still being guided by you as the leader on their journey. Which means you move on to making your Offer...

4. Offer

Your Offer is where you explain to your potential client the options they have to get the solution they want. The concept here is to explain how you work. How do you get your clients the results? What are the different options that they could choose? This isn't the detail of your actual technique or what you do in each individual session. It's the overall structure of your service, what they get and the expected end result for the client in each different option that is appropriate.

Something to remember when explaining the different options, your potential client has to get the end result they want. You are being paid because you are an expert in this area, and it is essential to give your expert opinion as to the option that is most suitable. You then need to explain why you think this. Sharing your expert opinion, then allows your potential client to make an informed choice because they have all the information. If you don't give your opinion, this is not serving your client because with less training and knowledge than you in this area, they cannot compare the options effectively or make an informed decision.

Now we know that some of you reading this are probably already thinking, "but I don't have different options. Clients just turn up and I work with them session by session until they stop coming in." Whilst this might be how you work currently; it is not the best business model for you or your client.

If clients are left to self-direct how often or when they have sessions without input or guidance from an expert, is it likely that they will get the best results? Of course not, yet it is how far too many businesses are run primarily because of fear of being too pushy or having clients go elsewhere. As we discussed earlier though, being the leader for your clients and telling them your expert opinion is what they are paying you for. Your clients don't have to like your recommendations, but they do need to know them.

To give you an example, something we tell all of our clients when we start working with them is this:
"Our job is to tell you what you need to know, when you need to know it, whether you like it or not. Are you ok with that?"

What this refers to is that sometimes, quite often, we find ourselves having to tell our clients things they don't want to hear. Common examples are, "You're not working enough to get the results you want", or, "Stop moaning about what's going on and start taking some actions to change it."

Whilst we don't like being hard on people, they are paying us to help them grow their business. It is far better that we tell them the truth and risk hurting their feelings, than let them continue down the path they're on where they'll end up in much more painful situations. It is this tough love that all of us experts need to sometimes employ and it's a key reason why we have a track record of helping our clients increase their income by £50,000 - £100,000 within 12 months of working with us. Tough love doesn't mean you don't care for your clients - it's the complete opposite. You give tough love because you care so much for your client's success that you're willing to risk them not-liking you as long as they succeed. Think of it like parenting. As a parent, we often say things our children don't like. However, we do it for their own good even if they cannot see that at the time.

When you are in the Offer step of the Heart Centred Sales process, your role is to explain all the options and the expected outcome of each, along with the investment required (how much it costs) and the option that you think will create the best result in this particular situation. This way, your potential client has all the information they need to make an informed decision whilst still having the freedom of making their own choice.

What type of options you have in your business depends on what you do? It could be as simple as saying something like this...

"There are two options available to you:

Option A is where you do the work yourself. I give you advice and a programme to follow and you implement it yourself at home. This option is free and will make a difference but is dependent on your following the advice and doing xyz every day or you won't get the results.

Option B is where you come in X number of times over the next X weeks and we work on this together. After X number of sessions, we review your progress and tweak your sessions as necessary to ensure you get the end result. The investment in Option B is £....and having successfully worked with X number of people in a similar situation to yourself, I would expect you to get xyz results within X time frame.

My suggestion is we move forward with Option B because you are much more likely to get the results within the timeframe you want. However, which option sounds best for you?"

As you notice from this example, the message and the options are very simple - either we work together, or we don't. If we don't work together, or if you want a free option, I'll still give you support and help to solve this problem, but it'll be up to you to implement it. If we work together, this is how it'll work, this is why you recommend this option, and this is the investment required. It then ends simply with offering a choice.

Please note there is almost no detail about HOW we will achieve the results. As mentioned previously, the actual techniques or skills are not relevant or necessary for most clients. Think of an airline...when you're buying that ticket to Australia, they don't break down every step of the flight. They don't mention the small seats, bad food or the 24 hours you'll spend cramped and trying to sleep. Instead they talk about being whisked away to your dream destination, where you'll wake up and find yourself magically transported to a land of sunshine, beaches and BBQs.

This is talking in terms of benefits not features. Features are the details, the HOW to get to the result. Benefits are the result itself, which is what people want when they come to work with you. If your Offer is made up of features, no one will buy it, regardless of how much they like you because it doesn't connect them with the end result.

Presenting the options as shown above establishes that you will be able to lead and support the client effectively on their journey. It also makes it very easy for them to understand their options and provides the clarity they need from which to make their decision. Of course, what you offer might be more complex than this example, or there might be many different levels and ways that someone could work with you.

For example, in his clinic, Chris had three different programmes that varied depending on how severe someone's back pain was and therefore how much support they would need to resolve it.

In our Mentoring Company, we have 5 different levels of support in our Mentorship Programme. The different levels are appropriate for different people based on factors such as business size, speed they want to grow, complexity of challenges they're currently dealing with and their financial resources.

We would suggest not having more than 5 different options otherwise it is too confusing for your potential clients. Think of menu dilemmas in a restaurant when there are too many choices. Most experts and practitioners are better off only having two or ideally three options until they reach the 7 figure and multi-person team level and even then, 5 options should be the limit.

The bit of the Offer that most people shy away from is discussing the price. This is because they are typically afraid of rejection and also, often, afraid of money itself, as we discussed before. Consider this, if you think your services are expensive, or are uncomfortable discussing money and payment, your clients will feel exactly the same way. This is one of the reasons we always advise our clients to use the word 'investment' rather than cost. We'll cover this topic in much more depth in Chapter 5, Money Mindset, however, recognise that your clients are investing in themselves not in you when they chose to work with you. They are paying money to you in order to get an outcome for themselves. This is a very different mindset for both you and them and it will result in much better results when you work together as they will be a more committed client. Also, the word price or cost is scary for a lot of people, so using the word investment helps prevent that fear clouding their decision making.

Here's a list of what has to be included when making your Offer:

1. State how many options they have
2. Description of each option that includes:
    a. Duration of option
    b. What is required of them - such as home exercises etc.
    c. Logistics, which includes:
        i. Number of sessions
        ii. Duration of sessions
        iii. Location of sessions
    d. Expected outcome
    e. Investment required
3. Your recommendation
4. Freedom to choose

ACTION STEP

Get clear on what your Offer is

Write down the options you offer a potential client

Review your options:
Do they feel expensive?
Are they easy to understand?
Is it clear what the differences are?

Practicing presenting them to a colleague and get feedback

5. CARE

The CARE step of the sales process is based entirely on customer service - a much overlooked and under-appreciated business concept in today's fast paced transactional world. A low price, mass-market business can probably skip this part of a sales process entirely as their clients don't expect much and their business model is not about keeping them happy. In a heart centred business, where you work with fewer clients and serve them to a far higher level, customer service is king.

In the CARE step, your potential client has just heard your Offer and is now making their decision about what path to take. Your job here is to help them with making that decision. This does not mean making the decision for them or pressuring them in any way whatsoever. Your expert opinion of what they should do has already been stated so there is no need to repeat this recommendation unless asked to.

There are several key areas of customer service to focus on in the CARE phase which will help them come to a decision and move forward:

- Answering questions

Sometimes something isn't clear, or the person just wants some extra information. Whatever questions come up, answer them simply so as not to add further confusion. Some people are very analytical in nature and will have lots of questions. Other people won't. Generally speaking, if your System and Offer were presented simply and in a straight-forward way, there typically aren't too many questions. If you always find you get lots of questions, perhaps consider reviewing the previous two steps so some of those questions will be answered without having to be asked.

- Objections and concerns

These might initially sound like reasons to not work with you but if you take the time to understand your potential client properly, concerns and objections are them saying they want to work with you and just need a bit of help to see how that is possible.

Not quite sure what we mean? Let us explain in a bit more detail...

We've found there are three main types of objections or concerns that come up.
Price - "It's too expensive", or, "I don't have the money"
Time - "I don't have enough time for this", or, "I want a quicker result"
Results - "Can you guarantee me the result?", or, "What if it doesn't work?"

All of these concerns have one thing in common: the person saying the concern wants to work with you which is why they have raised the concern. If they didn't want what you're offering, or wanted to go for a different option, it would be much easier for them to just say that. By raising the concern, they are telling you that they would like to make the choice to work with you but cannot see how it is an option until you help solve their concern.

At this point, your job is to help them resolve their concern so they have clarity on what options are available to them and can freely make their choice. Please note, resolving their concern does not mean resisting it or telling them they are wrong. If you try to convince someone that their concern or objection is not valid, you will come across as defensive and non-supportive. Instead the best approach in this situation is to ask them a question, or say something that helps them view their concern from a different perspective?

For example, if people say to us, "It's too expensive", our response is often to ask, "Too expensive compared to what?" This question has several benefits.

First, we want to know more information about their concern. What is too expensive for them? What or who are they comparing us to? What type of outcome would they want to make it not feel expensive?

Second, the question gets them to clarify whether they are comparing like for like. Something, they may not have otherwise considered. For example, comparing us to a business coach who doesn't have personal business experience or a track record of getting results to the level we do, would be like trying to compare oranges and apples. Both are fruit and both are usually round but beyond that they are incomparable.

Often, just by asking a question like this, it diffuses any tension and allows a proper discussion to ensue. Sometimes this discussion helps clarify the reasons to move forward together. Other times the discussion highlights that the concern is a deeper problem and that working together isn't appropriate, such as if someone genuinely does not have the money and it would be financially unsafe for them to start working with you. These discussions are hugely beneficial for both you and the other person as it gives clarity to them around their decision and it can prevent you from taking on clients who are not in the right place to work with you.

The good thing is, that because we know that pretty much all the objections or concerns that come up will fit into the three categories of Money, Time and Outcome, you can pre-plan some responses to each of these topics. This means that if an objection is raised, there is less risk of feeling defensive or reacting badly. Instead, your calm response will allow an opportunity for everyone to gain a deeper understanding.

ACTION STEP

Review the 3 common areas of concern for potential clients: Money, Time and Results.

Write down 3 objections your clients could make in each of these areas.

Work out 3 different responses to each of these objections.

Practice these responses until they feel natural.

- Asking for the Money and Taking Payment

Make sure to ask for the money. You might not expect this to be in the CARE section but without money being exchanged, you can't start working with them and therefore there is a limit to how much you can serve them. Now when it comes to asking for the money, there are a lot of practitioners and experts who avoid this topic completely and hope that clients will simply pay them later. This hope and pray strategy is not ideal. It isn't going to leave a client feeling that they will be effectively led on their journey.

A great example of this was one of our clients who is an excellent osteopath and Pilates instructor. She's so good we started seeing her ourselves for treatment. However, she never said what her charges were. We kept coming in for weeks and she wouldn't answer our requests about what we owed. Whilst on one level this might sound great, we were having sessions without having to pay for them. It was increasingly uncomfortable not knowing what level of debt we were accruing. Basically, her avoidance of the topic and promising to get back to us just felt weird and if we weren't more aware of what was going on, we probably wouldn't have continued seeing her.

Fortunately, we also started mentoring her privately on her business at this point and one of the first questions we asked was if she acted like this with other clients around money. When she said yes and admitted she usually just waited until clients just transferred whatever they wanted into her account, it gave us a good understanding why such an excellent practitioner was struggling financially.

One year later, after some pretty direct mentoring sessions, things are different.

- We're still having sessions from her every week and have a monthly standing order set up.
- She now discusses upfront with her clients what they need to invest before starting to work together.
- Her annual income has more than doubled from what it was before we started working with her.
- She is taking on team members and negotiating her second premises.

All of this came from no longer avoiding the money conversation.

Most practitioners and experts want to get paid higher amounts from their clients. Yet a surprising amount of them do not have a credit card machine in order to take payments. It's another great example of getting in your own way and not making money when you could.

Typically, people tend to say they don't have a card machine because of the fees associated with taking payments and it's cheaper to send the client an invoice instead. What they fail to realise is that once someone pays, they are more committed. The more time that passes before they pay, the greater the chance of them changing their mind and not paying at all.

Getting a payment from a client during the sales conversation might cost a small percentage in fees, yet it means the client is much more likely to stick to their decision and you can start work together. Sending an invoice often means many phone calls and reminder messages to get them to pay and they might not even come through in the end meaning all that time has been wasted. We'd pay a small percent fee to get a guaranteed client every time!

ACTION STEP

Review your payment process.

How and when do you ask for the money?

Do you have a Card Reader? If not, get one!

Next Steps
Once the investment has been taken care of, get the clients sessions booked in the diary straight away. This is hugely important as it solidifies their decision by making it real and increases their commitment to seeing it through. Make sure your new client understands the next steps and what to expect in their sessions with you and answer the door handle questions as they leave.

Door handle questions are the questions people ask as they open the door to leave. Ironically, these are often the most important questions the client will ask in the whole session as they are the questions they have been too scared or embarrassed to ask until now. The act of putting their hand on the door handle tells them they are out of time and they are forced to blurt out their question. Expect this situation and welcome it as leaving those questions unasked could sabotage the new client sticking to their decision

The final part of the CARE step is to celebrate. You have a new client. This is worth celebrating. Acknowledge the fact that by taking on this client, you have the honour and the opportunity to change their life for the better. This is amazing and we should connect with this reality every single day. You are changing lives!

It's also ok to celebrate that you are earning more money. A new client means increased income. It's ok to celebrate this because you're earning it in a way that is making a difference for someone. More money means you can do better for yourself and the people around you. You can contribute more and make a bigger difference in the world!

Celebrate. And then continue the process of serving your new client by following up…

Follow Up

Follow Up is essential to support your clients and grow your business. The fortune is in the follow up. This is true in sales and in any client interaction. If you are not following up, your clients are not being effectively served and you are leaving money on the table. Think of follow up as the ultimate in customer service and how you stand out from your competition. It can be done in person, via the phone, in a thank you card, a text or an email. How you do it will vary depending on the situation; however, the sentiment is the same: we value you as a customer/client and we're here to look after you.

For nervous clients, the Follow Up, or lack of it, is often where they finalise their decision to move forward with you or not. Ever had a great consultation with someone where it seemed like you were on the same page and excited to start working together? They just needed to sort out some finances or speak to their partner before committing and then you never hear from them or they don't show up for their first session? This can be heart-breaking because you know the difference working together will make in their life and you really want to help them. It's also expensive because you now have to find a new client to work with to replace the lost income. And finally, it can be massively time consuming in trying to get hold of the client when it's already too late.

To make follow-up effective, here are the guidelines we recommend to our clients and use in our own businesses.

Always tell people you will be following up with them and why you do this. It is important that they understand that the follow up conversations are part how you get your clients the results you do. Touching base in between sessions to gauge progress and answer any questions or concerns will keep your clients progressing and head off any potential disruptions to their journey. Let them know upfront that this is how you work best for them and get their agreement that this is ok.

- Always look to serve. Every bit of communication with a client should aim to serve them in some way. This isn't just a random call or email and it definitely cannot just be a request for a referral etc. Have a human conversation and explore how they're doing and if you can help or support them in any way. This is customer service. If you do need to ask something from your client, focus on service first, and only when you have served them can you make your request or ask them for something.
- Do what you say you're going to do. If you tell a client you'll call them tomorrow to check how they're doing, make sure you do it. If you don't, it undermines your position as an expert who can deliver what they're paying you to do. Of course, life sometimes happens, and things go awry. However, always communicate to your clients wherever possible and make it right with them if you let them down.
- Follow Up is always best-done human to human. A phone call is always better received and creates a better connection than a written message because it's a live in-person interaction. If you call and get the voicemail, always leave a message otherwise you're just a weird missed call who couldn't be bothered to say what you wanted.
- Handwritten messages such as cards or letters work better than electronic ones because it's rare nowadays and is more personal than what might appear as a mass marketing email. Taking the time to write and send something through 'snail mail' shows a much greater level of appreciation and works wonders to build your client loyalty.
- Text or SMS messages and email have approximately the same level of impact, but SMS messages are more likely to be opened because they show up on someone's phone and they are often perceived as more casual and therefore friendly. However, depending on your clientele, this could be a level of familiarity that doesn't work for them.
- Follow Up can be planned and expected, such as a typical follow up phone call after a session; or a card through the post on their birthday. However, the unexpected touch, such as a thank you note or an appreciation card that arrives unheralded is often the most valued and remembered.

With these Follow Up guidelines in place, the next question we most commonly get asked is, "When should I follow up and how often?" This question typically comes from a fear of rejection which is disguised under wanting to be 'reasonable' and not bother people. We would suggest being 'unreasonable' and acting differently to how everyone else runs their business. As long as you follow the guidelines suggested above, your clients will welcome rather than feel bothered by your attention.

As to when to follow up, here's our playbook for what we do and recommend...

After a sales conversation:
Follow Up within 24 hours by phone. Send a text/SMS as well as leaving a voicemail if you can't talk to the person directly. Doing this within 24 hours is essential to build on the connection you created in the sales conversation. We do this for everyone whether or not they decided to become a client.

If they have become a client, we congratulate them on their decision. Tell them how excited we are to be working together (if you're not excited to work with them, then perhaps you're not a match and you shouldn't be working together). Answer any questions they have and remind them of the next steps.

If they are still in the decision-making process, tell them how great it was to meet them yesterday and ask them what questions they have in order to move them forward in their decision-making process. Go back into the CARE step of the sales conversation and give them the support they need to come to a clear decision.

If they were not a match and you referred them elsewhere, ask them if they have made contact with whomever you introduced them to and check that they have everything they need in order to move forward. Wish them well on their journey and reassure them that they can always get back in touch if they want any further advice.

A great example of this happened with one of our clients Sara. The client had decided that they weren't a match and obviously, Sara was disappointed however she followed up and the person felt cared for. Then a week later, the client was back in touch asking if they would work together as the other person that they had been to see, that was cheaper, didn't offer the same level of service and they then had concerns over getting their outcome. With Sara it was clear what they could expect, and they were more than happy to pay a premium to get it having seen what the budget option looked like.

Your existing clients

Following up with your existing clients is essential. This could take place as a simple birthday card, a thank you card for being a client, or just checking in on progress in between sessions. Anything you can do to make your clients feel special and ensure they know they can reach out to you for extra support or guidance if they need it is worth doing.

Your previous clients

Past clients are a great source of new business - both in terms of repeat business if they need your services again, or in referrals or recommendations they make to other people about your services. The best way to make both of these business benefits happen is to simply go back to the principle of on-going customer service.

We suggest calling past clients one month after they finish working with you to check in and make sure they have everything they need and are progressing well. Then every three months after that. Whilst we know some of you might find this a lot, remember that the purpose of these calls is to explore how you can serve them, not to see what you can sell them. If you call people with this clear intention, the difference in how they respond and the gratitude they feel will transform your business and your reputation.

ACTION STEP

Create a list of all of your past clients.

Make a customer service phone call to 2 people on that list each day. These phone calls will probably take less than 10-15 minutes each. Once you have spoken to someone, put them into your 3-month customer service cycle so you continue to support them.

2 phone calls a day means you'll be contacting 10 of your past clients each week.

40 people per month.

480 people per year (depending on how big your client database is).

This consistent level of client engagement is guaranteed to massively grow your business!

Chapter Highlights

- ✓ Sales is essential to any business and is typically avoided because of a fear of judgement or fear of money. Without a sale, you don't have a business.
- ✓ Heart Centred Sales is all about finding a match and serving. It needs to be win:win
- ✓ There are 5 Key principles that underpin Heart Centred Sales that are all focused on you getting a better understanding of what is going on for your client so that you can most effectively serve them and fulfil your dreams.
- ✓ There are 5 Fundamental Steps in Heart Centred Sales. Set the Context, Discovery, Your System, Offer and Care.
- ✓ The Fortune is in the Follow Up so remember to complete your sale the way you started with service.

Chapter 5
Money Mindset
How to keep more of what you're earning

"Happiness is not in the mere possession of money; it lies in the joy of achievement, in the thrill of creative effort."

– Franklin D. Roosevelt

What We Think Creates Our Reality

By now, you've learnt how to get more clients through Attraction Marketing and how to earn more money using Heart Centred Sales. We now need to focus on keeping more of the money you make by working on your Money Mindset.

Have you ever had a situation where you have more month than money? It doesn't matter whether you have a good month or a bad month, there just doesn't seem to be enough money to cover everything? Or perhaps you have a number of good months and then something goes wrong and you're back at zero or below in your account? Any of these scenarios and a lot more can be ascribed to how healthy or otherwise your Money Mindset is.

Remember, as Henry Ford suggests, whether you think you can or think you can't, you are right. Whilst profound, this only scratches the surface of the powerful impact our brains have on our experience of the world and the reality we end up living. When it comes to money in particular, we have an internal mindset or belief pattern, reflected in our physical or external reality. By this we mean whatever you think and feel about money is reflected in the amount of money you have as your income and what you have in your bank account.

To take this a step further, it means that whatever you're currently experiencing with money, you have created it for yourself. Now we understand that some of you have just thrown your arms up in disgust saying something along the lines of, "It's not my fault that I have no money. He/she/they/it did this to me…" While we totally agree, life and circumstances happen to all of us. Bad relationships, losing jobs, cars breaking down, the boiler blowing up or any other unexpected expense... there are many ways that life can throw financial challenges at us. It is how we respond to those challenges that determines how much money we have.

For example, many of the self-made billionaires in the world today have lost all their money in the past and sometimes even gone bankrupt. Yet they are now billionaires. They had bigger challenges and sometimes faced more hardships than most of us will ever face. Yet no matter what life threw at them, they came out of it phenomenally successful. This is how powerful our Money Mindset can be and how much it influences how we respond to life's dramas. Elon Musk once said that he wouldn't partner with anyone who hadn't lost more than $1million. This is because the act of losing money and then making it back again demonstrates the quality of your Money Mindset. If you're going to partner with someone in business, you want to make sure they are going to react well to financial challenges. How they react is determined by their Money Mindset.

If your external world around money, or your bank balance and lifestyle isn't what you want them to be, we're sorry to hear it. On the plus side, whatever negative experiences you're having, you have created, which means you can change it. Now we understand you might not particularly like viewing things in this way. Of course, we all sometimes find it easier to blame someone or something else for what's going on in our lives. The trouble is, this is a victim mentality which means we feel we have no power to change things. Stepping into the alternative mindset that we are the ones who create our financial reality, gives us our power back. It's not what happens to us that determines how much money we have, but how we choose to respond to what happens. Remember, if you're having a negative reaction or emotion to any of this, fill in a Red Flag Sheet from the back of the book. Be prepared to fill out quite a few as we continue during this chapter as money can be quite an emotional topic!

Something to consider here is that we don't have money in our life because we deserve it. We have money in our life when we stop resisting it. We are the block that creates a lack of money through our mindset. Yet we often tend to believe that if we're good, we should have more money. Or perhaps the reverse, that only bad and unscrupulous people have money. Neither of these beliefs is empowering. Money isn't good or bad. Money is just coins and paper; or numbers in a bank account. However, if asked what money is, we are sure that you, like the thousands of people we've asked around the world at our events, would come up with a long list of meanings. Some positive meanings, such as: freedom, energy, a means of exchange, holidays etc. And some negative, such as dirty, greedy, corruption, the root of all evil etc. All of these meanings, however, are things that we have projected onto money - they are not what money is. If we don't address the meaning we have ascribed to money by working on the internal beliefs and mindset that created that meaning, our external reality of money won't reflect what you want or even the effort you're putting in to generate it.

Remember, the great example of lottery or inheritances where people are handed millions of pounds. The crazy reality is that 95% of lottery winners end up back to their previous level of money *or less* within 5 years. Now we know this seems crazy and like us, you're probably thinking, "That might be what other people do but I would be smarter with my money!" Or, "There's no way I would burn through millions of pounds in a couple of years!" Yet, 95% of people do. We might think we would be different but 95% is a pretty big statistic so the chances are, most people would be in that group rather than the 5% they might hope to be in. And, interestingly, this is the same across the world, so there seems to be no geographical bias on craziness. So is it craziness, or just the reality of the external world reflecting what is going on internally?

Remember, when we are talking about our internal thoughts and feelings about money, we are referring to our subconscious mind, not our conscious thoughts. This means that no matter how much you say to yourself, "I want more money!", or "I deserve more money!" it won't change anything if the little voice inside our head says, "I hate money" or, "I don't deserve money" It's our subconscious mind that directs our behaviours no matter how smart or powerful we think our conscious mind is.

Chris went through this for years, wanting to earn more money and working hard yet remaining broke...

It took years for me to realise and accept that I was the one who was keeping myself stuck. I used to blame everything else... it was a quiet month, I didn't have enough clients, the car needed fixing to pass its MOT, I needed that holiday to recover from working so hard, the interest fees are so high on my credit cards....so many things to blame before I started working with coaches who helped me too first understand and then start to resolve my self-sabotaging money mindset.

Why did it take me so long?
I guess I'm slow on the uptake and with my belief system, I thought that if I just kept working harder, I could solve my money challenges. After all, this is my family pattern - work all hours and all opportunities no matter what the personal cost in order to bring in money. The thing is, consciously working hard to make money while your subconscious mind is working hard to get rid of money is like trying to drive with the brakes on. Remember, it's not about deserving money. It's about not resisting it. I'm not saying that once I had my eyes opened that everything instantly got better. It still required a LOT of work to turn around my financial reality, get out of debt and start making real money. But by continually working to reset and improve my money mindset, the brakes are slowly eased off and the accelerator can take over. This is one of the reasons we suggest to our clients to focus on working hard towards what they want for five years. It can take more time than we think to do the inner work and for a long time, it might feel like nothing is happening. Then almost imperceptibly things can start to change before all of a sudden, your growth becomes exponential. The reason I've gone from a £20,000 a year income just six years ago, to owning multiple properties and a million pound turnover business today isn't just because of the work I've put in during these six years. It also includes many false starts and a lot of working on my internal blocks and self-sabotage patterns for two or three years before any financial growth happened whatsoever.

During those years of effort and growth, it takes courage and faith to keep going when you aren't getting any noticeable results. Think of it like the Chinese bamboo tree...
The farmer will plant the bamboo seed, water it, weed it and wait
Year 2, he's still watering, weeding and waiting
Year 3, more watering, weeding and waiting
Year 4, the same
Year 5, suddenly things start happening. Overnight the bamboo starts growing and can reach 80 feet in height within five weeks, growing at a rate of 1cm every 15 minutes!

So what was it doing for the five years when nothing was happening? Those 5 years were spent growing the extensive root network that is essential to allow such rapid growth. If at any point during that five year period, the farmer had stopped watering the seed, or stopped weeding and tending to ít"s patch of earth, the seed would have died.

Is the bamboo tree an overnight success? A lot of people would say yes, but the reality is that it is a five year overnight success. When it comes to making big changes in our lives and finances, we are the same. It takes a LOT of work under the surface, when you don't notice any changes, but this work is essential to making any growth happen.

So if you want to be in the 5% of lottery winners who keep the money they win, rather than the 95% who lose it, be like the bamboo, put in the internal work.

Step one is to get Clarity on what is going on internally and how you are blocking yourself from having the results you want. Once we understand the internal world, we can then review the external reality and start making some changes.

Your Internal Experience. Beliefs and Self Sabotage

We have all grown up with different experiences and different stories about money. You may have heard your parents saying things like:

- Money doesn't grow on trees
- I'm not made of money

- Money is dirty
- Money is hard to come by
- Money is the root of all evil

Alternately, you may have been luckier and heard phrases such as,

- There's always something left in the pot
- Things always work out in the end
- The love of money is the root of all evil
- You can achieve anything
- Money makes the world go around

All of these phrases build up to become our beliefs around money. They're formed in our childhood, when we absorb much of what we perceive about the world from our parents - both what they say and more importantly, how they act. This is why most of your money belief patterns, positive or negative, are the same ones your parents have. Your parents' Money Mindset is probably based on their parents' beliefs and so on. Just think, you are carrying around beliefs that have shaped your financial reality and they don't even belong to you!

This doesn't mean blaming your parents if you're not happy with how things have turned out financially. They have almost certainly tried to do the best they could with the deck of cards they were dealt. Remember, it is not about what happens to us but what we do with it that shapes our reality. Avoid the trap of anger or resentment towards family patterns. This will just keep you stuck. Instead focus on changing the patterns so you don't pass it down to the next generation. Break the chain by taking advantage of the huge amount of resources and support available to you in today's world of personal and business development and do what preceding generations were unable to do - consciously create whatever financial reality you want.

To make it easier to identify what's going on inside your head with money, consider whether your thoughts, action or relationships are creating the biggest issues:

Negative Thought Habits

For example:

- You might see someone getting into a nice car and think, "Rich bastard"
- You might discount the possibility of investing in the property thinking, "All landlords are taking advantage of people"
- You might avoid making investments thinking, "I'm bad with money and don't know what I'm doing"

Negative Action Habits

For example:

- You might have a habit of never looking at your bank account as it's too scary
- You might have a habit of spending money as soon as it arrives in your account
- You might have a habit of putting everything on a credit card irrespective of whether you have enough money in your bank to pay for it

Negative Relationship Habits

For example:

- You might have a habit of talking down success, saying things like, "Well he/she was born with money so it's alright for them"
- You might have a habit of sharing 'misery stories' with your friends, where you talk about how bad things are rather than exploring what might be possible
- You might have a habit of dating people who need rescuing financially

ACTION STEP

What are the typical phrases or sayings that might be typical of your family around money?

What negative thought, action or relationship habits do you have?

All of these negative habits create what are commonly known as self-sabotage patterns. Things that we do to ourselves despite the fact that we know better. Sounds crazy right?! That we would repeatedly make choices that end up in hurting us? However, we've all done this, and most of us more than once. For example, have you ever been in a bad relationship. Ever then repeated the same type of bad relationship with someone else? Knowing something is bad for us and doing it anyway, this is a self-sabotage pattern!

There are 5 main self-sabotage patterns that we have found most people have around money. These create the negative thought, action and relationship patterns we mentioned above and once you understand which patterns might apply to you, you can do something about them.

Sabotage Pattern 1. Rich people are Greedy

If you think that people with money are greedy, then it's unlikely you're going to want to have money. In fact, if you have it, or earn it, it probably won't last or stay as you will be looking for ways to get rid of it so that you can avoid being considered greedy.

Many business owners say they would like to work with people who can afford them, or that their ideal clients have to have money. And yet, if they approach these types of people with the attitude that people with money are greedy, this is a negative relationship that just won't work.

Now, of course, some rich people are greedy, some are not. Greed vs Generosity are two ends of a spectrum just like anything else and we all exist on this spectrum somewhere. The thing is, it has nothing to do with the amount of money you have. Money doesn't make people greedy. Money, like power, magnifies who we are. If someone is already greedy, give them a lot of money and they will become a lot more greedy. If someone is generous by nature, give them a lot of money and they will become even more generous. This is why we like working with heart centred business owners, because when they have more money, they do more good in the world with that money because that is their nature.

One more thing to perhaps consider with the concept of greed is that it is based on a feeling of scarcity or lack. To be greedy means you want more of something, or perceive that you don't have enough. In reality, wanting more of anything is totally ok, as long as it doesn't negatively impact anyone else if you have it. And this is where the problem comes in... a lot of people believe that by someone wanting or having a lot of money, it means that someone else has to go without. They think money is a finite resource and there is a limited amount to be shared around. For one person to have more, someone else has to have less and so people limit themselves to settling for less so that other people can share the limited resource.

This is not the case. Money is an infinite resource so there is enough for everyone to have as much money as they want! Not convinced? Governments are printing more money to boost the economy every day and no one knows how much money there actually is in this world. So it doesn't matter how much money one person has, there is always enough for everyone else to have whatever they want as well.

Still not convinced? What if we changed the concept from money to oxygen, or happiness?
Do people go round feeling guilty because they have used up too much oxygen meaning someone else has gone short. Do people kick themselves because they've been too happy and enjoyed too many smiles over and above the quota allocated to each person?
Of course not. So why do we do it with money?!

Wanting to have more money from a heart centred perspective is a good thing because you'll do more good in the world with that money. Wanting more money for you and your family's security is also ok. Even buying the expensive toys and accessories is totally fine as long as the money you spend has been earned from making a difference in people's lives. The problem of wanting more money comes about when that money is made in a way that hurts rather than helps people.

Sabotage Pattern 2. Money vs Spirituality

Many health practitioners, healers or people on a spiritual journey, believe that there is a conflict between money and spirituality. That you can't be spiritual and have money. People quote the phrase from the bible, saying, "Money is the root of all evil". And they put down money and earning money as below them.

The thing is, money and spirituality are totally unconnected concepts and so are perfectly fine to co-exist. Organised religion doesn't seem to have a block around money. They actively encourage followers to donate money. They know that with more money they can help more people and the wealth that religion raises across the world is staggering. Deepak Chopra who has spent a lifetime sharing his spiritual teachings with the world certainly doesn't have an issue here and has a personal net worth measured in the hundreds of millions.

And as for the biblical quote that people claim as the moral reason to reject money is a mis-quote. The full quote is, "The love of money is the root of all evil" This is a very different message. Nowhere in the bible does it say that earning money by helping people is wrong. Yet this is exactly what so many heart centred business owners do. By undercharging for their services and not earning enough, they don't end up helping as many people and often become in need of charity and support themselves.

This is perhaps a darker side of the search for enlightenment.... the traditional spiritual path of renouncing all worldly goods and occupations and withdrawing from society to go on an inward journey. Whilst noble in intention, people on this path can often become dependent on other people's charity and financial support to allow them to continue the journey of becoming 'enlightened'. This means they partly rely on other people staying non-enlightened (in their view) and earning money that they can take advantage of, so they can have the privilege of doing something different. Quite a different way of viewing it isn't it?

Sabotage Pattern 3. Money is Not Important

Money might not be important, and it might not buy you happiness. However, it certainly makes life easier and gives you more choice. Perhaps another way to view it is in the words of the late great Zig Ziglar, "Money might not be the most important thing in life. But in today's world, it is right up there alongside oxygen." Life without money today is very challenging. Try paying your rent, your bills or getting food without it. Of course money doesn't make you happy, but it can make you more comfortable while you're dealing with whatever life throws at you.

Those people who swear off money or earning more money because it's not important tend to forget that the main reason most marriages fail is money concerns. Of all of the things that could affect a relationship, arguing about money is the most common and the most damaging long term. That's quite an impact for something dismissed as not important!

If we behave in a way that suggests that money is not important, are we likely to keep it when we have it? Our energy flows to where our attention goes. By not paying any attention to money, we'll give no time or energy to its management. This could mean poor financial habits such as not checking regularly what is in your bank account, or spending money without thought of the consequences - habits and behaviours that almost guarantee that there will be no money left to manage after a while.

From a business perspective, if you believe that money is not important, are you likely to receive it gratefully from your clients? Or, like the salesperson we mentioned in the car dealership with Karene's parents, are you likely to behave as though it is a poisonous snake? How we respond to our clients' money will affect how they feel about paying you. If you are uncomfortable with it, they will be too and will start to go elsewhere so they can avoid the situation.

Sabotage Pattern 4. Waiting to be Saved.

Have you ever bought a lottery ticket or scratch card? Are you going around thinking that a man or woman, or your parents, or anyone else for that matter should just bestow upon you great wealth? This is magical thinking and is an attempt to absolve ourselves from the financial reality we have created.

Unfortunately, as the great phrase by Kim Kyosaki, says, "A man (or any person for that matter) is not a plan!" We need to take control of your financial destiny. Waiting around for someone to save you will lead to waiting for a really long time. It is also a position of helplessness that reinforces your financial reality. By waiting for someone or something else to act, your energy, thought and action isn't being focused on what you could do yourself to change your situation. Something every one of us sometimes needs to remember is that we are not victims, or at least we don't have to be. Recognise what is holding you back and change it, first through awareness and then action.

If we have someone solve our challenges for us, it might change our present reality, but we don't grow or learn. This means we will keep recreating the situation which is more damaging in the long run. The help we so desperately wanted to be saved by will keep us stuck in the long term and increasingly at risk. A great example of this is the caterpillar that turns into a butterfly...

When a caterpillar is ready to transition to the next phase of life, it builds itself a cocoon or chrysalis and shuts itself inside. Several days or weeks later, it is ready to emerge as a fully formed butterfly and it has to break its way free from the chrysalis. As a butterfly, it doesn't have the strong jaws or body muscles that it enjoyed as a caterpillar so the only way it can break out of the tough chrysalis that protected it during its transformation is by flexing its as-yet-unused wing muscles. This is hard work and takes a lot of time. When it's finally free, the new butterfly's wings have grown strong from all the work. This gives it the strength to fly so it can find flowers and get the nectar it needs for food.

If you saw a butterfly struggling to get out of its chrysalis and tried to ease its struggles by breaking it free, you would inadvertently be killing it. Without the struggle for freedom, the butterfly's wing muscles do not develop the strength or endurance needed to fly. This means it cannot reach the flowers containing the nectar it needs for survival, so it'll starve.

We humans are the same. If someone rescues us and eases our struggle, we do not develop the strength to tackle other challenges and although we (hopefully) don't die like the butterfly, we are forever limited to experience greater and greater challenges

Sabotage Pattern 5. I Can't Afford It

If you have ever uttered these words, then you are certainly not alone. We have all said these words at some point or had them said to us by other people. As parents it is sometimes very challenging not to say these words, even if you're aware of how damaging they are.

Karene and I have both had this experience with Mya when we admire a yacht, she as all children who have no idea about the value of money yet, asks something like, "Can we get one of those, Mummy?" Or, "Daddy, why do we fly Business Class rather than First Class?" The reality for us is that we're in the privileged position where we choose not to buy these things, rather than not being able to afford them. However, the instant phrase that still sometimes comes to mind in response to Mya's questions is, "We can't afford it" showing that this is a deep seated pattern that takes a lot of time and effort to shift completely.

Thinking with a limit of "I can't…" stops the brain from coming up with solutions. In effect we are telling our brains that it's not even worth trying to solve this, there isn't a solution. Although it may not always seem so, our brains are very obedient and if you tell it something can't be done, it becomes true. However, if you change the words to "I can't afford it yet…" This allows an opening, a possibility that although it might be like this now, it isn't set in stone and could be changed in the future. This is all the brain needs to get in action on your behalf to start puttering around to try and figure out how to make this happen.

However, an even more powerful re-phrasing of this question puts your subconscious brain into overdrive looking for a solution. Instead of saying, "I can't afford it", try saying, "How can I afford it?" This creates a resourceful state around money rather than a limited state.

Bear in mind, it is rarely a lack of resources that stops us, it is a lack of resourcefulness. This doesn't mean people should convince themselves they can afford something when they can't. Instead it's about stepping into a state where they can overcome their problems rather than live within their limits.

The list of ways we self-sabotage ourselves financially is endless. These 5 core patterns come up time and time again with our clients, friends and we too have had to work our way through most of them. It is changing these self-sabotage habits that allows us to create a new reality. Which of these self-sabotage patterns applies to you?

ACTION STEP

What of these 5 self-sabotage patterns do you recognise in yourself?

How do they show up?

What is this stopping you from having?

Your External Experience - Your Current Financial Situation

Getting clarity on your finances as we describe below, is very simple, yet few people take the time to do it. Get connected with how important it is for you to change your financial circumstances and use that as motivation to do these un-exciting, yet important action steps and you'll be amazed at the results you can create for yourself.

When it comes to our finances, we need to have clarity on the following four concepts:

#1 Your Income.

Sounds simple right, but do you actually know how much money ends up in your bank account every month? The figure we need to get clear on is your average monthly income, this way it covers any fluctuations you might have month to month - which is just part of running a normal business.

To do this, simply go through your bank statements and add up all your income over the past six or twelve months (the longer the time period, the more accurate the results will be). Then divide it by the number of months you reviewed. This will give you your average monthly income which might be higher or lower than you expected.

Employees often focus on their gross pay rather than what ends up in the account after tax and national insurance etc. We also find that business owners often work from an over-inflated income figure because they sometimes don't take into account the quieter months, the fluctuation in client numbers month to month, or the costs of marketing activities and other costs.

#2 Your Expenses.

How much do you spend every month? This includes fixed expenses as well as all those little unplanned extras such as cups of coffee, trips to the cinema, or those little extras that always sneak into your grocery shopping.

Again, the best way to work this out is to go through your bank and credit card statements and add everything up, including cash you took out from the ATM and see what it comes to. We often ignore the cash expenses because we don't notice how much money we withdraw from the ATM or how long it lasts. We also tend to forget the contactless card payments such as train travel, uber or the spur of the moment impulse buys.

We suggest doing this calculation for your personal expenses and your business expenses. Keep these separate but just recognise, that whatever you're spending personally, you'll need to pay yourself more than that out of your business each month. Please note, the amount you pay yourself needs to take into account how much tax you'll have to pay on that money, otherwise you'll get an unpleasant shock at the end of the tax year when HMRC come asking for what they're owed.

Once you know your average monthly income and expenses, you can now work out your Net Monthly Income

Net Monthly Income = Monthly Income - Monthly Expenses

Net Income refers to the amount of money you have left over after all your expenses are paid. Ideally, this is a positive figure meaning your expenses are less than your income. However, like far too many people, we have experienced far too many months when our Net Monthly Income was a negative figure, meaning we spent more than we earned. Obviously, this situation is not sustainable and is one of the main reasons people feel stressed about money. It is a horrible feeling to know that you are sinking each month financially and spending more than you are earning. We endured this, for way too many months before Chris finally (his words, not mine, took action to change things). By getting training and business mentors and coaches he put us on a path to earning more than we ever had before.

Living within your means whilst also increasing your means is the key to getting your financial house in order. Put another way, spend less and earn more!

ACTION STEP

What is your monthly income?

What are your monthly expenses?

What is your Net Monthly Income? If this is negative go back to the Attraction Marketing and Heart centred Sales chapters and find out how you can earn more whilst simultaneously reviewing your expenses to ensure that you are living within your means.

Once you know where you stand financially, you have the power to change it. There is no judgement to this information. As Tony Robbins says, "See it as it is, not worse than it is." The first step is to get clear on what's going on, so you can then decide what you want to change. Once you know that, you can then move onto the next steps of deciding what you need to do to change it!

Now you know your Net Monthly Income Figure, we now need to determine your Net Worth. This is calculated by looking at Assets and Liabilities:

#3 **Your Assets.**

This is the value of everything you own and is based on real values if you had to sell it today. For example, how much would your car be worth if you sold it today, rather than what you paid for it when you bought it?

Make a list of everything you own, and we mean everything. Beside each item, write down what you could sell it for today. To determine this, it might mean doing a search for a similar item on eBay or Google - obviously please avoid buying things during this price comparison search... it's NOT a shopping trip. Avoid the temptation to over inflate the figures you write down, no matter how depressing it is to discover that things are worth far less than what you originally paid.

Once you have everything written down, along with a price tag if you sold it, add everything together and get a total figure.

#4 **Your Liabilities.**

This is the total of everything you owe. This includes any outstanding balance on credit cards, personal loans, your mortgage and any other debts such as Student Loans etc.

Alongside the obvious debts, one component of looking at your Liabilities means going back to the Asset list you just created and write down how much you owe on every item on the list. It might be nothing, or it could be that you have a mortgage or outstanding debt on the item such as a car loan or purchase agreement. Obviously, this debt would have to be paid back if you sold the item so you might end up with less money than you think.

Just like your Asset list, add everything together so you arrive at a grand total for the amount you owe to other people. Now we start putting it all together...

Net Worth = Assets - Liabilities

Net Worth is how much money you would have if you sold everything right now. The value of everything you have minus any debts that need repaying.

Why is this relevant?

Well, if the worst-case scenario happened and you had to sell everything to cover some sort of emergency, you now know how much money you have at your disposal. We know this sounds depressing, but this is reality. Sometimes disaster will strike. Knowing that you have reserves in place, will go a long way to creating peace of mind.

Like the Net Monthly Income figure, sometimes the Net Worth comes up as a negative number, meaning you owe more than you can pay back. Obviously, this is not ideal and is not a safe position to be in, so we need to change this as soon as possible. If you are in this situation, we feel for you. However, remember to breathe. You have achieved the first step to getting out of this situation by first of all getting clear on where you are.

ACTION STEP

Calculate your total Assets.

Calculate your total Liabilities.

What is your Net Worth?

What actions can you take to increase your Net Worth? Do you need to put in place a debt reduction plan, do you need to work towards increasing your savings or buying more assets so that you increase your security?

Do you need to put contingency plans in place? Do you have insurance in place particularly if you are self-employed with a dependent? It is best that you seek independent advice for your circumstances and the types of insurance you might be looking at would be: Death and Disability, Income protection etc

The last bit of external clarity is your Wealth Number. This takes your net worth figure and brings a bit more reality to it. Your Wealth Number refers to how long you could survive financially if you were no longer able to earn money. This might sound unlikely, but just imagine if you got sick, or had an accident and couldn't work; or something happened to a loved one and you had to give up work in order to look after them. These unfortunately are very real circumstances that could happen to any of us and knowing how long we could survive financially either gives us reassurance and a measure of insurance; or it will (hopefully) light a fire under you.

Wealth Number = Net Worth divided by monthly expenses

Now if your Net Worth is negative then you have no security if something goes wrong. Please consider getting some insurance in place asap as a safety net whilst following the suggestions in this book to increase your income and net worth.

If your Net Worth is low, your Wealth Number isn't going to be a big number. This means that you need to both work on growing your net worth and also make sure that you have a backup plan in place.

If you have a reasonable Net Worth, then Wealth Number could be 6-12 months which is a good start of financial stability and responsibility.

True financial security means your Wealth Number exceeds the number of years you're likely to continue to live for. When you reach this stage, you can now focus on leaving a legacy for the people or projects such as charity that you want to support when you are gone.

To give you an example,
If you had a Net Worth of £1,000,000 and your monthly expenses were £10,000 then your Wealth Number would be 100 months.

100 months divided by 12 = 8.3 years.

You would be able to survive for 8.3 years before you ran out of money. Whilst this might not sound all that long when you think about it, hopefully in this amount of time, you would figure out some additional sources of income meaning you could continue to survive after this point.

ACTION STEP

What is your Wealth Number?

It might be that the actions you need to take here are covered in your last action point or this may have created the impetus for you to revisit your action plan?

If you don't like what this clarity has brought up, as we said at the beginning of this chapter, we're sorry to hear that and it's also great because now that you have clarity, you can change things.

Your Money Thermostat

Now that you have clarity on your internal and external reality around money, how do we go about changing it? One way is to look at your financial set points.

The easiest way to think about a financial set point is to think in terms of a temperature setting on a thermostat. We all have different temperature settings we find comfortable in our house or a room. For some of us this will be 21/22 degrees Celsius, for others 25. Some like it hot, some like it cold and some people will fluctuate day by day. To control this temperature in a room, we use a thermostat. This is the control box on the wall that allows you to keep the temperature at your desired setting. For example, if you want the room to be 21 degrees Celsius, and the sun comes out and heats up the space, the thermostat will turn off the heating and turn on the air conditioning to cool the room down. As the room cools down and goes below 21 degrees, the thermostat turns off the air conditioning and turns on the heater to bring the temperature back up.

Financial set points work much the same way as a thermostat, they however, are controlled by pleasure and pain instead of hot and cold. Too much pain or too much pleasure will lead our set point to pull us back in the other direction. Think this sounds bizarre? Just consider this for a moment, have you noticed that you've had periods where you seem to consistently end up earning roughly the same amount each year. Individually the years are very different and there might be huge fluctuations in monthly income. However, overall, they all seem to end up around the same amount. This plateau of income is a financial set point.

Imagine you are following the actions suggested in Attraction Marketing, you are out talking effectively to more people, perhaps networking, or constantly asking for referrals. You're doing well at this and you increase your client numbers and start earning more. This moves you towards pleasure and it feels good.

You then implement Heart Centred Sales and start earning a lot more and life is getting even sweeter day by day. However, at some point, your set point kicks in and you start to subconsciously think, "This is too much pleasure, I'm not comfortable with this." And so you self-sabotage, you stop asking for referrals and stop networking so you don't get any new clients; enjoying the high life, your monthly expenses exceed your income; or the car breaks down and your income steadily decreases down to your normal levels before perhaps continuing towards pain. It will continue to decrease until it gets too painful, forcing you back into action so you build up your clients and revenue again. This pattern keeps repeating for most of us where we subconsciously bounce back and forth between pain and pleasure.

To work out what your actual set point is, look at what your average annual salary was for the last 5/10 years? As we've discussed, Chris had a very different Money Mindset to me and was stuck around £20,000-£25,000 for many years. My set point was very different and hovered around £150,000. However, once we started working on the inner game of money and learnt how to change our set points, we moved quickly toward £250,000, then £500,000, then £1million and now we are aiming for £5million turnover. Remember the bamboo, our income and current set point is not an overnight success or a lucky break. Rather more like the luck of Thomas Jefferson…

I'm a great believer in luck, and I find the harder I work the more I have of it.

We spent years putting in the groundwork while nothing noticeably changed on the surface. Looking back, our journey seems both short and long. Long, because we remember all the long days and hard work. However, it was also short, because it was only six years ago when the bamboo-like growth of our finances first poked its head above the ground. six years really doesn't seem that much time to radically change your Money Mindset and financial reality forever!

ACTION STEP

What is your financial set point?

So, how do you change your financial set point? There are five levers that will change your financial set point including:

- Knowledge
- Actions
- Mindset
- Community
- Mentor

Knowledge

We need to be educated or have the information necessary to change. Most people don't have a financial education. It is certainly not something that is covered in school. Most professional qualifications pay lip service to running a business and certainly not the ins and outs of money.

Kylie, one of our clients, joined our Mentorship Programme having completed four decades in a wonderful career of education and leadership most recently as a Head Teacher. However, she came to realise that during all those years, she was in effect, financially illiterate. She in her own words says that she has been on a roller coaster ride of emotions, self-reflection and personal development. She now has the tools to launch what has previously been a hobby and dream, to begin her own business with an empowered Money Mindset, no longer having a fear for her financial future.

Similarly our client Samantha, the acupuncturist from Essex who illustrated early on in the book how it is possible to earn £1million readily admits that she, despite being in practice for almost two decades, fully booked with a waiting list, had no knowledge of how to manage her cashflow. She had to rely on credit cards etc if she wanted to take her family on holiday or have work done in the house. She has now learnt how to run her practice as a business. She's been able to afford nice family holidays and pay for work to be done in the house without credit. She's also been able to save some cash and afford the odd massage and facial for herself - Something she never thought possible before. She now feels much more financially stable. This stability has taken away a huge amount of stress and she has been able to give more to charity.

When Chris did his Osteopathy degree, he remembers only two afternoon lectures where they were given business training. The topics covered were how to set up as self-employed and how to pick your price point. Nothing on money, how to make it or how to keep it. This is the fundamental reason why we created Heart Centred Business and speak at business and financial conferences around the world. Too many people need the knowledge we learnt the hard way, so we are thrilled to be able to pay it forward and share our expertise.

Actions

As Dale Carnegie says:

***"Inaction breeds doubt and fear.
Action breeds confidence and courage.
If you want to conquer fear, do not sit home
and think about it. Go out and get busy."***

JFDI - When it comes to action, Just F***** Do It. There are thousands of reasons we all tell ourselves why not to take action. And these reasons all keep us stuck exactly where we are. Action is the only thing that will move you forward because it is how you implement every other component of growth.

For example, as we tell our clients, they have access to the best strategies and knowledge for heart centred business growth on the planet, yet if they don't take any action, nothing will change no matter how much they wish/hope/pray/visualise.

Taking action will help conquer the fears that typically keep us stuck because motion and progress change our emotions. This combined with the feedback we get in response to the actions we take, is how our brains can permanently overcome fears. Action also builds momentum which is what's needed to create success and repeatable habits in any area of life and business.

One of our clients Ruth, a Pilates instructor in London, excelled in the area of taking action. She had what seemed like the entire bag of fears and challenges when we started working with her and her Pilates business was still a dream as she trained for her qualification whilst working in a demanding corporate job. With a bit of motivation, work on her mindset, and a clear series of action steps to take, she got underway and managed to take her Pilates exams three months earlier than planned. When she took the plunge and left her corporate job to launch her business full-time, she was scared at how long it might take to build her business. However, following the right system and putting in the work, in the first four months, she earned over £7,000 in a single month, twice. Within six months, she was completely fully booked. And we mean really fully booked...read looking through her diary desperately trying to find spaces to fit extra hours in weeks in advance. Month seven she enjoyed her first month earning more than £9,000!

What was Ruth's secret? She just got in action in spite of her fears. Was it comfortable? No way! However, taking daily action no matter what, has meant she is now living the life she just dreamed about 15 years ago!

Mindset

We've looked at the fact that your mind can work for you or against you when it comes to most things in life and money is no exception. Remember we talked about the Lottery winners or those who received their money through inheritance? They hadn't sorted out their beliefs around money so when 'gifted' large amounts 95% of them they lost it all or more within a year. Shifting your mindset is about understanding your internal thought patterns and beliefs so that you can change them to ensure that you can keep more money.

Start with getting clarity on what's going on for you internally around money and perhaps who or what influenced you and contributed to these patterns for you. From here, connect with the concept that anything is possible and allow yourself to dream of what you want. Remember that before Roger Banister ran the mile in under four minutes, it was considered impossible. Once he achieved it, it made it possible and more than 1,400 athletes have achieved it since. It was the same with running 100m in under ten secs. Until it was done once, it was considered impossible. This is why it is so important to fill your mind with positive influences of people achieving far more than you might believe is possible. Books, YouTube videos, seminars etc. anything positive that reinforces ideas around what is possible so that it becomes possible for you.

Community

Who we spend time with is who we become!
We are the average of the people we spend the most time with. This is true in all areas of life ranging from relationships, weight, health, energy levels and our finances.

For example, if the five people you spend the most time with are all overweight, the chances are you will be too.

If the five people you spend the most time with are all struggling financially, then you probably will be too.

Why is this the case?
'Birds of a feather, flock together'

We naturally gravitate towards people who are like us and who share our values and viewpoints in life. As we discussed earlier in the book, this is a heritage of the tribal mentality that kept us alive in cave-man times and is hardwired into us. In those days, to be alone was to die, whereas a tribe offered protection in a harsh world.

We still exhibit the same behaviours today, even going so far as to limit our own growth in order to stay the same as the people we hang out with. This sounds crazy right?! Why would we limit our own growth just to fit in? Especially if we want to change something that is hurting us, such as not earning enough money?!!

The thing is, safety is a deeper need than happiness. We can cope with discomfort or even pain, but a lack of safety might kill us. Think about it, in cave-man times, being happy was a luxury whereas being safe and therefore alive was a necessity.

So, we limit ourselves in order to fit in. But what's even more crazy is, we subconsciously limit others so that they don't leave us behind. If one of the people you spend the most time with starts changing, that triggers the deep parts of our brain to react. If they change, we might be left out and be 'tribe-less' and so we try to bring them back down to our level. Now of course this is nonsense but remember, this is subconscious.

A great example of this is crabs in a bucket. If you catch one crab and put it in a bucket, it will climb out. You have to put a lid on the bucket to keep the crab in. However, if you put two or more crabs in the same bucket, you don't need a lid and none of the crabs will get out. Sounds strange right? Why would more crabs mean none can get out? Crabs demonstrate the same tribal safety mentality that we do - they are just more open about it. If there is more than one crab in a bucket, and one of these crabs tries to climb out, the other crabs will pull it back down and stop it escaping. If the crab persists in trying to climb out, the other crabs will even go so far as to break off its legs to stop it climbing. It is a very harsh example of how a group limits the actions of the individual members in order to all stay the same. Of course, it's self-destructive, however, it's what we all do automatically without even thinking about it.

Have you ever got excited about something you were going to do that would change your circumstances? Perhaps you were going to get fit, run a marathon, lose weight, start a business, change your relationship, earn more money... anything at all that would move you forward in life.

Did anyone close to you ever try and talk you out of it? Or express concerns or doubts that took the edge off your excitement or even made you reconsider your plans?

This is a human example of crabs in a bucket. We may not break off each other's legs, but we are just as threatened when one of our group tries to change and we bring them back down to our level in just as destructive, although more subtle ways. Unfortunately, we have all been guilty of this at some point and we guarantee that there are people you currently spend time with who will do this when you announce you are going to change your financial circumstances. You know the ones I'm talking about... those people who have a problem for every solution. Also recognise that these people genuinely believe that they are keeping you safe. So thank them and then get on with changing.

How do we change this, and escape being trapped in our circumstances?

Get a different community!

Remember that the people we spend time with will shape our reality? So, start spending time with people who live the reality you want to live. To make more money, start hanging out with people who have more money. Spending time with people who are already living the life you want to live will pull you up rather than keep you down. This is the importance of our Heart Centred Business Community for our clients. Having a community of passionate business owners who share the same values and support each other to massively increase their income, is very different to what most people have in their own lives.

Find people who share your values and your ambitions and spend more time with them. Yes, this could mean decreasing the amount of time you spend with some of the people you currently hang out with. We're not saying cut them out entirely, although you could if you want to. However, recognise that who you spend time with is who you become. If you want something different for yourself, put yourself in a different community. One great way we've discovered are seminars. Attend a seminar to learn something you want to improve in your life and you're automatically going to be surrounded by people who want to improve the same area and they will support rather than limit your growth.

Jeannine is one of our clients in Brighton who works with food and body issues. Since we started working with her, she's tripled her income to just under £100,000, whilst still being a full-time single mum. She credits getting straightforward and honest feedback from a community of wonderful human beings and business owners as the key reason for her success.

Mentor

As we've discussed earlier in this book, for us, mentors have been a key ingredient in our success. Without having mentors, neither of us would have achieved what we achieved in our previous careers and we most definitely would not be enjoying the success we now have.

A mentor is someone who has been there and done it. They have experience in the area you're looking to grow in and have previously solved the challenge you are wanting to solve. They also have a system with which to apply it to others. Sir Richard Branson, for example, who has been a big influence on us since Chris spent time with him in Singapore, is someone you can learn from because of his track record of success. However, he isn't a mentor, as he will readily admit, because he has no system for people to replicate his success.

Mentors also need to have failed in the past, otherwise they have no appreciation for how hard it can be. Without having done it themselves, they also don't personally know how to bounce back. We mentioned earlier that Elon Musk, the founder of Tesla, won't partner anyone who hasn't lost $1million. I guess since we have only lost £100,000 ourselves, we're not yet ready to partner with Elon on anything. However, the point is that if you have lost a lot, come back from it and you're still interested in mentoring others, then you exhibit certain powerful characteristics.

For us, mentors also need to be mission or purpose driven, meaning there is something bigger in their life that they're committed to. This is perhaps more of a personal preference as we want to be inspired by the people we spend time with over and above the work we're doing together.

A mentor can apply their experience to anything that you want to change or improve in your life, even learning to ride a bike. I mention this as our experience demonstrates that even when you know what will deliver success, sometimes we all need a reminder. Mya, aged four, got her first bike complete with stabilisers, streamers and doll carrier on the back. She was so cute wobbling along with her helmet on her head and favourite doll strapped in behind. We were not riding regularly so quite a bit of time passed with her riding with stabilisers before we took her to the park to teach her to ride without them.

Both Chris and I were taught how to ride a bike by our parents. We've been riding for years and so we should be able to teach Mya how to ride straight away, right? Wrong! In the course of trying, we explained how it would feel for her, we provided her with support in the form of Chris running along behind her bike and yet, it didn't work. Mya got really frustrated that she couldn't do it and no one enjoyed the experience. Ironically for an Osteopath, Chris put his back out from an afternoon of running along beside a child's bike, bent over sideways and holding Mya upright. This was the icing on the cake. Yet it wasn't until Chris was injured that it dawned on us that we should try something different. I mean, we know first-hand what creates success and yet we weren't applying it in this situation. We needed an expert or a mentor who had a system for teaching children how to ride bikes.

So we went online and discovered the Pedal Project. Here was a bike riding mentor.
He had a system and track record of success with teaching children to ride.
He had testimonials.
He had a guarantee that if they couldn't ride without stabilisers or support in three lessons, he would work with your child until they could.

These are all key components we have in place for our clients in our mentoring business - well, except for the children and stabilisers part. And they're what we look for when we're selecting our own business mentors.

And guess what, after three one-hour sessions, Mya thoroughly enjoyed the experience and could ride a bike without stabilisers or support. Chris' back is fixed and out of danger and everyone is happy.

A mentor will change your financial set points much faster and easier than you will be able to do it alone. You still have to put the work in, but you can learn from their experience and put your effort in the right place to get the best results.

ACTION STEP

What is your set point?

What area do you need to focus on to change your set point?

Are you Missing Opportunities?

Another way to change your mindset around money is to stop thinking like a customer and start thinking like an investor?

Customers are focused on how much things cost. Investors are focused on what they get. An example is where you are in a shop buying a suit and you read the label and notice that it is £400 or more. Now, I have some of these priced suits and looking at them like a customer, I could certainly think "How much?" no way am I paying that and go off and find somewhere that I can buy a suit for £150. Or I can look at the suit as an investment and work out that if on average I was going to wear it 2 days a week for a year and I work 48 weeks a year that would be 2 x 48 = 96 wears in a year and because it is a quality suit it will last 2 or 3 years so that would be 192 wears. So then if we divide the cost of the suit by the number of times it is worn £400/192 = £2.03 This means that it 'costs' £2.03 per wear which I don't think is terribly much. Now you might be thinking if you just paid £150 using the same calculations, it would only be £1.63. However, is it likely to last that long? Will it go shiny or lose its shape or just not feel as good?

An investor is focused on "What do I get?", whilst a customer is focused on, "How much does it cost?" Investors are looking for long term benefits, customers are focused on short term gain or pain. Working through the numbers helps all of us see the real difference between these two mindsets and what you get and it is a useful concept to use with your clients. Here's an example from Chris' clinic...

Several years ago I had a client called Patrick, who'd had back pain for the past 25 years. Every six weeks or so, his back would go into spasm and he would spend the next few days lying down, unable to move. To get him back to feeling normal again he would have a couple of sessions of treatment and then be fine again for the next six weeks. He had tried treatment from Osteopaths, Chiropractors, Physiotherapists, Massage Therapists, Acupuncturists and all manner of other professionals and all gave him the same result, so he had resigned himself to this was how life was and got on with things.

When I met Patrick he was limping and when I asked what was wrong he said he was just getting over his regular spasm and told me the whole story. Curiosity piqued, I suggested he book in for a consultation so we could explore what was really going on and why he still had his back problems after seeing so many other practitioners. Although sceptical that we would find out anything different, we scheduled a consultation for later that week.

When I examined Patrick, yes it was clear his back had some long standing issues. But what was more clear to me was that he also had a major weakness and imbalance in one of his ankles. This meant he was not standing evenly on both legs and was twisting slightly which meant he had a twist going through his lower back and pelvis. This twist was putting a strain on the joints and muscles, making them tighter than they should be which was leading to his back spasms. When I explained this, I asked him if he had ever injured his ankle. After several minutes of reflection, he suddenly remembered that he had sprained his ankle really badly in his early 20's about six months before his first episode of back pain.

Now we knew the probable cause of what was going on, I was curious if anyone had worked on his ankle before to try and fix the underlying problem. Patrick's answer was a confused, "No, they just worked on my back because that was where the problem was." Which explained why he still had the problem 25 years later. Everyone had just worked on the symptoms, which to be fair were very dramatic, rather than addressing what was causing the symptoms. This is what we were referring to in Heart Centred Sales when we discussed better serving your clients. Always look to address the deeper problem rather than just the initial symptom or issue as this is where the long term benefits for the client are.

Fortunately, this was what I specialised in and I had worked with thousands of clients like Patrick so I was confident we would get a good result. The only challenge was that it had gone 25+ years untreated so it would take time to fully resolve. Based on my experience, I estimated it would take six months to fully resolve Patrick's ankle issue and get his body realigned so his back was no longer going into spasm. My clinic was based on getting clients results, or I would work with them for free until they did. To make sure clients were as committed to their success as I was, they paid upfront and a six month treatment plan was £6,000.

I explained all this to Patrick and gave him his options:

1. I can patch you up like you've had every time up until now and then see you every six weeks when you spasm up again. This option will cost you about £100-£200 each time depending on how many sessions you need. Or...

2. We can work on fixing the root cause so your back stops going into spasm at all. This is a much longer journey and will take approximately six months of working together. This option is £6,000 payable upfront. If things take longer than six months to resolve, I'll work with you for free until you get the result.

Of course, Patrick was shocked at the price of the longer term option but very intrigued by the idea he might be able to resolve the underlying issue. I then asked him two simple questions, "How much had he spent on treatment sessions for his back until now?"

After a lot of thought, he estimated that in the past 25 years he had probably spent around £15,000 on all manner of treatments that kept patching up his back and getting him out of pain. However, none of them had solved his problem, as he had kept on having back spasms every six weeks in spite of spending all that money. Being in his late 40's this meant he could look forward to spending another £15,000 over the next 25 years whilst still being in regular pain.

The alternative was to pay more money upfront than he'd ever paid another practitioner. Yet, this would hopefully mean he would be able to live the next 25 years without having back pain at all. So actually, the choice was £15,000 paid over time and still be laid up unable to move every six weeks; or, pay £6,000 now and put in the work for six months to then enjoy the rest of his life. Suddenly, option two didn't look so expensive!

Patrick paid his money and we got down to work. He had one back spasm during the six months we worked together, and then one more approximately three months after we finished his six month programme. The regular spasms stopped entirely and he returned to doing things that he hadn't been able to do for years. Which, unfortunately, is what caused his second flare up after we had finished our work together. He had been feeling so good for so long, he decided to move some concrete patio furniture alone rather than waiting until his team could come and help him and he strained his back while lifting it.

With all of my clinic clients, this was exactly how I worked. Find out what the root cause of the problem they had was and work out a plan to fix it. Almost certainly this was more expensive than their regular sessions, however, it was focused on long term outcomes rather than just short term gains. I then presented the options and gave them the choice. People who thought like customers wanted the short term option which cost them less upfront even though the solution was far less satisfactory and more expensive in the long term. These people I referred to other practitioners who specialised in providing quick fixes like this. People who chose to work with me, thought like investors and like me, were committed to getting a long term gain from our work together. These are the clients that make up a premium service heart centred business and personally I find them much more fun and engaging to work with.

However, to attract these types of clients we need to think differently ourselves. To test yourself, as to whether you think like a customer or investor, let's look at a non-business example. Karene, Mya and I were wandering down Oxford Street a few months ago and we went into Watches of Switzerland. This is a shop that contains a lot of very beautiful and very high-priced watches. Karene has always liked Rolex watches so Mya and she started trying a few on for fun, and probably to drop hints to me of what they would like for Christmas. After trying on several different styles, the shop assistant noticed that both Karene and Mya are rather partial to a diamond or two. Let's rephrase that... they're like magpies. If it glitters, that's the one for them. So, with all due aplomb, the assistant brought out a Rolex that was covered in diamonds. The watch face, the strap, the hands, everything. It was dazzling in every sense and of course, both girls fell head over heels in love. The watch retailed for £153,000 and we then had to explain to Mya how much money this actually was. This watch was worth more than some of our investment properties. At this point, I very politely thanked the staff and firmly escorted my two ladies back outside without the watch and we continued our day. However, what if the story took a twist here...

Let's pretend that Karene couldn't sleep that night because she was dreaming of that diamond encrusted Rolex and the next day, she snuck back to Watches of Switzerland without me and bought it. Feeling a million dollars (yet £153,000 lighter), she arrived home wearing the watch and suddenly it hit her... buyers remorse. She was worried about what I would say if I knew she had bought the watch instead of an investment property and decided she had to get rid of it immediately. Let's pretend she couldn't get back to the shop and therefore has to sell it privately as quickly as possible for whatever she can get so I don't notice. She offers this watch to you with all its ownership papers and box for just £50,000. Would you buy it?

Now it is helpful to see what comes up for you at this point. For those of you who wouldn't buy it, why not? What would stop you? Is it that you don't like diamonds? Or you'd prefer an Omega watch instead? Or some other equally expensive brand? You don't have £50,000? You can't imagine when you would ever wear it? I am sure that at least some of these came up, yes?

Remember, there's no right or wrong here, you're just observing what comes up for you. Now, if you wouldn't buy the watch at this point, you are thinking like a customer.

For those of you who would buy it, what are you going to do with it? Sell it and make a profit! If it retails for £153,000 and you have only paid £50,000, you could even sell it for £100,000 and make £53,000 profit. But we know some of you are saying, "But I don't have the money" Could you find it? Does it have to be your £50,000 or could you borrow it from someone and split the profit? Could you get £5,000 from 10 people or £1,000 from 50 people? All of these creative options would allow you to make money and take advantage of an opportunity.

Now, let's be clear, Karene didn't buy the watch (thankfully) and so this is not a real offer to buy it for £50,000. However, this concept could apply to anything and highlights the importance of thinking like an investor, "What do I get?"

Remember, it is never a lack of resources that stops us, just a lack of resourcefulness. So how can you train yourself to be more resourceful? These logic problems can help and then there is the real action of putting it into practice by exploring what other people value. If you're curious to challenge yourself and have the chance to grow exponentially in a very short space of time, here's a bonus action video:

www.heartcentredbusiness.com/book-offers

This is a short video Chris recorded several years ago for our Mentorship clients to give them the chance to explore conversations around value and what's important to the people they know.

To whet your appetite, one of our clients, Tom, an Osteopath, did this exercise on two separate occasions. Now, Tom hates getting on the phone. It was one of his biggest fears. However, the first time he did the exercise, he got a new client out of it who paid him £600. 8 Months later, he used this same exercise to raise £197,000 in 3 weeks to buy his third house. Obviously, we aren't suggesting this will be the case for you, however, it will definitely give you the chance to think differently and explore being resourceful as you look to support people in getting what they want.

ACTION STEP

Watch the video and take action.

Thinking like a customer or an investor will also have influenced how you set up your pricing. When Chris was starting out at an Osteopath, he was told to Google other practitioners in the area and then set his price somewhere in the middle. This is a customer way of thinking and firmly placed him as a commodity service. However, when I was starting out as a coach, my approach was different and I priced myself from an investor perspective. By this point, I had firmly connected with the fact that people working with me were going to be learning the skills, tools and strategies to allow them to conservatively earn £100,000. If they paid me £10,000 to help them get that result, that is a 10 times return, which is the result we always aim to provide our clients with. It is worth considering in your own business how you could do the same with your clients. With this focus on client outcome, I wasn't looking at what my hourly rate was or comparing myself to other coaches too see what they charged. Rather, I was looking at what my clients were going to get and as such it was a completely different conversation and a completely different pricing approach. Remember that customers ask, "How Much?" and Investors ask, "What do I get?" When Chris and I are investing in our mentors, we ask ourselves, "What do we get?"

Apply this to your business. If you're just setting your pricing relative to your competitors, your clients will look at you as a commodity and having worked with you in this book through Attraction Marketing and Heart Centred Sales, you most definitely are not a commodity my friend. You are a specialist and should be charging for the specialist result you help your clients attain!

Now you have a better understanding of the impact that your thoughts have on your external world, you can be more circumspect about your thoughts. You have also learnt that if you don't like your reality, you can change it. Money is such an emotionally charged issue for many of us, that without sorting out your Money Mindset, all the mentoring, business coaching or knowledge in the world will have limited impact as you will just sabotage all of your good actions.

If you aren't able to sort out your belief patterns yourself, perhaps find an expert in changing these beliefs to help you. Both Chris and I have had to do a lot of work with various money mindset experts to clear some of our personal blocks. We view working on your Money Mindset so important that we include exercises to transform money blocks and limiting belief patterns in all of our events and client work. If you recognise that you perhaps could benefit from some support in this area, book a strategy call with one of our Coaching Team and explore what's possible if you transformed your Money Mindset. Please now visit

www.heartcentredbusiness.com/book-offers

and book a strategy call.

Chapter Highlights

- ✓ Your external reality around money is a reflection of your internal beliefs, habits and relationships around money. This means that if you don't like your reality, you can change it.
- ✓ Getting clarity on the key financial measures of Income, Expenses, Assets and Liabilities as well as your Wealth Number, is key to understanding what you need to tweak or change to reach your goals.
- ✓ There are 5 typical self sabotage patterns that disempower us and result in our being less resourceful around money. Remember that there is never a lack of resources, just a lack of resourcefulness.
- ✓ We all have Financial Set Points much like our own money thermostat which we can adjust with Knowledge, Action, Mindset, Community and Mentor.
- ✓ You can choose whether you think like an investor and look for opportunities or whether you remain stuck as a customer, missing them. Thinking about what you get vs what it costs will shift your and your client's mindset!

Chapter 6
Confidence
How to Be Seen in the Way You Want

"Almost every successful person begins with two beliefs: the future can be better than the present, and I have the power to make it so."
– David Brooks

Confidence is something that nearly all experts and practitioners could use more of. Belief in ourselves is necessary to do effective work with clients. It is also necessary for your clients, as without belief that you can help your clients, your clients won't believe that they can make any progress.

Most practitioners struggle to believe that they are good enough despite the great work they do. They subsequently keep their prices low with the belief that they'll increase what they earn as their skills increase. This is why they tend to do course after course, getting more and more skills, yet never feeling confident enough to increase prices because they still lack confidence.

In order to develop a premium heart centred business where you work with fewer numbers of clients and serve them to a much higher level, as we discussed earlier in this book, you need to be positioned as a specialist and ideally an Authority. An Authority is someone who is not just a specialist but is the go-to person for xyz problems. This is the reputation we want you to have in your local area, so your ideal clients seek you out, rather than you having to chase them - which is why it's called Attraction Marketing after all!

The trouble is, it doesn't matter how good your marketing message is, or what person, problem, solution marketing message you use, if you don't come across as a confident expert, no one will believe you.

We assume you already have the expert bit sorted - whether you believe it or not. Of course, you can always get better and should always be striving to improve. However, you are already an expert because you are qualified in something and/or have knowledge and skills that can help people. If you are still training for your first qualification, great, keep going and build your skills and confidence. If you are just at the stage where you are considering starting a business, work out what you need to do to get enough skills to make a difference for people. This is what people will actually pay for.

Confidence is challenging for most people. And is what leads them to doubt their expertise. The thing is, confidence is a two-part game:

1. Inner confidence and self-belief
2. The outer perception that the world sees

The inner world of self-belief and confidence, this is something that builds with time and experience that builds our trust in ourselves. However, we can speed up this process by focusing first on the outer perception of confidence. Imagine what it would be like if you were a confident, well-respected authority in your area of expertise? What would you look like? What would it feel like to be this person? If you walk, talk and think like you're that person right now, you will start the process of becoming them.

Yes, this is just a mind trick. However, neuroscience has shown the brain doesn't know the difference between imagination and reality. This means whatever you imagine or see in your mind, the brain thinks is real. If we imagine something that doesn't exist yet, the unconscious brain works to bring it into reality because it thinks it already exists. Think crappy thoughts about life, the brain works to make this true. Think positive or life-enhancing thoughts and this becomes your reality. Now of course, just thinking happy thoughts doesn't magically make everything better, but it certainly goes a long way to helping.

The first step to building confidence is to walk, talk, think and act like the person you would be if you already had it. Which leads us to the second component of confidence - the outer perception.

The more confident the world thinks you are, the more this will be reflected back to you. This in turns builds your inner confidence leading to a greater projection of confidence externally. It becomes a virtuous circle.

When it comes to projecting confidence outwardly, there are several essential components and fundamentally it all comes down to creating your personal and business brand.

ACTION STEP

Write down a vision of yourself as a confident, expert who was known as the go-to Authority in your area

What would you see if you were this person?

What sounds would you hear?

What would you feel physically in your body?

What would it feel like emotionally?

What would you taste and smell if you were this confident expert?

The more detail you add to this exercise, the more it builds this vision in your brain and your unconscious will start to recreate it in the real world.

You Are Your Brand!

How you show up in the world creates how much you get paid. Being heart centred and basing your business on better serving your clients is one component of this. But how do we create a good first impression with people if they have never heard of you before, or have no idea of the ethics with which you run your business? How do we show up as a confident expert or Authority, so our ideal clients are attracted to work with us?

This is where your brand is so important. And we know that some of you will immediately say you're too small to have a brand; or you'll point to your logo and say this is your brand. This is all part of the misconception that exists around what a brand is, what a brand can do for you, and how to create your own brand that establishes you as an Authority in your area (which we know might be another area you're having a crisis of confidence... we'll work with you to solve this as this chapter progresses).

So, as always, let's go right back to basics in order to create something substantially more impactful than what you may have been doing up until this point… let's answer the question, "What is a Brand?"

Many people think a brand comes down to the words you use, the colour or shape of your logo, or the corporate image. Whilst these can all be important factors, a brand is much more fundamental than this...

"A brand is a promise kept"

This perspective on a brand completely changes the priorities when it comes to creating a new brand or redefining an existing brand. Ask yourself, what is the promise you and your business make? And do you always keep that promise?

Think about some major brands you know:
Nike, McDonalds, British Airways, Burberry, Ferrari, L'Oréal
Think about each company, what is the promise they make?

Take Nike for example. We all know the Nike swoosh - the tick symbol. Most people would probably also recognise their tag line: 'Just do it'
So what is Nike's promise? With big companies, this is easiest to see in their vision and mission statement:
Nike vision is "to bring inspiration and innovation to every athlete in the world." While its mission statement is to "do everything possible to expand human potential".

Compare this with their main rival Adidas… "The Adidas Group strives to be the global leader in the sporting goods industry with brands built on a passion for sports and a sporting lifestyle."

What's the main difference? Nike's vision is about others - inspiring people and expanding human potential. Adidas's vision is about themselves - to be number 1.

Regardless of whether you like Nike or Adidas better, a company driven by a guiding philosophy like Nike's is going to take different actions and use different metrics to determine if it's delivering on its promise compared to a company that is merely looking to beat its competitors.

And does it make a difference? Well, looking at the size of these two competitors, whilst they are both very successful multi-billion dollar companies, Nike is nearly twice the size of Adidas ($39billion vs $26billion in 2018).

Bringing this back to you and your business, what is the promise you're making? What is your vision and mission statement? This is the message that needs to be shared in the world. Yet, ironically, for most experts and practitioners, this message doesn't need to be written down, or incorporated in a company brochure. This is because there are two types of branding in the world... corporate Branding and Personal Branding.

Corporate branding is about your company or business, whereas Personal branding is you. An example of this is Virgin. Virgin is the corporate brand whereas Richard Branson is the Personal brand.

Both Corporate brands and Personal brands are important, but unless you are already in Phase 2 and earning over £100,000, or you have a large team of people working for you, you don't need a Corporate brand as the Personal brand is all anyone is going to pay attention to as YOU are the business. After all, in Phase One, you are doing the work with your clients. You are doing the marketing and the sales conversations. It is YOU that people are buying into, so YOU are the brand.

The good thing about this is that Personal branding is much more effective, quicker to create an impact and better to grow a community compared to a Corporate brand. This is because Personal branding is about you ....a human. And remember, human to human connection is what people crave most. Developing a corporate brand in a Phase One business is just putting a barrier between you and your potential clients and decreasing the human connection. Even large companies have realised this in recent years with many more CEO's allowing their names and personal lives to become more central to the company marketing. Think of Apple and Steve Jobs, Tesla and Elon Musk, Amazon and Jeff Bezos. All these companies have done so well partially because the leader behind the company became visible and allowed customers to feel a human to human connection.

As always, the key is to do the right things in the right order - first develop your Personal brand, become known as an authority in your area and grow from a Phase One business into a Phase Two or Three business before creating a corporate brand.

Both Personal and Corporate branding have at their core the concept of a promise kept. So, in order to build an effective Personal brand, first recognise that YOU are the brand. This means we need to explore what you stand for? What is the promise that you keep?

Some people find this challenging to answer so we're going to give you a little help to figure this out.

First, we'll give you an example from our life and then we'll have a stab at figuring out what you stand for.

In our immediate family there are three of us: Chris, Karene and Mya. As we've mentioned before, Mya is aged seven at the time of us writing this book. Several months ago, we all sat down and worked out our family motto. Just as we tell our clients in their marketing - if a 7-year-old can't understand it, then it's too complex. When Karene and I decided we wanted to create a family mission statement, as in what do we stand for as a family, we had to do it in a way that included rather than excluded Mya.

Now why do we need a family mission statement or motto, you might be wondering? In the same way that focusing on our core values in our businesses has helped direct our decision-making process and actions, leading to dramatically increased growth; we wanted this same outcome in our family. Obviously, we aren't measuring our family relationships in terms of revenue etc. However, by getting clear on what was important to all of us, we knew this would strengthen and grow all the things we already love about our family.

The words 'mission statement' or 'core values' are quite a big concept, so we went with the phrase 'family motto' as this was familiar territory for all of us. We sat round our dining room table, we all put forward words and phrases that meant something to us and after a laughter filled hour or so, we had condensed everything we had come up with down to three simple words that have become our family motto.
Courage
Curiosity
Kindness

Courage because it's ok to be afraid sometimes in life. In fact, you can't be brave unless you are afraid. The key is always having a go and getting back up when you fall down.

Curiosity because there is always more to learn, always ways to improve. Life is much more fun and rewarding if viewed through child-like wonder and questions .

And Kindness because without this, nothing else is worth having. Kindness to ourselves so we look after each other. Kindness in everything we do so we leave the people we meet and the environment we're in better than we found them. For example, we carry a bag to pick up litter whether we're going for a run around London or walking on the beach.

This motto is written out and stuck to our fridge and we all remind each other of it frequently. It is how we deal with challenging situations and it directs our behaviour and actions.

What do you stand for? What might your mission statement or motto be? Without having worked with you yet, we don't know what you do. However, we're pretty confident we can make some pretty accurate assumptions about you and your business methods since you've read this far in a book about building a heart centred business…

Your business is based on service of others
You are an expert at what you do (even if you don't fully believe that yet)
You make a difference in people's lives
You go above and beyond as a rule rather than the exception
You are well respected by others (even if you don't believe this yet either)

This makes for a pretty compelling set of values. It also means we're pretty confident you can deliver what you say in your Attraction Marketing message of Person, Problem, Solution. And that your service for your clients and solutions you could offer them wouldn't stop there. This means you're able to keep the promise you're making to your clients. Now we just have to project that to the world in a way that says this within the first three seconds of someone meeting you.

ACTION STEP

What do you want to be known for?

What three-five words would you use to describe yourself or your business?

Create your own personal and business motto or mission statement.

Make a Good Impression!

A first impression is formed within seconds of meeting new people. Once formed, this first impression is very difficult to shake, so we want to maximise the chances of it being a good one. To do this, we need to be aware of the main factors that contribute to making a favourable impression and one that gives us the credibility and projection of confidence we want to have.

First, we need to stand out. Now we know that a lot of you have already cringed when we said that. Something along the lines of, "But we don't want to blow our own trumpet" perhaps going through your mind?

Whilst we understand that sentiment (we are British after all), as Rowan Atkinson says in the comedy TV series, *Blackadder Goes Forth*, when he finds out that George is secretly a highly gifted artist and doesn't want to blow his own trumpet, "You could have let on that you had a trumpet!" If people don't notice you, or you don't come across as an expert, how will the people who need your expertise be able to find you? We want you to stand out in the right way that promotes the impression you want to make.

This is achieved through the five Pillars of Impact:

- Dress
- Posture
- Voice
- Greeting
- Energy

#1 Dress

This obviously refers to what you wear. Do your clothes promote or detract from your expertise?

Clothing is the first area to focus on because what we wear can be seen from a distance and will influence someone's impression long before they speak with you. Whether we like it or not, we all judge people instantly based on what they're wearing, so make sure you're judged the way you want to be. Here are a couple of suggestions to upgrade how you look and come across:

- Dress smarter. Most experts and practitioners do not come across as credible experts in their field because they do not look the part. If you're a bodyworker or healer and you need to wear loose fitting clothes that allow you to do your sessions, do not wear those clothes outside of your workspace, otherwise it'll look like you're wearing pyjamas.
- Putting on a suit jacket or blazer will uplift any outfit and instantly raise the appearance of professionalism. It doesn't mean you have to wear a full suit and tie but a jacket will give you credibility that

just a shirt does not. For years, in his clinic and our mentoring company, Chris wore smart jeans, a button-down shirt and a suit jacket and this was his work uniform. Smart, professional, comfortable and most of all, he felt good about it.

- Find your own style. You have to feel like yourself whilst still projecting a professional image
- Stop wearing anything with rips, tears, wrinkles, scuff marks or general tatty-ness. This doesn't mean becoming someone you're not. Just review what you wear and ask the question: does this promote the level of professionalism I want to be regarded with? Of course, in your non-work time you can wear what you like. Just be aware that you could still meet potential clients when you're out and about...just saying.
- Wear plain colours. Avoid stripes, checks or any patterns. We want to avoid distracting attention away from the face because this is where the most connection is made between people. The human eye is instantly drawn to areas of high information density and peoples gaze will focus first on the patterns you're wearing rather than your face which then delays the speed of connection.
- Avoid ostentatious jewellery for the same reason as above - it distracts attention away from the face.
- Wear Pink, Blue, Yellow or White. Not a whole suit in these colours or you'll look like a clown. However, a plain shirt or blouse, or a tie or scarf, in any of these colours will create a more immediate connection with people on the subconscious level.
- Hilary, a copywriter in south London, one of our clients bought a pink scarf to drape over various handbags, jackets and through the belt loops of her jeans on client meets. This allowed her to feel a better connection to potential clients and, in her own words, "to feel irresistible to them all as their new Copywriter".

ACTION STEP

Review your work wardrobe.

Does it reflect how you want to be seen?

What needs to be upgraded, tweaked or replaced?

What key items of clothing, such as a suit jacket, do you need to add to your wardrobe?

If needed this can be done very affordably through charity shops, or whilst on holiday in economies/exchange rates that are cheaper than our own.

#2 **Posture**

How you stand impacts how you feel and most definitely the impression that you give others. If someone is standing hunched over, shoulders drooped and looking at the floor, what would you instantly think about their mental and emotional state?

You'd think they're depressed right? And it's unlikely that you'd automatically leap from this conclusion to thinking, "Wow, they must be an expert at what they do!"

Yet, whether they are depressed or not, a lot of people adopt this posture when they go somewhere new as a way of trying to hide and avoid attention. Unfortunately, though, it attracts exactly the wrong kind of attention and has people forming a very different impression of what you might want. Furthermore, our physiology and how we hold our body also affects our mood and our mindset. When we look down, we start to feel down. And with that downward body language and perhaps inner dialogue comes inner bio-chemical changes that bring us down emotionally. By standing in a depressed posture, we will create a depressed emotional state. We'll cover this later in the Energy Pillar but take it from us, low energy will be detrimental to you and anyone around you.

So what's the alternative?
We need to stand tall. This doesn't mean stiff military posture, nor does it have any reference to how tall you are. Standing tall means standing up within yourself. Think of it more as being lifted by a bit of string attached to the top of your head. Your head raises and gently pulls the rest of your body up with it whilst remaining relaxed. By lifting the body by the head and remaining relaxed, we fully inhabit the space and we will have more presence. By looking up, lifting our head and our body; it impacts our thoughts and emotions and we release a whole new biochemistry. Endorphins to lift us even further. Look at the sky, the sun, the stars, the clouds, whatever is up there right above you right now. If it's just a blank ceiling, imagine looking through it to the heavens above. Feel that connection to all that is. There is glory, wonder and answers up there.

Walking into a new environment and meeting people for the first time with this sense of lift through your body, will change how you feel, and it will have a very different impression on the people you meet. What you communicate through your movement and your posture speaks volumes about you and your expertise long before you open your mouth and speak.

Karene recently had a great reminder of this concept whilst watching a behind-the-scenes rehearsal of the English National Ballet (ENB). One of our clients works with the dancers and knowing how much our daughter Mya loves doing ballet, gave Karene and Mya the opportunity to go and watch a rehearsal. Watching from chairs in the front of the class as the dancers worked through a particular piece from Gisele, it was truly insightful how we are always communicating through our body language whether we realise it or not. The ballerinas first do the entire run through without music and with no speaking. They are just counting the beats and practicing the moves and the stage positioning. After approximately ten run throughs,only then did they add the music. Without speaking and without music, these phenomenal dancers had spent over an hour communicating and creating a masterpiece that told a story.

Consider how you communicate through your posture and your movements.

How do you stand?
How do you move?
Are your hands relaxed by your side, stuffed in your pockets, or tightly holding your drink to your chest?
Do you fidget or have any nervous gestures or habits?
Often these traits are unconscious so it's a good idea to ask people who know you for feedback. Ask them to share how you appear to them so you can learn what you might not be aware of. Does this represent the expert you are and the authority you would like to be known as? If not, what could you do differently?

ACTION STEP

Practice standing tall by imagining a piece of string gently lifting you from the top of your head.

Breathe slowly and allow your shoulders to relax down while your head is lifted.

Pay attention to how you move and act and try to reduce any nervous or unconscious habits .

Ask five friends how you come across and for feedback about what you could do differently.

#3 **Voice**

Your voice is a very powerful tool and for many of us it is underutilised or taken for granted. Being international speakers on stages all over the world, we are only too aware of the importance and the power of voice. The voice, so much more than the words themselves, are what people connect to.

Chris once lost his voice during the first day of a three day Training we were running for a large room of business owners. I had left the event to go and collect Mya from school and Chris was presenting the last section of the day alone as he usually did. Walking Mya home from school, I received a frantic phone call from our Team saying I had to come back to the event urgently as Chris couldn't speak. Knowing it was important or they wouldn't have called me, I quickly organised a babysitter for Mya and headed back to the event, thinking it couldn't be all that bad.

When I arrived back at the event, I found Chris on stage, still presenting to our full-packed room of participants whilst struggling to even whisper through his microphone. People couldn't properly hear him, and his voice was deteriorating further every minute he continued to strain it. When you run a speaking business, this is a bit of a problem. Fortunately, with there being two of us and a great support Team behind us, we were able to get Chris off stage and look after him whilst continuing to deliver our Training for our participants. Although Chris was incredibly frustrated at being unable to help or get involved for the rest of the event, the event turned out just as successful and profitable as ever.

There were multiple lessons for all of us from this experience. One is the power of having a great team to support you in business - and a wife who can step in and save you. But perhaps the key learning was how important the voice is and how much we all take it for granted. Chris had taken a 20-minute nap in between speaking slots because he wanted to preserve his energy for the rest of the event. When he woke up, he had no voice. This had never happened to him before, there were no warning signs and he was unable to speak for the next six days.

Consider what would happen in your business if you were unable to speak? How would you continue to serve your clients? This was such a big wake up call for us, we have since spent countless hours working with voice coaches and health experts to train our voices and ensure it never happens again. Being able to talk is such a key tool in being able to communicate and build connections with people that it is not something to leave to chance.

Your voice is also key to making an impact or having people take action. If you talk in a very soft voice and you are trying to get people to take action, it is unlikely that you will be taken seriously let alone get people to move forward. Similarly, if you have a tendency to talk fast or quite high pitched, this is likely to get people excited, however, it isn't going to have them listening to you or following your command.

There are three key voices for effective communication in life and business. We need to be able to flow between these three voices depending on the situational requirements. For example, sometimes we need to speak as the authority and have people listen and follow what we say. Other times, this voice of authority would prevent us from connecting or building rapport with someone or prevent people from having fun with us. The three voices are:

The Warrior Voice: This is the voice of command and direction

The warrior voice is a deeper voice and is expressed in clipped sound bites. It doesn't need to be loud, because like all true authority, if you have to shout, you don't have the authority. Instead it is direct and very clear. There is no ambiguity or vagueness in the warrior voice.

The Heart Voice: This is the voice of connection and rapport

The heart voice is rounded, softer and warm. It's the type of voice you would use in a heartfelt conversation with a friend or someone you care for. The voice that says, "Come in, I've just put the kettle on"

The Head Voice: This is the voice of excitement and energy

The head voice is higher pitched and faster paced than the other voices. It's high energy and would be the voice you naturally use when talking to a child about an exciting activity they're going to do.

Each of these voices is very different, yet we all have access to them, whether you speak fast or slow, deep or high pitched. Everyone probably already uses these voices, but it is most likely unconscious, which means they might not be using them in the best way. The key is having awareness of the different voices and using them appropriately depending on the situation and the outcome you want to produce.

For example, we were having a family play day in Battersea Park a couple of months ago. At some point in between hanging from the monkey bars and chasing each other around the sand pit, we saw a man trying to put a lead on his very young and very excited dog. After watching him chase his dog around and around whilst repeatedly calling its name, Mya leaned towards us and said in that serious and disapproving tone only a 7-year-old can muster, "He's using his head voice. He should be using his warrior voice, or his dog isn't going to listen to him!"

Having joined us at our events where we've taught the power of voice to thousands of business owners, she had learnt about the different voices herself and was quite right. The man was using his head voice, the voice of excitement and energy, and his dog thought this was a wonderful game they were playing and so kept running away. Dogs, much like children, respond to the tone of our voice more than the words we use. Use the playful head voice when telling your children, "It's time to go to bed", and you'll end up chasing them round the house in a great game of 'Avoid the parent'. Say the same words in your warrior voice, the voice of authority, and your children will start heading upstairs to bed before they even realise they're moving.

ACTION STEP

Play with the three voices and see how comfortable each voice feels.

Become aware of how you use your voice in different situations and explore using one of the other voices to see if it creates a different result.

#4 Greeting

How you greet someone is where the impression they already have of you gets cemented. Either this is good and our greeting reinforces the positive things they're already thinking. Or it goes the other way and it confirms the less than positive impression they've formed so far.

Despite this dramatic description, greeting another human is one of the most natural things in the world and is easy to do right. Of course, what's easy to do, is easy not to do. We have met MANY people whilst networking who seem to struggle with this most basic of human interactions so it's definitely worth making sure your greeting has the impact you want it to have.

A greeting typically has three stages to be effective:

Smile

Connect

Engage

This may sound simple but as discussed, your greeting is what reinforces the impression someone has of you. Once a first impression is formed, it is very difficult to change so we want to make sure you are using every tool at your disposal to create the connections you want.

1. It all starts with a Smile

Smiles are what connect us universally with other humans. A smile tells the other person I am non-threatening, and it is safe to connect. Of course, this only refers to genuine heartfelt smiles. We can all spot the phoney, pasted on smile a mile off and it doesn't do anything to connect us to the other person. However, the real deal, where someone is smiling from the inside can light up a room and is contagious in a way that people can't help but respond in kind.

You all know the type of smile we mean. That person you pass as you walk along the street who is just smiling at life, grinning at something that has happened to them and their happiness is bubbling out of them. You don't know them, and no words are exchanged but seeing their smile, you smile too just looking at them.

We have a client like this called Olivia, who's a massage therapist and reflexologist from Bristol. Olivia is one of the most down to earth people we know, and she has a warmth and smile that's like the sun coming out. You can't spend time with her without feeling an uplift in spirit. Harnessing this in her business is one of the reasons she now is able to charge nearly five times what she was previously charging. Granted, she was woefully undercharging when we first met her and admitted she could have given up her business and earned more claiming benefits than she was earning herself. Yet her growth in confidence has meant that she can now help even more people and feel proud of earning enough to support herself and her husband.

A smile is your key to instant rapport, however, if left at a smile, nothing else happens. Think of the person walking past you in the street, you smile and move on. The next necessary step after and during a smile is connection

2. Connection starts with eye contact.

Poets have often said that the eyes are the windows to the soul. Whatever your personal belief system, it is eye contact that builds on the trust and good feelings generated by your smile. Eye contact changes a random connection into a personal one and is necessary to build rapport. Eye contact is often missing in today's world, especially in big cities where people seem to have retreated into the defensive culture of looking down and not making eye contact, usually fixated on their phone.

Eye contact will reinforce confidence in your expertise because someone who can't meet you in the eye is rarely going to be someone you trust as an Authority. It doesn't mean entering into a staring contest. However, holding someone's gaze for long enough to properly see them, and be seen, is something that connects us to people in a way that is difficult to put into words.

Something to remember, everyone has different comfort levels around eye contact, much like we all have around personal space. Some people like to stand right up close to you, whilst others almost seem to exude a space around them so no one can get close. Eye contact is the same with some people comfortable holding your gaze, whilst others prefer to only look you directly in the eye in brief glimpses. Notice the other person's preferred style and follow their lead in order to build rapport. Whilst this might mean you're not entirely comfortable; experiencing the world through the other person's habits, and at the same time making them feel more comfortable with you, is going to help you better connect and understand their perception of the world, as we discussed in the rapport building section in Chapter 4, Heart Centred Sales.

If you have exchanged smiles and made eye contact with someone and don't then do anything to further connect within three seconds, it creates a level of awkwardness, even if only unconsciously. The final piece that brings everything together is to engage.

3. Engage to build upon your connection

If you have exchanged smiles and eye contact, you have someone's attention. The natural next step is to engage them in some sort of conversation. This usually starts with an introduction of some sort and ideally physical contact. Now let's be clear, physical contact needs to be professional and appropriate for the situation. Launching in for a hug might not be the best move unless that's standard procedure in that network. Always best to go conservative first and the most universally acceptable form worldwide is a handshake. And this is also where far too many people fall down and would have been better going for a hug or not touching at all.

Physical touch builds connection far faster than anything else. As humans we crave touch and it will either make us feel safe or unsafe depending on how it's administered. Take a handshake, for example, we've all experienced various forms of this greeting that leave us with very mixed feelings.
There's the alpha male bone crushing squeeze.

The floppy hand that feels like you're trying to catch a limp fish.
The weird grasping of someone's fingers when they haven't reached out as far as you have.
The enthusiastic two-handed grasp.
Or the firm and sure shake that acknowledges you whilst keeping a respectful distance.

Think back to the worst handshakes you've experienced and ensure you never repeat them. Sometimes due to circumstances outside your control, you end up in one of those handshakes. For example, the person moved their hand awkwardly and you ended up with a partial grip. Or you were nudged by someone else just as you were reaching out and gripped too hard as a reflex. What should you do, because the longer it goes on, the worse impression you leave the other person with?

Chris has got into the habit of simply calling it for what it is. If he gives or experiences a bad handshake, he now just says directly to the other person, "I'm sorry, I'm totally doing this wrong and this is a terrible handshake. Let's start again." He then disengages his hand and re-presents it so the other person can take it and have a proper handshake. It doesn't matter if it was his fault or theirs that the first handshake was bad. He takes responsibility for it and creates another chance for a first impression, along with bringing some humour to the situation. This might seem extreme, especially to us socially uptight Brit. However, the handshake is so important to reinforcing a good or a bad impression that Chris decided to ensure it always went the way he wanted.

ACTION STEP

Practice Smile, Connect and Engage with three people every day.

Each stage of the process can be practiced separately many more times each day. However, using all three stages deliberately in the correct progression, will massively improve your skills and levels of connection with the people around you.

#5 Energy

Energy = Success

The biggest similarity between the successful people we've spent time with, is their level of energy. The multi-millionaires, the billionaires, the Olympic athletes, the serial entrepreneurs, the hugely successful people from many different walks of life... they all have huge amounts of energy and focus on what they're doing.

This energy is palpable when you meet these people and it infects everyone around them in the same way a smile does. When you meet someone with that level of focus and energy, it releases something in you too. Without necessarily realising it, you start to step up more, to aspire to more, to take bigger actions in order to achieve what you want. This is one of the key reasons we make time to meet and spend time with people who are more successful than us. We want to get uplifted and inspired by their energy. We are also those people for our community and network.

Conversely, we've all met people who just drain you. Without saying a word, they seem to suck the energy out of a room and bring you down to their level where everything is hard work and it seems like the world is against you. We said earlier that energy is infectious and this is true of both positive and negative energy. It's one of the reasons we are careful to maintain our own energy at a high level, so we benefit, rather than harm the people around us.

Your energy level is crucial to achieving anything in life or business as it will determine your entire mindset, your focus and your willingness to overcome challenges. It is also essential to creating a good impression with people and being perceived as an expert. Having a high level of energy does not mean constantly jogging on the spot or wearing Lycra to prove how fit and sporty you are. You can be standing perfectly still yet have a vibrancy and energy inside you that people can feel and connect with.

If you feel yourself flagging in energy when you're talking with someone, focus 100% of your attention on them and what they're saying. One of the secrets to having more energy is to be fully present in what you are doing and who you are with. Giving someone or something, your complete attention and energy will raise both your and their energy and result in you both having a much better conversation and experience. This works equally well for conversations as well as tasks. For example, writing these words right now, Karene and I are sitting at our dining room table and it's 3:05am on a Saturday morning. We have been writing past midnight for the past 10 days straight to complete our goal of writing this book in two weeks and fitting it around the running of our multiple businesses and being fulltime parents for Mya. Yet, despite the huge amount of effort and it being the middle of the night, we are firing on all cylinders, highly focused and enjoying the process of getting these words down on paper for your benefit. It all comes down to energy and giving the task 100% of our attention. These two things are something everyone is capable of and the more you apply them to your life and business, the better you will come across and the more you will achieve.

One method we use to gauge if our energy where we want and need it or not is to ask ourselves where we are on a scale of 0-10 (0 being practically dead and 10 feeling on top of the world). Anything less than a 9 or a 10 means we have work to do because lower energy than this is ineffective at helping other people to raise their energy or to accomplish our own goals and dreams.

We know this might seem an extreme way to look at things but just ask yourself, how important is it that you achieve what you want to achieve? If you know that your energy levels are crucial to your success, it makes sense to focus on them yes? So, here's how we use the 0-10 scale and what the different levels mean…

A self-rating of 0-5 means something is obviously wrong, such as being sick or physically unwell or feeling stressed and overwhelmed. Whatever the cause, people are usually pretty good at identifying what they need because it is quite obvious they are struggling. If left unaddressed, this level is going to be pretty non-functional at moving anything forward so the focus is on self-care and building health and energy quickly.

The real danger zone is a score of 6, 7 or 8. These numbers usually indicate you feel ok, not perfect, perhaps a bit tired or a bit under the weather but nothing serious and overall life is fine. This is the comfort zone which is where most people exist all the time. They don't feel great, but the niggles and minor upsets are not big enough to spur them into action, so they just put up with them. Which is why the comfort zone is so dangerous and ultimately so uncomfortable. It is also not an energy state that engages people or inspires them. Your energy, your passion and ultimately your effectiveness, will be lower in everything you do at this level which only reinforces the average level feelings.

Anyone rating themselves at a 7 is just hiding. 7 is the most common number to pick too rate anything and is a way of being non-commital towards something. If you ask someone to rate a restaurant, or a movie or anything at all, if they don't have any particularly strong feelings, then more often than not, they will say '7'. We have a plan that if anyone asks us to do something, we rate how we feel about it. If we say 7, we know it means we're pretty ambivalent and probably haven't rated it lower due to a sense of obligation or niceness. Our response once we realise this is to politely decline. If the score isn't above a 7, why bother doing it?

Alternately being at a level 9 or 10 means you are progressively more engaged, energised and feel on fire. You are connected with what you are doing, looking forward to what's coming and will be a beacon for other people as they are drawn to your energy and enthusiasm. Just in case you're thinking this is only for extroverts, everything we have just described could be happening under the surface as someone sits or stands quietly. It is how the person feels inside that counts

If you're not a 9 or a 10 out of 10 right now as you read this, what could you do to get to this level now? What could you do to be at this level every day because this is the level that you will positively impact the world around you and create results you've previously only dreamed of?

Ask yourself every morning, "What's my score?" Anything less than a 9, put in the work to make yourself feel better and you'll create much better results in your life and business!

ACTION STEP

Ask yourself every morning where you are on a scale of 0-10.

Make 9/10 or 10/10 your new normal and put in the work each day to make this happen.

Actively spend time each day with people on a similar energy level.

Whilst these five Pillars of Impact are focused on making a good impression on the people you meet and establishing yourself as an Authority, the more you use them, the more your confidence and self-belief will increase. Remember that everyone has doubts and concerns with whether they are good enough or not. It's part of being human. Focusing outwardly on how you interact with other people, will build the perception in the world of who you are, and it will in turn help you to start to believe it yourself.

Pay it Forward

Giving to charity is one of the most overlooked ways to both build confidence and grow a heart centred business. After all, why do we give people presents? We give presents for the joy of seeing someone else's happiness with what we've given them. At the root of doing good is that it feels good to do good. This is a reciprocal benefit or a win:win situation.

Feeling good about what you do will give you confidence in yourself. It will also reflect in your business because your clients will know that there is more to you than just getting another client and making money.

An example of this is that Chris has worked closely with the charity Teens Unite Fighting Cancer for years now. He was a Trustee for the charity for 3 years and now runs a committee working directly with the teens to explore how the charity can continue to improve how it supports them.

Giving back to teenagers going through cancer has been hugely important to me ever since my own experience of having cancer aged 16 and 17. Whilst cancer, and the subsequent chemotherapy etc sucked, and I wouldn't wish it on anyone. It is also one of the best experiences of my life and I am truly grateful for it. Cancer set me on the path I am on today. Without it, I don't know if I would have discovered my passion for helping people overcome challenges, or improving their health and their lives.

Obviously, whilst I was going through it and experiencing chemo (losing all my hair, constant nausea and my body weight plummeting to less than 8st or 50kg) I was a long way from the grateful position I am today. This mindset and my realisations came much later. However, it could have come about sooner if I had had support or guidance to open my mind to what cancer had taught me about myself and what therefore could be now possible.

I wanted for years to help others transform their traumatic experience into the gift it had turned out to be for me. But I was so financially stuck and working so many hours trying to stay afloat, that I didn't have the time or the money to do anything. One of the first things I did, once I grew my clinic business over six figures was to start researching to find a cancer charity to support. I didn't want to just give money to a research charity because although these charities do great work, I wanted to make a difference for the individual with cancer rather than just cancer itself. This is when I discovered Teens Unite

Fighting Cancer founded by Karen Millen and Debbie Pezzani. They don't do any research or work to reduce cancer. Instead they provide a community where teenagers with cancer can just be normal and perhaps most importantly, they provide on-going community once you go into remission.

Think about it, being a teenager is a pretty crazy period of life. Hormonal changes, mind and body growth, changing social dynamics - being a teenager has enough challenges and then you throw cancer into the mix. You're suddenly thrust into a world of tests, treatments, stigma and challenge. Dealing with all that is hard enough but then when the doctors give you the all clear, tell you you're in remission and to just get on with your life, this is where a lot of the challenges become even greater. How do you go back to being 'normal' after something like that? Forget the fact that as a teenager, you don't even know what normal is. You've just been through something that, no matter how hard they try, none of your peers can understand. No one really understands the worry about whether it'll come back, or how self-conscious you might be around how your body, voice, appearance etc may have changed. The truth is that any traumatic experience ages you. Being forced to confront life and death situations forces us to grow up no matter how old we are. To experience that as a teenageer just increases the difference between you and everyone else around you.

This is where Teens Unite comes in - they provide a community who understand what you're going through when you're experiencing cancer because they've been there themselves. And also it's a community for when all other support stops and you're told that you're 'normal' again. Providing activities, support, skills training, Teens Unite allows these teenagers to just be normal, to not have to explain or justify their illness in any way. And this was exactly the type of charity I wanted to support. When I found them on Google, I arranged to meet them asap. Whilst this of course led to donating money ourselves and raising donations from other people; by far the most rewarding aspects of our engagement has been the work I have done with the teens themselves. Providing mentoring, running motivational events and generally joining in the activities the charity provided for the teens, fulfilled me in ways that my work in clinic didn't, even though I was helping clients overcome pain and health challenges everyday. I would come home from a Teens

Unite activity or motivational day I'd say to Karene, I almost felt guilty because I was so inspired, so 'filled up' and so grateful to be working with them that it felt an unfair exchange.

Bringing this charity component into our businesses then added another dimension. Once they heard that a percentage of our revenue was being donated to Teens Unite, our clients started getting interested and a lot of them started donating either time, money or both to the charity. It has led to a deeper connection and conversation with our clients about what causes matter to us and to them. Revealing a vulnerability from my past as a strength and reason to contribute to others in the same situation opened the doorway for our clients to connect with their own journeys and explore what they had learnt and how it could similarly benefit others.

On a financial level, donating tens of thousands pounds ourselves and raising more through our network and our businesses, we've made a difference for the charity and the teens. However, it has also unexpectedly benefited us. Either through direct connections and people who became clients; or by conversations and collaborations with people we've met through the charity who have upgraded our mindset and provided us with inspiration to do and be more.

The fulfilment, the inspiration, the connection with others and a bigger purpose, the pride of being able to contribute; all these components lead to a greater connection with what you're doing in your business and a greater confidence in who you are as a person. This will come across to everyone you meet and reinforce the positioning of you as an expert and an authority in your area.

Our only regret regarding charity is that we didn't connect with the concept and start contributing sooner. We let our previously limited mindset around time, money and our personal circumstances block us from being able to contribute. No matter what stage you're at in your business, find a cause you're passionate about and connect with it. Give what you can financially. Ask other people to donate. And most importantly, try to give your time and directly meet the people you're supporting. It will transform a nice action into something altogether more powerful and lead you to step into a much greater reality for yourself and others.

Katherine, one of our clients from Amsterdam who we mentioned earlier, found exactly this in her life. After creating success using our systems and scaling her Osteopathic and Physiotherapy business to multiple locations, she started to connect more with what was important to her and discovered this was working with children. Initially, this started as opening a specialist children's clinic in London, however, it rapidly progressed into organising medical visits to Africa. She's now exited her previous business entirely, and works remotely with clients in order to spend more time with her family and charity projects which have progressed to building hospitals and training local people in medical techniques so they become less reliant on foreign aid.

ACTION STEP

Spend some time thinking about what causes you are passionate about. What difference would you like to see or make in the world outside of your business?

Find some charities or organisations working in this area and explore how you could get involved and support them.

Commit to giving time, money or both regularly.

Let your clients know about your charity/cause and why it is important to you.

Comparative Thinking

This is perhaps one of the most damaging things we humans do to ourselves. We compare ourselves to others and it NEVER ends well.

Our view of ourselves can be quite low. Perhaps we don't weigh what we want to, or we're not as successful as we'd like to be, or we have negative and unkind thoughts about others and ourselves. There are countless reasons why we might not be happy with whom we are. The reality, of course, is that we judge ourselves far more harshly than we would ever judge anyone else. Let's face it, if our best friends ever spoke to us the way we speak to ourselves inside our own heads, we would definitely no longer be best friends!

We never let on to other people though what we really feel about ourselves. To everyone else, we promote the best version of ourselves. We only share the positive things and keep the self-doubt and negative aspects locked away in our heads for only us to know about. It's why we do our hair and put on make up before leaving the house. We want other people to see only what we are comfortable with them seeing.

This is the same for every human being alive and we all know this is the case. Yet when we look at others, we allow ourselves to judge the worst aspects of ourselves against the best image the other person is portraying of themselves. Despite knowing that this best image may also be covering up the same type of negative thoughts, feelings and anxieties that we're having, we still allow ourselves to make this unfair comparison.

This is why so many people get caught up in variations of 'keeping up with the Joneses'. For example, it might be that you're completely fine not skiing. You've never missed it or wanted to go and you're not even fond of the cold. Yet when you meet someone who's just back from a skiing holiday talking about how great it was, you immediately feel bad that you've never been, that you don't have the money to go, and that you've probably left it too late to start skiing anyway. I mean, doesn't everyone start when they're a child?

We see this with our clients all the time. They see lots of people posting their successes on our Private Mentorship Forum, such as:
"Doubled my income!"
"Best month ever!"
"Closed 3 new clients today!" etc etc
Seeing regular successes like this, automatically triggers some people to judge their own progress. It doesn't matter whether it is a fair comparison or not, the judgement is automatic. For example, it might be that someone doesn't even have any staff or associates. But if they see something like "Reduced my hours, expanded my Team and made an extra £75,000" such as our client David posted recently, it's all too easy for them to think, "I'm working more and not less and I don't have a team, maybe I should give up!"
Or, "My income hasn't gone up as much as his has. I can't be as good as him and I must be doing something wrong"

Comparing ourselves with others is completely pointless as we always come off worse. Comparisons typically dent our confidence and motivation and leads to a decreased effectiveness and focus. This then reinforces the negative opinion we had of ourselves because now we are achieving less. This obviously will have an effect on your confidence and how you come across to the people around you and you continue to spiral downwards...

Recognise we are all running our own race. No one's journey is the same and we all have different challenges. We cannot know what is going on behind the scenes of someone's success and don't have enough information to make any comparisons accurate. Far better to focus on whether you are on track on your own journey to make the progress you want to make in each area of your life.

We truly believe that making progress is one of the key components of happiness. It doesn't matter how big or small that progress is - as long as it feels like you're moving something forward, you'll feel better about it. Well, at least you will until you compare yourself to others.

I recently shared with Karene a conversation I'd had with one of our clients who is going through a bad patch. She's coping with a LOT of family drama, health concerns and past trauma. All leading to her being unable to work or even get out of bed sometimes. This is obviously having a knock on effect on her business and finances. She was concerned she was not succeeding in the same way the rest of our clients were and from reading about their successes, it reinforced her feeling that she was failing.

Along with various other strategies and bits of advice, one of the things I told this client was to view progress differently. She wasn't in any state to start setting bigger goals such as going networking or making lots of phone calls. Instead, I got her to focus on what she could do. Perhaps just getting out of bed in the morning when the alarm clock went off was enough. With where she was at the time, this was a big deal. Doing this each day would be progress. This could then lead to other things and step by step she could work her way out of where she was. Whilst not the cause of the challenges she was dealing with, comparative thinking had kept her feeling less than her problems rather than bigger than them and so she had stayed stuck longer than she might have otherwise.

ACTION STEP

Notice when you are comparing yourself to others.

Notice how you feel when you do this
and how long this feeling lasts.

Notice how effective you are while you feel like this.

Make a conscious choice to stop comparing yourself and
catch yourself and others if you notice it happening.

Chapter Highlights

- ✓ Your Brand is a promise kept. Build your Personal Brand and determine what you stand for. What is your vision/mission?
- ✓ Confidence is an inside job built up by how the world views you. Walk, talk and think like the person you want to be
- ✓ Five Pillars of Impact: Dress, Posture, Voice, Greeting, Energy. Focus on what you could tweak or upgrade in each of these areas to better create the impression you want people to have of you.
- ✓ Pay it forward. Find a charity or project you are passionately committed to and explore how you could support it. Let your clients know why this matters to you and be open about your vulnerabilities so they can explore this for themselves in their own lives.
- ✓ Comparative Thinking is the road to unhappiness. Remember to run your own race and let other people run theirs. Focus each day on making progress, no matter how small and you'll feel happy while also creating the life and business you really want.

Chapter 7
Sexy Systems
How to Free up your Time and Increase your Income!

"The bad news is that time flies, the good news is that you're the pilot."
– Michael Altsuler

How Can You Have More Time?

Wanting more time is a universal need so how can you have more of it? How many times have you said to yourself or a loved one, "I'm sorry, I don't have time"? The key reason that we don't have time is because we fail to prioritise.

When we look at the challenge of time most business owners face, this is primarily created by the fear we all have of missing out. This Fear Of Missing Out has become so ubiquitous that we even have an acronym for it: FOMO. People become unconsciously terrified if they say "No" to something or someone. They might miss out. This could be a missed client, a missed opportunity, a missed connection or anything at all. It all comes down to a fear that if you miss out on something, you might miss out on being part of the tribe. Remember the fundamental fear in all of us, coming from caveman times, is the fear of rejection? If you're not part of the tribe, it makes us feel we are at risk of dying, so we tend to say, "Yes" to everything to avoid missing out. Knowing when to say "No", however, is a critical step to free up time or make time.

How do you know what to say No to? It's all about priorities. And how do we set priorities? We get clear on what you're doing things for, or by connecting to your "Why". When you are clear on "Why" you are doing something. you can more easily know what will move you forward towards your goals, what is a distraction and what will support someone else's goals. You will then be able to make conscious decisions about how you are spending your time. This will allow you to prioritise and therefore free up your time.

As a set of action steps:

- Get clear on your "Why" and your goals.
- Say Yes to things that move you towards your goals.
- Say No to things that don't.

Before I met Chris, working took up an awful lot of my time. There were a number of years when I didn't even take holidays. In fact, I remember once I was forced to take a month off, as I had accumulated so much holiday leave and had to use it or lose it. I was a classic workaholic. I was also hiding because I was young and I had a large amount of responsibility and thought I was going to be 'found out'. I was also convinced I didn't have enough time to plan things. Holidays, social activities, relationships, were always an afterthought or because it was easy.

I look back at the young me and realise that in many ways I was fearless and in others, I was completely terrified. There was an awful lot of self imposed, as well as very real pressure to deliver on some very critical projects. Not exactly life and death, however, it felt that way at the time. My coping mechanisms were a combination of running, making myself sick and out working everyone else. Even now, I am reluctant to share this as I would rather maintain the image that I've done everything perfectly all of my life.

I can paint the happy rosy picture of life then; travelling around the world in business and first class, dinner at the House of Lords, tea at 10 Downing St, corporate hospitality at Twickenham, Wimbledon and seeing Madonna. I had some amazing experiences and opportunities. And I was also deeply unhappy at this time and working all hours in order to deliver on the expectations everyone, including me, had of me.

The only thing that I thought I had control over was my body. I would run every morning telling myself I was having some 'me' time when really it was just punishment. Similarly, I would socialise and then go home and very privately make myself sick. I'd like to say this was a short period of time, however, this lasted years and years. I felt trapped not being able to tell anyone, as I thought this would bring down all the walls I had tried so hard to build. Even now, when things are particularly emotionally difficult, I can recognise the impulse to still be 'perfect'. I am not sure it ever goes away, however, I definitely wouldn't consider making myself sick or punishing myself through exercise anymore. I have developed much healthier coping mechanisms and far better relationships and I genuinely love myself now.

When I met Chris, things had already started to change as I had realised I couldn't continue at the same intensity and more importantly, didn't want to. I had discovered yoga, and I was still super intense however, I was starting to be the real me. Ironically, in the journey to becoming a serial entrepreneur, I probably work harder now than I did in a job. My mother reminds me of this often. She also knows how different it is, how much more I enjoy it all and how rewarding life and work now are. I couldn't have possibly imagined how much better life could be and we're just getting started really.

When Mya arrived in our life, my focus completely changed. I wanted and needed to spend my time with her. This meant I became much more focused with my time. She was my motivation and the reason I wanted something different. She was and continues to be my "Why". I take her to school and pick her up almost every day. Even when we are running Training events, we have engineered things to allow me to be 'mummy' and business owner.

In addition to Mya, I have also discovered my ambition to do more and be more and have learnt to be super time efficient. Sure, I still waste time and there are days when I don't feel productive. However, more often than not, I get to do what I want to do and more importantly, I support other people in doing this too. That is the best gift.

One of our client's, Peter, a fertility expert in South England, has a different story however he also highlights the importance of knowing your 'Why". He had lost his love for what he did and it had become a job. He was finding working with clients very draining and had a part-time job because he wasn't earning enough. When we worked through his values and he reconnected with his "Why", he created a balanced lifestyle that he truly enjoys. He's fallen back in love with working with his clients and has grown his business enough to give up his part-time job.

Being clear about your "Why" allows you to fit in more, because you are reducing your decision-making time. This allows you to be hyper-focused. When you aren't clear on "Why", you don't know when you say no. You might agree to things that take up time which leave you feeling like you haven't done anything, or you have been unproductive. You might do things that you should be leaving for others to do. What this is really a reflection of, is that you haven't done what is important to you.

If you are clear on your "Why", you can choose how you spend your time appropriately. For example, if part of your Why is 'making a difference', then doing things for other people and helping them achieve their goals and dreams will fulfill you at the same time. It is very rewarding to support others in the achievement of their dreams. So much so that Chris and my businesses are built around just that.

Do you know what you "Why" is? Are you clear on what motivates you and what you are working or living for? If you are, awesome. It will be very easy for you to now get clear on your priorities and free up your time. If not, then use the following Action Step to get clear.

ACTION STEP

How to discover your personal reason Why!

Find a quiet place with no distractions - a setting that allows you to get in touch with what's important to you.

Take your time with this process. Don't rush through it. Your personal reason Why, may come to you in an instant or you may find you want to think about it over time.

1. a) Ask yourself "What is my reason for wanting a successful business?

   Think about:

   What would you do if you never had to work again?

   What if you had all the time in the world to spend exactly as you wanted?

   How would your life be different if money were no object?

   b) Write down everything that comes up

2. a) Ask yourself again, 'What is my deep-down core reason for wanting to be successful? Look deeper

   b) Write down everything that comes up

3. a) Ask yourself again, going deeper, "What is my innermost, heartfelt reason for wanting to be successful?

   b) Write down everything that comes up

Continue to ask yourself the question again and again going deeper within yourself each time until your personal reason why is crystal clear.

Once you are clear on your 'Why', you will be able to prioritise your time management. Sure, you can force yourself into being productive to a degree through scheduling and other time management tools. However, how many times have you created a schedule, only for it to be ignored and things to take longer than expected? Times when the schedule just doesn't seem to work? We come across this a lot with our clients. Once they have connected with their 'Why' however, it isn't so much an endless battle with time. Perhaps it is now just a small skirmish from time to time.

Unreasonable Deadlines

We're not going to say it's always easy to stick to schedules, as it seems to be the human condition (or perhaps just ours) to try and do too much. Writing this book, for example, has been a major priority for us. However, we don't have the luxury of locking ourselves away to write it. We have a child, extended family to support, multiple businesses to run, people to manage and hundreds of clients to serve. To make this book happen, we had to make time. This resulted in three weeks of very late night/early mornings, fitting in our writing around all of our other commitments, and we got it done. Looking back, what made this happen was single-minded focus and really connecting with what this book means to us, to our business and, most importantly, what it might mean for you, the reader. This is how we managed to fit in what was needed to meet the unreasonable and unrealistic deadlines we set.

Speaking of deadlines, setting unreasonable and unrealistic deadlines can be a great way of creating time and fitting in impossible tasks. When we say unreasonable and unrealistic this refers to what most people would say when you tell them your goal. In life or business, if you only do what is reasonable or realistic, you are guaranteed a result of mediocrity at best. For example, one in five businesses fail in the first year and 50% of those businesses that survive year 1, fail before their fifth year. If you were starting a business today, this is a realistic and a reasonable assumption. Yet, our clients regularly create unreasonable results, precisely because they set 'unrealistic goals'.

Ruth, the Pilates Teacher we mentioned earlier, is a great example of this. In the first four months of going full time in her business, she had earned over £7,000 in a single month twice. Ruth's business success is unrealistic if you don't have proven systems to follow and a drive or "Why" to make it happen.

Our actual goal for writing this book was to complete it in one week. This was the big unreasonable and unrealistic goal that drove us to put the necessary effort in. However, we failed. It took us two weeks to write and one week more to self-edit what we wrote before sending it to our publisher. We failed to hit our target, yet achieved so much more than many people thought possible. The late nights, the extra stresses and challenges were all totally do-able because writing this book was an exciting process completely connected to our passion to help more businesses better serve more people. What goal would motivate you enough to be unreasonable and expect more from yourself?

> ACTION STEP
>
> Is there a task where you could set an unreasonable and unrealistic deadline to create momentum and get something done?

We know that setting unreasonable deadlines isn't for everyone and in fact, some people find it completely debilitating when they fail to achieve lofty goals. Another way of creating more time is about making it easy to make good choices. We tend to talk about things being both easy to do and easy not to do. If you want to skew your choices toward good, make the bad choices harder to do.

Make Good Choices Easier

The 30 second rule is a great example of this. When it takes you more than 30 seconds to organise something to do, unless you really want to do it, then you probably won't. We instead, opt for what we might consider to be a less good choice. One of Karene's mentors had a great strategy to play guitar more and give up TV.

It was easy after a long day to come home and turn on the TV, however, he really wanted to play more guitar and it wasn't happening. Following the principles of making the preferred choice easy, he removed the batteries from the remote control and put them in another room. He also made sure that his guitar was out and immediately accessible. Then, when he arrived home after a long day ready to 'relax', it was far easier to do this with his guitar than rummage around looking for batteries to watch TV. Eventually, playing the guitar became his new habit and he didn't have to hide the batteries any more.

What might you apply this to? What are you not doing, despite your best efforts?

Similarly, what distractions or 'bad choices' that don't move you forward, could you make more difficult? How can you make sure that the 'good choice' wins? For example, getting your running/exercise gear out the night before so you're ready to go in the morning. Moving the alarm clock across the room so you have to get out of bed to turn it off. Removing social media apps from your phone so you have to access them via your browser or only when you're at a computer or similar. The possibilities are endless. What might this look like for you?

ACTION STEP

Where might you be able to stack the odds in favour of your good choices or something you really want to do? Where might you be able to make distractions or bad choices more challenging?

Being More Effective

Another way to create more time is to be more effective in doing tasks. Here are some simple things that might allow you to do things differently so you can fit more in when you perhaps thought you didn't have time.

- Listen to a piece of music on repeat whilst you are doing a task. This allows your brain to focus differently. You may have heard references of people being in 'The Zone' where they are hyper productive. This is one way of artificially creating your own 'Zone' particularly if you aren't in the mood and just need to get something done. Try this with email or a proposal or admin you'll be surprised how effective it can be. Chris and I have done this a lot. We don't have a soundtrack or song we have used exclusively in the writing of this book, however, there are many other projects where we do.

- Leave books in the loo/washroom. Ladies, where you always sit down, if you even just read half a page every time you visited the bathroom, you'd be surprised how many more books you can get through. Gentlemen, the same principle applies, it just requires more dexterity or simply sitting down.
- Take regular breaks. Movement, change of position, fresh air etc will all increase your effectiveness and focus.
- Make sure you are managing your time. Most tasks will expand to fit the time you have available. If you limit the time, guess what, the task takes less time.
- What can you combine? Perhaps you can listen to an audio book whilst commuting or cooking or cleaning? Can you have walking meetings to get movement into a work activity and also achieve an exercise goal? Chris and I have a daily walking date after we drop Mya off at school where we walk to Hyde Park, do a lap around the Serpentine Lake and walk back home. Whilst enjoying being outside and exercising, we use it as our planning time for both life and business. As I write this now, I am standing at our breakfast bar, marching on the spot whilst typing to get in my steps for the day.
- Speed things up. Any audiobooks can be listened to at 1.5 times their normal speed and you can still take it all in, for some authors who talk particularly slow this can even be 2.5 times. For one of our clients, Kelly, she has trained herself to listen to most things at 6 times their original speed. It is amazing how much she gets through. Personally, we find this a little fast as we tend to sync our breathing rate with that of the presenter and 6 times speed makes us a little anxious and slightly hyperventilating. However, how you listen and absorb information is a skill that can be learnt just like everything else.
- Set things up the night before so you have more time when things might be tight. For example, getting kids to school and yourself out the door in the morning can be challenging. What can you do the night before to make it easier?
- What can you prepare in advance? Snacks, a big jug of water, easy to cook or heat up dinner for weeks when there is a lot going on? Make it easy to make good food and dietary choices.

- Schedule your time. This is one of the biggest mistakes we see with clients who believe being self-employed is all about freedom. They don't set up regular working hours and they don't have structure around when they will meet with clients or not. Their diary's become so unstructured, they don't have time to fit things in and end up wasting a lot of time. One of our clients, Alexandra, is an Osteopath and Yoga Teacher. By connecting with her "Why" and looking at how she structured her working life, she has freed up a significant amount of time just by being clear about her client facing days vs time working on the business. This has created better boundaries with her clients and now has time to pursue more projects she is passionate about, such as training other Osteopaths how to use Yoga to help their patients..
- Put a timer on when you go onto social media. We get it, sometimes you have to be on social media for marketing activities, if that is the phase of business you are in. Yet remember, social media platforms are set up to distract you and keep you on them, so that they can attract more advertisers. Limit your exposure by setting clear time boundaries to bring you out of the social media trap. Also remove Facebook from your phone. Karene did this and apart from freeing up a lot of storage on her phone, it has meant that she has to make the conscious choice to check things, rather than just reacting to notifications.
- Turn off your notifications. Those little red numbers or beeps or vibrations will distract you, so turn them off. The world and people existed without the speed of response that we now offer. Re-educate your clients around when you check your email or respond to posts etc and then stick to it. This means you plan where you are spending your time rather than being at the whims of your notifications and other people's time requirements. By all means have a method where you will respond to urgent requests, however, give yourself some control over your time. It is very liberating.

You now have a lot more options for making time. How can you implement some of the items on this list above and free up some time? What could you do more of, or what could you start doing that you may have previously thought you didn't have time for? As humans one of the ways that we feel successful and happy is by making progress. So get progressing!

ACTION STEP

Using the list above as inspiration, write down three ways you are going to help yourself create more time for what you really want to be doing?

Even with more strategies, some of you might still struggle with time, so what else might be going on for you? For example, do you know what you are going to do with any extra time that you create? If you aren't clear what you want more time for, you will never have it. We all get 86,400 seconds in a day and we get a do-over every single day. Still so many people end up wasting time. Have you ever written down what you would do if you had time? If you haven't then now is a good time to.

ACTION STEP

Write down all the things that you believe that you don't have time for.

How might you make time for these things?

What do you want to do that you aren't currently doing?

What would having more time freedom really feel for you? Just like money, sometimes it is our beliefs around time that stop us from having more. Do you have any negative thoughts, actions or relationship habits around time? What are your stories around time? Would having more time and not being busy make you anxious?

This is something Chris recognised in himself over the last couple of years. He noticed he wasn't allowing himself the time to sit and read books, because he felt guilty to be just sitting 'doing nothing' when there were so many important things requiring his attention. With this mindset, having more time would just make him busier rather than less. With more time, he would find more things to do because of the drive to be 'busy'. So the key, as Chris discovered, isn't actually to just create time freedom. It is to create the mindset around time that will allow you to enjoy it the way you want to.

To understand the mindset or stories you might have around 'time' consider the following:

Are you perhaps constantly repeating negative phrases like:

- "I just don't have enough time"
- "I can't seem to find time to…"
- "I wish I had more time to…"

Are you perhaps attached to some more negative thoughts and behaviours around time including:

- You might see people talking about all the things they get done thinking, "Well, it's alright for them..."
- You might have a habit of planning out your week and then never looking at your diary as it's too scary
- You might have a habit of spending time doing the things you enjoy and then you are rushed doing the things that have to happen. This then reinforces the idea that what you have to do isn't a 'fun' activity.
- You might have a habit of putting everything on a to do list, regardless of whether it has to happen this week or not. This will artificially keep you stuck in overwhelm and repeating patterns and thoughts that whilst unpleasant, are perhaps familiar and therefore normal.
- You might have a habit of talking down how much time you have available, because if you had time it might mean you aren't 'busy' and therefore you aren't 'successful'
- You might have a habit of sharing 'misery stories' with your friends, where you talk about how bad things are rather than exploring what might be possible?

- You might leave everything to the last minute to create artificial deadlines to make you do things. Whilst effective it means periods of massive pressure and time scarcity.

You have now read about the power of your mind to create your relationship with money in Chapter 4, Money Mindset. Do you think that perhaps the same could be true of time? What does your external world look like around time? Do you have mountains of things piling up that you aren't getting done? What do you think is going on in your internal world if this is the case?

ACTION STEP

Write down all the stories and habits that you currently have around time. Based on what we've shared in this section what can you change?

Leverage Your Time

When you first start a business, you end up doing everything, or almost everything, because you either haven't got anyone else to do it or you can't afford them even if they do exist. Once you start earning money and getting busier, it is important to revisit this so you can free up more time. As a recovering perfectionist, I am all too familiar with the trap of thinking, "I'll just do it because it will be quicker than explaining it to someone and I will do a better job anyway" Whilst this may be true, Chris often reminds me that this is hampering our growth and will keep me stuck doing everything.

Just imagine, someone does some of your tasks 80% as well as you do, and you get 100% of your time back. This means in the time that you would otherwise be doing everything, you can instead focus on the things that are the most fun and earn you the most money. This means you can pay other people to do even more of the tasks that are better suited to someone else.

If this sounds like a utopian ideal right now and you can't imagine it happening, chances are you need to start letting go. If you don't, you will at some point burn out, lose the fun in what you do, feel overwhelmed, stifle your growth, or all of the above.

Roger, an Osteopath client of ours, was earning 6 figures in his business in Leominster, and recently shared with us that letting go and leveraging himself better, has been one of his biggest revelations. He was very busy and didn't realise that just being busy didn't equate to a successful business. He thought he needed help to make himself even busier in order to earn more money. Being a devoted parent with three young children, this wasn't an ideal solution. In working with us, he discovered a different way of thinking and leverage, meaning he can earn more, have more time to spend with his family, have a clearer direction and use his current business as a stepping stone to something much bigger and more successful than he thought possible.

So, if you need to be like Roger and let go of being busy, a quick and easy way of working out what you could start giving to someone else to do is to create a "Not to Do" list. What are all the things you do that you either don't need to do, don't enjoy, or could pay someone else to do at a rate that is less than what you earn working with your clients?

For example, ironing. You can find people to do this in your home, or a pick-up and delivery service that would remove this job from you for a quite low level investment. What could you be doing instead of ironing? If you saw an extra client each week instead of doing the ironing, how much better off would you be?

Or perhaps for you, it's your accounts. If you are in business and you don't have a bookkeeper, you need one. When we had dinner with Robert Kiyosaki of *Rich Dad, Poor Dad*, the key piece of advice he had for any business owner was to get a bookkeeper. He views a bookkeeper as so essential and something that so many people neglect to do, that in the couple of hours we spent with him, he must have said this at least 8 times. There are great tools out there that automate receipt capture and put it directly into your account software etc, however, you will still need to reconcile things. This is where a bookkeeper comes in and these people love doing this kind of detailed number crunching work that you might hate.

It is great to see people really enjoying what they do because they will do a better job. If there is anything that you are lukewarm about at best, put it on your "Not to do" list and spend your time doing something else. When you have a collection of things being taken care of by other people, it is amazing how much time you will get back. For us, this list is always expanding and currently includes:

- Cleaning and ironing
- Housekeeping tasks such as changing the sheets on the bed and doing the dishes
- Bookkeeping and accounting
- Printing or shredding
- Washing the car
- Booking holidays and booking any travel
- Picking up and dropping off dry cleaning
- Grocery Shopping
- Tenant finding for our rental properties
- Gardening at rental properties
- Handyman jobs
- Organising Marketing events
- Finding venues for training and events
- Appointment booking
- Phone answering services
- Cooking meals in advance

This is by no means an exhaustive list, however, it does give you a flavour of the type of things you might put on your list to outsource. Also, it highlights you might not be able to find a single person to do all the tasks. For example, cleaning and housekeeping tasks such as washing the dishes and changing the beds, we have sorted with a cleaner/housekeeper who comes three times a week. For appointment bookings, however, we have an automated online solution people can access 24/7 to book into Chris, our Team or my diary within our set availability. Similarly, grocery shopping, I can do on my computer, it is delivered on a day when my cleaner visits and is all put away without me having to be involved.

What does your list look like? Once you have created your not-to-do list, look at what the best option for you is to get these tasks completed whilst still managing them. Remember, even with someone or something else doing your tasks, it will still require management and oversight to be successful. This is a key mistake many people make. They are so excited to get rid of doing something themselves, they just dump the task on someone and run. Even with someone else doing the task, you are still responsible for it being completed the way you want. You might need to check in with said person, or set up rules for how to deal with exceptions, or create some other form of guidance to ensure you benefit from the experience rather than regretting it.

ACTION STEP

Create a Not To Do List.

Write down all the things that someone else could do better or more cheaply than you, or just the things that you don't particularly like.

Work out whether these would be better done by someone else or in a different way.

Another way to understand what other people could do within your life and business is to get clarity on what you do now and also want you want to be able to do.

The easiest way to start understanding what you do and what you are spending your time on is to keep a time diary. Just like if you were going to a Personal Trainer or Nutritionist and they asked you to write down everything that you eat in a week in a food diary. You need to understand everything that you do in a week. The good, the bad and the ugly and how long each item takes. How long are you just checking Facebook? Or cleaning? Or playing with the kids? Or doing the dishes? We might have a feeling about how long we spend doing these things, however, it is important to get clarity. Once you know how long things are taking and how you are actually spending your week you can start to do something about it.

ACTION STEP

Create a Time Diary.

Depending on whether you are a paper and pen kind of person or you like everything online, the principles are the same:

1. Choose a week to record, if you are prone to putting things off start right now wherever you are in the week (for some of you just getting started without planning etc will be a breakthrough so just do it).
2. Start with the date at the top of the page and start recording. (Lawyers or anyone who typically bill by the hour or in six minutes intervals will already be used to this). If you can carry around a book/your phone notes page, note when you start a new task or activity, when do you start and when do you stop? Alternatively, at the end of the day, go back through your calendar and record what you have done and some rough timings.
3. Do this for seven consecutive days, this way you can record weekdays and weekends, so you have a better idea of what a typical day looks like.
4. At the end of the week list out the discrete tasks and add up the time that you spent on them.
5. Work out the rough breakdown of:
    a. work/business, family and social activities and chores.
    b. Within Business/Work see whether you can split this into Marketing, Sales and Delivery .
6. This data will give you a great start for working out where you are spending your time and what might need to change. You should be spending 60% of your time on your main focus. If you're not, then you know what will need to change.

7. Ask yourself the following questions:
    a. Am I happy with this mix of time?
    b. Is there anything that I am doing that someone else could do better/cheaper?
    c. What makes me happy and how can I do more of that?

Creating Leverage by Building Your Associate Team

By keeping a time diary, you will have a better understanding of what exactly you do with your time. Clarity, as we have previously mentioned, is very powerful. Armed with this knowledge, you can create your outsourced team to free up your time. The next step is how you can leverage your time with your clients and build up your client service team. Now we get it, not all of you will want to build a team, or you might not think it is possible. As you get busier with clients, if you don't want to have a team, then there are still several options available that allow you to continue to grow such as a waiting list, increasing prices and programme options, and referring to other similar businesses to name just a few. However, most people, at some point, benefit from building some form of team.

One of our clients, Penelope, a Physiotherapist specialising in long term rehab work for stroke victims, has grown her practice to an extent that she has had to start turning people away and wanted a different option. She's now exploring the choice of whether to just refer people to other practitioners she knows, likes and trusts; or whether she wants to build a team of associates, even if in a loose association so she still manages her client experience and levels of serving. This is still a work in progress for Penelope, however, it is a nice challenge to have, right?

In our experience, there are three different ways of taking on associates to create a team-based delivery structure in your business. Each of these will have a variety of advantages and disadvantages. However, each of these individually could be their own chapter, so we're only going to cover off the basics here.

Percentage Associates

Firstly we have a percentage arrangement, which is a very traditional approach used in the health industry. The idea being that revenue from clients is shared between the business owner and team members based on a pre-agreed percentage split, such as 50:50, or 60:40 etc. If the associate doesn't have any clients, there is nothing to share and therefore nothing to pay them. This makes it low cost and can be set up very simply. Although, please make sure to use proper contractual agreements otherwise it will lead to challenges in the future.

As a business owner, whether or not you make money from this arrangement is usually dependent on how busy you get the team member. Typically, associates in a percentage agreement will assume that work and new clients will be 'given' to them rather than generated by their own efforts. It is key therefore, that the business has enough work and a solid marketing system such as Attraction Marketing to get the new person going.

We notice a lot of business owners adopt this model too soon because they have an extra room and assume that the extra pair of hands will be self motivated to get busy. Unfortunately, too often this isn't the case and just leads to resentment on both sides. If you have a spare room a much better option is to rent out room and continue to focus on building your business whilst getting a regular and guaranteed income from the room.

Renting room space is the basis of Loris, one of our client's, entire business in Farnham. She herself is passionate about wellbeing, and is studying massage. She bought a business with studio space and multiple treatment rooms which she rents out to other practitioners and teachers. She does offer her rental clients some marketing support, however, the relationships are set up very clearly that the room renter is responsible for marketing their own business. This is something not often communicated effectively and is perhaps one of the reasons renting space to other experts can sometimes seem hard work.

Alternately, Simone and Adam, our clients and clinic owners in Purley, have built their business and augmented their expertise by adding two additional staff members who are less experienced than they are. In exchange for being mentored and having clients referred to them, their associates get paid 50% of the revenue they generate. Simone and Adam demonstrated that as long as you have an effective marketing and business system in place, the percentage associate model can be started quite early in a business life. It all comes down to doing the right things in the right order.

Something to note is that the percentage you pay associates can vary and needs to be based on what it costs the clinic to get and serve a client. If you are just creating a percentage based on what you think is fair, or what other people in your industry do, you are at risk of not having enough money left for yourself. This is the trap far too many business owners find themselves in because they follow what everyone else does rather than working out the specific requirements of their own business. Do the numbers (if this is challenging, get a bookkeeper to do them for you)!

Subcontractor Associates

Next, is the subcontractor arrangement. Typically, this is where the business owner agrees to pay a wholesale rate for which a subcontracting team member will serve your client through their expertise. This might be the same expertise as you deliver, or it could be an additional service that complements what you do in order to provide a more complete solution for your clients. We suggest paying a wholesale rate for subcontractors instead of the retail rate they charge their own clients, because you provide them with the client. They don't have to do any marketing or sales, they just have to show up and deliver their expertise. Your wholesale discount pays you for providing them with the client and for maintaining the client relationship. This also allows you as the business owner to make money by having a team of subcontractors working for you. If you paid full price, you might as well do the work yourself as there'd be no profit in it and it would cost you money to have subcontractors.

For example, the builders who we use to renovate our investment properties have a subcontractor arrangement with various plumbers, electricians and painter decorators. We are served by the builder and pay them directly. The builder organises and pays the subcontractors. For us, it is a complete service so we don't have the hassle of finding all the separate tradespeople to manage and coordinate. Our builder, who we are sure charges us a premium for finding, managing and providing us with our desired outcome, has a bunch of subcontractors to fulfil my requirements. The benefits to him of having subcontractors rather than employees are that he doesn't have to pay them if he doesn't have work, meaning there is lower financial risk.

There are a couple of potential issues to be aware of with this model. One is availability to get the work done. This is something that needs to be managed, as the subcontractors will also have their own clients or business. This can be worked around with some planning and clear boundaries. The other potential issue with this model, which really needs to be addressed upfront, is if the subcontractor establishes their own relationship with the clients and decides to cut you out of the deal. Very simply, you need to make it clear that if they undercut you or take on your client themselves, your relationship is over. With a breach of trust like this, you cannot work with them again and also we suggest you share their poor behaviour with other business owners you know who may also be working with them. This will protect others from suffering a similar situation and ensure that there are consequences for the poor behaviour. Being this upfront about the rules of engagement will help prevent this behaviour from happening, and if after this clarity, your subcontractor still acts like this, they are making it very clear that they have different values to you and you are not a match to work together.

Chris interestingly experienced this situation in his clinic a couple of times with subcontractors before we realised the importance of setting up effective boundaries...
When I first started taking on subcontractors, I initially started working with practitioners I knew well. I thought because we were friends, we didn't need formal agreements. However, over the next few months, several clients came back to me saying they felt uncomfortable that my subcontractors had offered them lower priced sessions to work with them directly. Not ideal. Ultimately, I lost a couple of friendships, however, I am very grateful for these practitioners highlighting the need for formal agreements. If you want to work with your friends, great.

We work with a lot of our friends today in several different businesses. However, we protect our friendships by setting clear boundaries right from the start in our business relationships.

There are a number aggregator services that bring together multiple subcontractors under a 'trusted' banner. It provides the user with a level of quality assurance if trying out someone or something new. In some instances this also facilitates an anytime, anywhere service. These aggregators typically turn the services provided into a commodity. Where the person delivering the service is selected based on availability at a fixed cost to the user. Ultimately, this drives down what the subcontractor can earn, although it might give them more clients if they don't know how to build their own business.

Employees

The final option for a team structure is to take people on as employees. By paying a fixed salary, you own their time so they will be 100% dedicated to you. You will have higher fixed costs initially, however, you are likely to have better margins than a % share. The greater security of a job, with all of the benefits that this entails such as sick pay and holiday pay, mean that an employee will typically be paid less than a subcontractor or % associate. For the employee structure to work effectively for all parties involved, you will also need to create a team culture with associated training, support and management systems.

David, one of our clients with a Phase 3 business in Portsmouth, has recently moved all of his team from a percentage share to full-time salaried employees. His staff now have a renewed level of commitment and security. With more support, he has managed to reduce his own client facing hours. And with this extra time, and the extra profit he is now making from having employed and engaged staff, he can offer his staff a better level of management and training. He can plan his cash flow better and everyone including David is happier and delivering better service and results for their clients.

Regardless of what structure you adopt, ensuring that everyone is aligned to your values and service expectations is key. It is best therefore, to hire slow and fire fast to protect your business. Remember our discussion in Chapter 6, Confidence, your brand is a promise kept.

Key Business Systems

Based on the last couple of sections you will now be armed with lots of strategies as to how you have more time. You will also have a better idea of where you can introduce other people into your life and business to better leverage your time. If you are using more people however, how do you make sure that they do the right things in the right order? This is where systems come in and when we talk about systems, we don't always mean automation or a computer system or programme.

A system can just be a set of rules, or steps for how you do things to achieve an outcome. If you don't know what systems you have in your business, then chances are, you are the system. This might be fine when your business is just you, however, you then become the single point of failure. If something happens to you, there is no business. This is also why it is key to identify and ideally document the systems within your business so that when it grows, there is at least the possibility of some form of exit otherwise, you are forever tied to it.

The amount of detail that you go into in your systems depends on what you need. It might be that you start with a high level picture of what happens and refine this over time. You may initially capture the basics and then move onto McDonalds levels of repeatability and consistency. McDonalds is a great example of a business that has very clear systems. Regardless of how you feel about McDonalds personally, their systems mean they can provide a consistent customer experience wherever you are in the world no matter what staff they have. If you haven't seen the movie "*The Founder*", the story of the McDonald brothers and Ray Croc, it is well worth a watch. McDonalds, like a lot of chain restaurants and retail chains, and many larger service-based businesses, have a large amount of staff turnover. At the extreme end of the spectrum, a store could have a completely new set of staff every three months. Imagine what that would feel like in your business right now? If every three months, you had to train an entirely new set of employees. This is only possible if you have very well documented systems and training in place. Whilst we are not suggesting you will need this level of sophistication, it does help to focus the mind as to how understanding and then documenting your systems will enhance your customer experience, your ability to take on staff or associates and leverage yourself, or sort out your not-to-do list.

To further bring this to life, perhaps it would help if we shared the system for washing the dishes in our house. Yes, there is no limit to the detail your systems can go into!
Dish washing in our house:

h. Pack as much as possible that is 'dishwasher safe' into the dishwasher.

i. Chris to repack the dishwasher from everything that has been stuffed in

j. Put everything else on the right hand side of the sink with glasses at the back so they don't get knocked over and break.

k. Hope it's the day the housekeeper is in so she can take over. If no housekeeper, move onto the next step.

l. Turn the tap to hot, fill up the jug until you get hot water (we like to save water in our house so rather than just letting water go down the drain until it runs hot, we fill up a jug with the cold water and then use it to water the plants and fill up our water filter or the iron)

m. Get washing up liquid on sponge

n. With hot water, wash the dishes, starting with glasses then moving into chunkier items, wipe everything with the soapy sponge and then rinse off with hot water.

o. Stack washed item on drying rack to the left of the sink.

p. Dry dishes using clean tea-towel to make space on the drying rack as needed.

q. Put dried dishes away into cupboards

I am sure that we could go into even more detail here, however, it gives you an idea of what to do and what not to do in a clear and easy to follow format if you are ever washing the dishes at our house. Learning from my experience as a landlord, when our new cleaner started, I took photos of all of the rooms of our house and listed off all the key things that I expected in each room. I could just as easily have talked this through; however, we were experiencing a number of different cleaners in a short space of time and I didn't want to have to repeat this process each time someone new turned up. We now have a more regular set up, however, I always have the manual if we ever need someone new.

There isn't necessarily a right or wrong to automating systems or not however as you can see from the example above, we don't put glasses in the dishwasher because when we did, they broke. Additionally, if you automate something that isn't working, it will just happen faster, which could create more problems. For those of you familiar with "*Santa Claus the Movie*", this is highlighted when Patch the Elf, creates a machine to put the toys together, which obviously is quicker than a series of elves doing all the work by hand. With his 'new-fangled' invention, he generates a much larger volume of toys than previously possible. As they increase the speed, the quality suffers and suddenly screws are missing their holes and parts aren't painted properly and it all goes terribly wrong. In the end, the toys break, and children send letters of complaint to Santa for the first time ever. In disgrace, Patch leaves the North Pole... now don't worry, it does get better for Patch, however, we're not going to spoil it for you here, just go and watch the movie, it's one of our favourites. The point is, automation is not always the answer.

"The first rule of any technology used in a business is that automation applied to an efficient operation will magnify the efficiency. The second is that automation applied to an inefficient operation will magnify the inefficiency."
– Bill Gates

The easiest way to capture the systems in your business, is to go back to the key functions of the business. Whether you are augmenting your team or not, having your systems defined will help you do things more effectively and also potentially add to your customer experience. Anything that adds to your customer experience has the potential to enhance your business and earn you more money and a better reputation. The key areas all businesses need to have systems in are:

1. **Marketing**
2. **Sales**
3. **Delivery**

From here you can look at what repeatable processes you have within each of these areas and what opportunities there are for streamlining and automation whilst delivering a premium service. For each of these key areas you need to identify what you and your team do. There are a number of different ways to do this. The easiest is similar to the time diary, for a week, write down all of the tasks that you do in this area. Then spend some time breaking down these tasks into the individual action steps in the same way we described our family's system for doing the dishes.

Another option is to map out your customer experience. This might sound more complicated and it can certainly get that way, however, what if you simply imagine that you are a client and walk through your business. Make a note of everything that happens good and bad on that client journey. From here you have clarity of what you might want to change or improve.

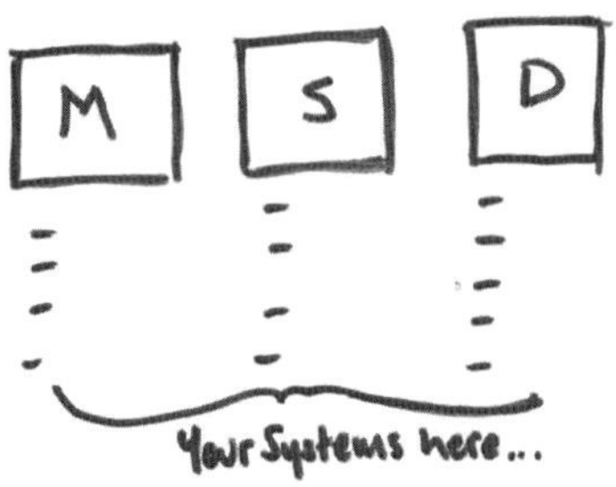

Marketing

What are all the different ways that someone can find out about your business:
Email, networking, social media, referrals, leaflet, t-shirts, billboards, newspapers, articles and the list goes on. At our two-day Client Mentorship Training specifically on Attraction Marketing we fill at least two flip charts with all of the various options that are available to market a business. As we mentioned in Chapter 2,Attraction Marketing, you need to work out what is right for your specific clients in your particular Phase of business.

You probably have some form of conversation with potential clients, whether written, in person or face to face, that determines if they would like to find out more. You would then book them in for this 'Sales" conversation.

Sales

What does this look like for the client? Is it on the phone, some form of video or online chat, or in person? Where does this happen and what are the logistical requirements for you and the client? Are there any logistics or pre-session emails, texts reminders etc that go out and any follow up etc required?

Following your sales conversation, they have either become a client, or a referral to someone or something else at this point - what happens for each of these options? Emails, appointments booked, introductions to someone/something else?

Delivery

How do you deliver your service? Is it in person, hands on, speaking, completing a report, editing or fixing their copy, sorting out their interior design etc? Does it happen in a particular location? on the phone or all online. How many sessions do clients usually have? How are these sessions organised and what is the format of these sessions? Are there other people or services involved, if so what, who or how many?

Follow up

What happens when they are finished working with you? Is there a next step with someone else? Or do they go into your database so you follow up with them at regular intervals to see that they are still ok? How else could you support them or anyone else in their community? What is your follow up procedure, phone, email, text, post? And what frequency?

Once you have answered all of these questions for your business and worked through this, you will have a 'map' of your business. This will be the start of your policies and procedures document: the process steps and user manual for your business. When it is just you, this is less necessary. However, having at least an outline of the inputs and outputs of each step means that if you were to either hand over tasks to someone else, or use an external service to deliver something, you have a better idea of what that might look like.

ACTION STEP

Keep an action diary for a week and create a list of tasks and actions.

Map your customer experience for each of the key areas of your business.

Expand on each of these so that you are clear on how everything works.

Create your business user manual.

There are so many different tasks and ways of doing things in each key business area as you will have discovered above and from the preceding chapters that each area could have their own book. For completeness and to give you some more ideas, whilst by no means exhaustive, we have tried to capture some of the more obvious repeatable tasks in each area that you could focus on to gain improvements in your customer experience or time efficiency.

Marketing

There are lots of systems and opportunities that you can introduce around marketing including and certainly not limited to:

- Introductions - you can have draft templates set up, so you are just cutting and pasting the names of the people you are introducing rather than writing a new email every time.
- Follow up - 'nice to meet you' and 'thank you' emails all ready to go with clear next steps.
- Your marketing calendar - if you are using social media do you have your year mapped out for posts? What topics are you covering? Are you offering seasonal solutions or promotions?

- Nurture sequence - how does a potential client move through social media, email, face to face meetings through to a sale conversation? Create a consistent and duplicatable step by step journey.
- Funnels - as discussed in Chapter 2, Attraction Marketing, funnels are simply how someone goes from first hearing about you to becoming your client. They can be very simple or complex and getting clear on what funnels work best for your particular business is both an important and often time consuming task.

Automation options for marketing might include having some form of customer tracking system, this could be a spreadsheet or a customer relationship management database. Referred to as a CRM, there are lots of free and paid for versions of these available and we suggest that you work out what you need and then pick software so that you are clear on what you want rather than having to work around a system or tool.

You might also have an automated email or postal mail distribution tool which may or may not be built into your CRM or delivered by a third party. Similarly, you might have someone or a tool that automates your posts etc on social media platforms.

There are also lots of tools and people for content creation, whether that is copy, audio, video, memes, photos or the like. Your business may be that of a copywriter or digital marketing specialist and still need you to do all of this for yourself.

Although an admin task, diary management is key for all of your in-person marketing meetings and conversations even when virtual, also having an automated booking system will greatly reduce wasted time here and make sure that you can fit everything in.

ACTION STEP

Write down all your Marketing Actions.

Explore all ways you could automate or streamline these actions.

Sales

Sales is itself a complete system as we discussed in Chapter 4, Heart Centred Sales. Here we will look at some of the subtasks that would be good to focus on:

- How is your room or space set up?
- Is your sales process consistent every time so you can see what's working and what doesn't for continuous improvement and growth?
- Do you have your programmes or client service options written out? Of course, you can modify them for a more personal experience depending on what individual client's need. However, if you have a framework you can more easily move someone forward in the sales conversation rather than having to go away and create a proposal. Anything that reduces the time to getting clarity as to whether you are a match to work together or not, is a bonus.

There isn't a lot of opportunity for automation in sales, rather the process of tracking someone's first contact through to being a client can be automated as well as the interactions, reminders and additional content you deliver to them.

Again, diary management is key here to form habits around follow up and ensure consistency.

ACTION STEP

Review your Sales Process.

Where could you create more consistency?

Have you got your programmes or service options written out for simplicity? If not, do this.

Delivery

Delivery can be separated into two subsections:

1. Client Facing Delivery, or your area of expertise (the work you do with your clients)
2. Non-Client Facing Delivery: The associated admin and compliance required outside of your client facing time.

Client Facing Delivery - Your expertise

Most people excel at delivery which is what they spend years and hundreds if not thousands of pounds training on. However, you may not have thought about your system. Chapter 4, Heart Centred Sales talks about the importance of having a delivery system that you can simply and easily describe to your clients. In addition to this being great for your clients, it will also help you transition to having a team. If you are clear on how to deliver your services, then if you need to augment what you do then having a system is key.

We have a 3 Step System, Knowledge, Mindset and Community in Heart Centred Business to get the results for our clients, as illustrated in the picture below:

There is limited automation in client facing delivery because, if you could be replaced by a programme or app, then you are more likely to be at the commodity rather than premium service end of delivery. It might be that you use automation and tools to augment what you offer such as a series of videos or other tools to support your client's experience. The focus may also be on how to automate the tools to support your service delivery such as video conferencing, webinars, closed groups, membership sites etc.

Non-Client Facing Delivery: Admin/Compliance

Whilst necessary, most of us aren't fans of admin and it becomes something we just fit in when we can. This is fine whilst you are relatively small and don't have a team. However, it won't allow you to scale, manage your cash flow or manage many of the key metrics within your business.

At the very least you need to be focused on the elements of admin that add or detract from your client experience and also those that impact your cash flow. If all you manage is activities around these key areas, then great. Ideally, however, you will progress to everything else as well.

Key activities you need sorted around your client experience and also cash flow is anything related to taking money and billing. Also understanding your numbers as you move from marketing, sales and delivery: how many people do you have at each stage and what is your % success moving them to the next step. These are referred to as conversion ratios. To support this, there are five metrics we recommend all our clients track as a minimum:

- Number of Referrals given and received
- Number of Curiosity Conversations
- Number of Sales conversations
- Number of New Clients
- Number of Follow Ups made

There are a lot of opportunities for automation here, however, this is certainly an area to start small and messy so that you get into the habit of doing it before getting lost in technology. There are a lot of diary management tools that will allow you to track some of these numbers. A spreadsheet is a good option here and old-fashioned paper with tally marks might also be an option. We've used all these different versions and have to admit, the easiest one to use was just pen and paper.

ACTION STEP

Start tracking your key metrics so you can understand how successful you are at moving from one step to the next. If any of these percentages are less than 10% then go back to the chapter that focuses on this area and see what you can tweak or change.

You will now have a better idea what areas you might focus on within your business and where there are opportunities for automation. Obviously, without knowing the specifics of your business, it is hard to make too many recommendations. Our intention here was to perhaps challenge your thinking or offer alternatives that might support you doing things differently and therefore getting a different result.

You

Whilst we're capturing and documenting business systems to remove single points of failure, we have to acknowledge that for many people, 'they' are the single point of failure in their business. If you are a Phase One or Two business this will be particularly true. Even in Phase Three, we tend to build things that require at least some of our attention, oversight or decision making. Even if you have set up your business to be ready to exit, you'll need to think about what comes next, so it is helpful to have a system for Health and looking after you. After all, if you are the single point of failure and something happens to you, where's your money going to come from?

Health covers a lot of areas including mental, emotional, physical and spiritual wellbeing. You might already make great choices around your health, however, in our experience, most experts and heart centred business owners are so focused on giving to other people, that they neglect themselves in some way.

Remember, we discussed that the key to having more time was to prioritise? This is particularly true for health. If you have limited time and health isn't a priority, you will probably make compromises. Convenience vs healthy food options; skipping a workout for some extra sleep; work vs relationships; work vs sleep etc. We've all done these things at some point and made decisions that negatively impacted our health. We just need to make sure that from now on, these are conscious choices knowing the cost and benefit of the choice both in the short and the long term.

ACTION STEP

What is your current approach to health?

Is it a priority?

If it isn't and you are your business, does this need to change?

What are you doing to ensure you are the best version of you each and every day? There is a growing movement of people focused on morning routines to answer this question. Both Chris and I have always instinctively had some form of morning routines. If you don't, perhaps this is an area you might want to look into and it doesn't just have to be the morning perhaps some of the things we will now discuss you can do before bed, so you recap your day and are set up for tomorrow.

Who wouldn't want to set themselves up to have your best day everyday? I think that this quote encapsulates the benefits.

"People often say motivation doesn't last. Neither does bathing—that's why we recommend it daily."
– Zig Ziglar

There are many different ways to energise and motivate yourself which creates a system for health including exercise, meditation, affirmations, visualisation, journaling, gratitude and making your bed. All of which we incorporate to a greater or lesser degree into our own routines and we hear time and time again from our clients, these work.

One of my property mentors is a huge fan of morning routines, however, he was also older and wasn't juggling children and a husband. As a mother, I have always read people fitting all these things in and wondered how on earth it was possible? It is possible, yet it takes a little more organising, some flexibility and forgiveness of yourself when it doesn't work out. You also need firm boundaries. Chris and my morning routines have morphed and changed with the various different phases and requirements of our daughter Mya, however, we have always had something.

So we can be practical about this rather than disappearing into some utopian ideal. We'll go through suggestions for energy and motivation based on what we ourselves do or have done and what our clients have shared works for them so that you can find some answers that suit you. I know I have read a lot of personal development books and thought, yes but how do you do that with a child/family etc etc. I would be lying to say it is always easy and sometimes it just doesn't happen. We have worked with Mya for her to understand how important it is for both of us and her to have a routine to get us going and this has made a big difference.

Looking first at Exercise; this is a huge priority for us and particularly me, as I just work better with some form of exercise. I know that this isn't the case for everyone so find what you enjoy. Even when Mya was a baby, I fit in exercise by doing yoga with her, or putting her in the buggy and taking her for a run. When I was training for the marathon and had to go on longer runs, this was particularly challenging as she was at an age when she wanted to get out of the buggy and totter around. I had to work out ways to let that happen and still do what I needed. I would love to say that nowadays she will ride along on her bike whilst I jog, however, that doesn't typically happen. Chris and I either get up early and take it in turns to go for a run so one of us is home with Mya, or we alternate home exercise and going out for a jog. Even on holiday, we work something out which is more family oriented so we are always present parents whilst fitting in the essential exercise.

As mentioned earlier, we have also implemented a daily walk after dropping Mya off at school and using this as a planning meeting for the day as well as an opportunity to get moving before we get started for the day. When you have a predominately desk based job it is always helpful to get out more. You might work from home and need to walk around the block so you have a commute to 'get into work mode'.

Chris has a daily meditation he combines with stretching that he uses to start his day. Ever since I met him, meditation and breathing have always been part of what he does. In part he started this to cope with some major health challenges he was having and it just became a habit because he felt better doing it than not. Meditation, or finding space to turn off your conscious mind, has great health benefits. There are also a large number of different options, silent, with repeating words, guided meditations, the list goes on. Personally, I struggle with sitting meditation. I've tried it in many forms, however, if I am really honest, it doesn't work for me. I know all the theory and have seen how it works for so many people and that is great. I seem to get more benefit though from a moving meditation. This is what yoga, jogging or walking is for me now. Recognise there isn't a 'one size fits all' option here and you need to find what works for you too. This could be a trial and error approach until you find your perfect mix.

Affirmations can be a super tool for supporting goals, changing beliefs or just reinforcing positive thoughts to change your state. If you aren't familiar with affirmations, they are the repetition of a short outcome based phrase, every day, out loud whilst moving in some way. Whilst you can say affirmations silently in your head, or just by being still, we have found combining words and movement the most powerful option.

Phrases such as "I am a genius, I am applying my wisdom", "I am a money magnet, money comes to me", "Stronger and Stronger everyday in every way" are some of the options that Chris and I have used over the years. Chris had a habit for several years of taking a mini trampoline into the garden at 5am and bouncing for 10-20 mins while saying these affirmations. I'm not sure what the neighbours thought but it coincided with massive growth in his mindset and financial and business success so that's worth taking a few odd looks.

There are entire websites with massive lists of possible suggestions for what you could use in any given circumstance. We will leave it up to you to choose what wording works for you. Saying a chosen phrase or number of phrases everyday, like brushing your teeth will become a habit if you stick with it. Most days, when I leave the house, I find money of some sort on the street which I pick up. It can just be pennies, or more occasionally pound coins or even notes. Is that a result of my money magnet mantra, who knows?! However, it could be, so I keep on doing it the affirmation.

We have mentioned visualisation early on in this book when we were talking about our friend Tom and his Ironman Triathlon. As it is such a powerful tool, it's definitely worth another mention. Our brains don't know the difference between real and imagined so making something real in your mind and engaging all of your senses in that imagining, allows you to make it a reality. You can do this every day simply by imagining your goal like we did at the very beginning of the book, or through guided meditations where someone walks you through the process. You can visualise your day going well, or an interaction with a client or loved one. The applications are endless. I am a bit more hit and miss with this, however, I will do it before our larger events to visualise the outcome I want for our clients and ourselves. Chris though does visualisations everyday as part of his meditation. Again this is personal preference, find what works for you.

Another helpful health system is writing things down or journalling. At the very least, the physical act of writing, engages a different part of your brain. You might find that it helps to:

- Get ideas or issues out of your head.
- Gain clarity over an issue or problem.
- Record what you were doing/thinking/feeling on any given day.
- Find the good in others and record it for them or you.

Chris and I have used journaling at various points: for gratitude, issues, thoughts and ideas. This is typically an end of day activity for us, it is also something that we are probably the least consistent with and that is ok too.

Gratitude is another great tool you can incorporate daily or weekly, or when you remember. As the saying goes, "Gratitude, changes your attitude". When you are really truly grateful and seeing the good in others, a situation or whatever, you can't simultaneously be anything else. Try it the next time you are feeling frustrated, angry or depressed, it just isn't possible to hold those two emotions at the same time. Now we're not suggesting this is a panacea to all negative emotions. However, it might give you the necessary space to change your reaction. It might just allow you to recognise one thing that is ok when everything else isn't. To get to where we are now, there have been some times, days, weeks, and even months that haven't been great on our journey. We have made mistakes, so many mistakes and been disappointed, heart broken, sad, angry and everything else in between. Being able to check in with something good that happened that day, no matter how small, has been a really helpful reminder that there is always something to be grateful for.

Following on from gratitude would be the importance of making your bed. "What?" We hear you say. Yes. making your bed is very much something that we would recommend. This comes from a great 2014 commencement speech by Admiral William H. McRaven to the graduating class at the University of Texas. The idea being that even if nothing else goes well, you have achieved one thing and you have a nicely made bed it hop into at the end of it all. It works. In our family, it's non-negotiable even for Mya. No matter what type of day we've had, or how big the challenges have been, we all get into a nicely made bed each night and that's both something to be grateful for as well as a level of comfort and consistency that will help to move you forward.

Once you have decided on a health system, and put it into practice, do it for at least 30 days. This will allow it to become a habit. Once a habit, you will get that feeling that you have forgotten something when you miss it, much like brushing your teeth. This is when it really starts to work for you!

ACTION STEP

What of these techniques/tools do you already use?

What might you now like to use?

If you have heard of these previously and haven't tried them before what stopped you?

What can you do to change that?

Remember if you want something to change, you can't keep doing the same things and expect something different.

Chapter Highlights

- ✓ Having more time is all about being clear on "Why" you are doing something. Once you have this, you can say no and prioritise freeing up your time to do more of what makes you happy and moves you forward.
- ✓ There are a number of strategies to be more effective, make good choices easier, set unreasonable deadlines and get more done. There is no one size fits all and you will need to find what works for you.
- ✓ Time like money can be influenced by your Mindset, if you aren't clear on what you need more time for and you are perpetuating negative thought patterns around time, then it is unlikely you will create more.
- ✓ Leverage is key to creating more time as you grow and realise that you don't have to do everything yourself. Being able to have people do tasks even 80% as good as you and give you 100% of your time back is one of the quickest ways to 'buy' time.
- ✓ You need systems, repeatable ways of doing things, in your business and life to ensure that you and others are doing the right things in the right order.

Chapter 8
What's the Plan?
How to get in Action and Move Forward

"The only question is whether you're going to do it today or tomorrow. If you keep saying you're going to do it tomorrow, you'll never do it. You have to get on it today." – Warren Buffett

It all Starts with a Single Step...

Little and often is a success mantra for getting things done. Many people think they have to take massive action to change things and that success needs some grand gesture. However, to make change sustainable, small daily actions to create the right habits are what will keep you moving forward in the direction you want.

The big actions reset or kick-start your new course or direction. Big actions may also bring something to life quickly. It's the small progressive steps however that will sustain all of this. Small consistent actions will have a greater impact long term to move you forward, although they seem far less impressive. Look at nature: wind and rain erosion can carve out mountains given enough time. You too can create the life and business of your dreams with this consistency of effort.

To achieve our success to date we have used a combination of massive action steps and daily sustainable habits. One example would be writing this book, we used a combination of the two. Our massive action was setting a date for release. We chose our next Training event which happened to be approximately five weeks from when we made this commitment to get started. We worked backwards, understanding how long it was going to take to get it formatted, published, printed etc and then worked out we had approximately a week to get it written.

During that week, we committed to writing ten A4 pages a day. We created up the table of contents to give us a structure to follow and then wrote on a shared document, keeping the commitment was 10 pages a day no matter what. This commitment meant going to bed around 1-2am most nights for several weeks for both the writing and editing process.

Yes, we didn't need to take quite such an extreme approach, however, we wanted it done. We then put in place actions to ensure we kept going. I announced it during one of my morning videos. We posted a poll on the closed Facebook Group we have for our clients asking them to vote on book cover designs and announcing the release date. We also kept our Mastermind updated with our weekly actions and whether we were fulfilling the commitments we made so they could hold us accountable. We gave up any of the relaxing evening activities we would typically do and even 7-year-old Mya started telling us that sleep was important and we should really start to go to bed earlier. Fundamentally, we took massive action as well as daily consistent steps and guess what… you're reading it now, so it must have worked!

Yes, we had a number of conversations about what else we could be doing and it produced a lot of challenges we didn't expect, however, it was all worth it and we would absolutely do it again. It set a great example for our daughter and clients and we hope for you too, of what is possible if you challenge yourself to achieve more.

If our book writing approach is too extreme for you then think about a lovely country walk or perhaps a hill that you might climb. You will only get to the top of the hill one step at a time. A little while ago, we were on a family walk with some friends and their dog. Mya's legs were only marginally longer than the dog's. To get to the pub and the table we had booked for lunch, we had to walk 2.5 miles there and back. This was a pretty big ask for a 6-year-old in wellies across muddy fields and steep hills. So we played tag, we played eye spy, we skipped, we ran, we walked, we sang songs, we climbed trees and we made it all fun. We got there one step at a time. Mya walked the entire way and yes there was some whining at one point, however, that was mainly Chris because he was hungry. We had the same return journey which included rolling down a hill just for fun. When we were back in the car and we told Mya she had just completed a five mile walk, she was so proud of herself, as were we. How did she do it? By breaking the task into manageable chunks. By making it fun. By having a supportive community doing it with her and having the reward of a great lunch in the middle.

All of these strategies can support you in getting things done. How might you incorporate them into your life and business?

ACTION STEP

Identify what you need to change to get more done.

Do you need to break things up, add rewards, fun, music, a community, accountability?

We have covered some of these strategies for taking action in the Chapter 7, Sexy Systems, specifically around time and will cover the remaining strategies in detail here to show you how to apply them to your situation.

Goal Setting

Existing in the world today without knowing that goal setting is something that we 'should' be doing would be a challenge as it is universally accepted that you need to have a goal or goals in all areas of your life to achieve success. Just in case you missed this trend, goal setting very simply is articulating how much of what you want, by when.

A good way to explain the importance of having a goal or at least knowing where you would like to end up is the interaction between Alice and the Cheshire Cat in Alice in Wonderland. Alice is asking the Cheshire cat for directions and the Cheshire Cat is asking Alice where she wants to go. Alice doesn't know so as the Cat points out, it hardly matters which way she goes. It is the same in life, if you haven't set out a goal or started with the end in mind then where are you going? Chances are you are spending your time pursuing someone else's goals.

Georgia, one of our clients, realised that despite being in her mid-40s and previously having had a successful corporate career, she had never sat down and made a plan for what she wanted to achieve in life. Most of her previous decisions were based on what made her feel comfortable rather than leading to a sense of fulfilment. In her words, she has said being on the Mentorship Programme, has been life-changing in that it has opened her eyes to leading a life driven towards her goals, rather than living a life based on taking the easiest option. It is more challenging, but she can genuinely say she is happier at work than she has ever been and has a true sense of purpose. The changes have positively impacted her personal life. She is braver, more content, more grateful and has much more fun doing things she loves with people she loves. Oh, and as an aside, she earns 50% more, works the same hours, and her clients are getting awesome results too!

Now we've established why we need goals; we will go through each area of life and sort out some goals. The key areas that we have found that work best for goals that cover most things yet keep it simple, were shared with us by Randi Zuckerberg. Yes, she has a very famous brother. We spent time with Randi in the Green Room whilst waiting for our turn to go on stage at the Empowered Woman event in Sweden in 2018.

As an aside, she inspired Mya to try computer coding because who wouldn't want to be a tech nerd when they have cool shoes and sing modified versions of Little Mermaid songs on stage in front of hundreds of people like Randi did? Mya was backstage at the event with us so similarly had a very personal experience of meeting Randi, admiring her shoes and then watched her on stage.

In Randi's book, *Pick Three*, there are five key areas that she highlights that we all aspire to fulfil in our lives. Her book is all about the fact that in trying to do all five, we set ourselves up for failure. We totally agree that trying to do too much in one day just leads to disappointment. As such, looking at how you fulfil these key life areas over the longer term is a far healthier approach. We have borrowed these five life areas to use as the basis for goal setting. They are:

- Family
- Friends
- Health/Fitness

- Work/Finances
- Sleep

What would you like each of these areas to look like? If you are struggling with this, remember Richard Branson's wisdom, first design your life, then design the work and income to support it. What do you want in each of these areas? Be as specific as possible.

For some people, articulating what you want can be quite challenging. If you're someone who finds it hard to articulate what you want, perhaps try working out what you don't want or what you want to avoid. Once you have this defined as what you don't want, translate this into the positive.

For example, if you know that you don't want to live at home with your parents, great, does that mean that you want to share a place with friends? Have your own place? Where? How big? (Remember to fill out a Red Flags sheet, if you're already having a reaction) Working through goal setting can be challenging, however, without it, you have no idea of what you're aiming for or what actions to take.

Take the time to work out what you do or don't want in each life area and write it down. Make sure when you write them down, you only write the positive version. Our brains don't recognise negatives. By this I mean if I were to tell you "Don't get hurt", you would have to imagine yourself getting hurt to then imagine staying safe.

Not convinced? Let's try it out. "Don't think about a purple elephant." We mean it, "Really don't think about a purple elephant!"

How did you get on? To not think about it, you have to picture one, right? It is the same with our goals. If your goal is to be debt free, then you have to imagine the debt to be able to imagine being free of it. The brain will then focus on seeing you having debt and will keep recreating this situation. If, however, you imagine you have £50,000 savings in the bank, this is a positive image that your brain can imagine without any negatives and therefore work towards making it real.

Something to note, is that neither Randi or we feel it's possible to focus on creating success in all these five areas at the same time. It's unrealistic and trying to do everything typically leads to mediocre results that doesn't mean that you should set goals in each of these areas.

For example, if you are focused on becoming an Olympic Athlete, you don't have enough time or focus in your day to be the perfect friend or build a business. These things are still possible, it might just take longer to fulfil on all of them.

If you're a new parent, with a baby who won't sleep; focusing on your family is exactly what you need to be doing and sleep, friends, fitness and work might all suffer during this phase of life.

Another aspect that a lot of us struggle with is to actually dream big enough. We tend to avoid saying what we really want in case someone judges us. So what? If you don't dream it or set a goal around it we can guarantee it will never happen.

It is also worth remembering that you will not necessarily reach all of your goals. Oh yes, we don't like to sugar coat things so it is possible if your goals and dreams are crazy enough then you might not get there. And that doesn't matter because the person that you become in the pursuit of them will be able to reset the goals and keep going.

Also, recognise that experiencing or fulfilling your goals might not turn up in the way that you expect. Chris and I have always dreamed of living on the beach. The idea of being able to open the doors, walk down to the sand, feel it between your toes, hear the waves, smell the salt and feel the sun on your face. Now that goal has not materialised yet. What has materialised is that we now spend nearly three months of the year away from home staying near beaches. Every year we visit my parents in Australia and spend most of that time at the beach, we rent a house on the beach on the south coast in England so we are closer to Chris' parents and we also spend the whole summer in Sardinia, an island off the coast of Italy with beautiful beaches and a wonderful community of people that we have now made friends with. So, we might not own the beach house however, we own the experiences and it has opened up an entirely different community and opportunities we might not have otherwise had.

What goals might you have already achieved that you have discounted because they didn't show up exactly the way you had wanted them to? What goals could you now achieve by looking at how you could fulfil them differently?

ACTION STEP

Write down your goals in the areas of Family, Friends, Heath/Fitness, Work and Sleep

You may have short medium- and long-term goals in each of these areas that you then break into annual, quarterly, monthly, weekly and daily goals. Think also about how else you might achieve this goal. What other options are available for you to have the experience?

There are lots of great resources specifically on goal setting and whilst this is enough to get you started if you need more detailed support, join our Facebook group

www.facebook.com/groups/HeartCentredBusiness

And check out Karene's daily videos.

Goals can also be tricky because…As Jack Canfield says, "everything we want is on the other side of fear". And this fear can be quite debilitating. If this is you then you might need to address this with something we use with our clients called a "fear setting" exercise. The idea being you get over the fear by imagining the worst and then repairing and preventing it, as well as working out the positives of taking action and the cost of inaction. Armed with all of this you will have a great tool to conquer those fears and have everything you want. As Fear Setting isn't as readily know about, or used, we thought it would be helpful to work through an example.

Firstly, we need to understand what you are afraid of. You might not be aware of what exactly you are afraid of, so it is easier to pick an action you are avoiding. For example, you might be avoiding putting your prices up. This is one of the key actions most service businesses need to take to earn more money. During our Training events, it comes up time and time again, this is something most people are resistant to. There is the fear of rejection that all clients will leave. Fear of judgement that whatever you do isn't worth it or someone else is cheaper. Fear that you don't deserve it. And so many more fears wrapped up in this one simple challenge.

Let's ignore all of this for a moment and focus on what is the worst that could happen if you raise your prices or whatever action you have chosen? List everything, every bad result, such as...

- Lose clients.
- Lose confidence.
- Have no money.
- Lose family.
- End up homeless or living with parents.
- Clients laugh at you.

These are real things our clients have articulated when we have worked through this and you can see some of them are quite extreme. If you really believed these things might happen if you raised your prices, it's understandable you would avoid taking action.

Now, let's assume you raise your prices and these worst case scenarios all happen. How might you repair things? Examples could be...

- Offer a discount for blocks of sessions or a programme to return prices to near original prices.
- Get a job as an associate.
- Get some temp work.
- Get a mentor who has gone through this before and can give you a system for repairing this situation.

Let's assume we want to avoid the negative consequences and we still take action, how can we prevent this worst-case scenario? Such as...

- Only raise prices with new people, as they don't know what the old price is. Whatever you tell them is just the price.

- Increase the value for your clients before raising prices.
- Give existing clients a loyalty period/discount.
- Learn heart centred sales so you can have better conversations with your clients.
- Get a mentor and learn how to raise your prices.

So, from this, you can see there are lots of options to safely take action and either repair or prevent whatever you imagine the worst-case scenario to be from raising prices. That however, is only half of the equation.

The other side of the equation is about the positive results from taking action and the cost of inaction. What are all the good things that would come from raising prices. Again, list everything out, such as...

- More money.
- Happier clients as you are solving bigger problems.
- More committed clients. In our businesses, clients that pay a lot, pay a lot of attention and tend to get the best results because they have a different level of commitment. Those that are focused on the cost are still looking for things to fail or go wrong and they just aren't committed. We're sure you've experienced, like us, working for clients for free and finding they don't value our efforts.

There are some great things here to motivate you to take action. If this still isn't enough to get past all those fears though, what about the cost of inaction? For some of our clients this alone is enough to get them in action. Let's see what might be the cost of inaction for avoiding raising prices; emotionally, financially, physically:

- Your finances stay the same or get worse as they don't keep pace with inflation. You are at risk of not being able to afford your lifestyle, let alone building a safety blanket or security for the future
- You start resenting your clients who you might feel are taking advantage of you
- You start believing you are worth less and your confidence is diminished.

- With decreased confidence you do less marketing and progressively have fewer and fewer clients.

With these costs of inaction, added to having a safe way of navigating the challenges, taking action and the positive outcomes to connect with, you will be able to smash through any fears. And if you still have fear, great. If you are never afraid, you can't be brave.

Whilst we have used raising prices as an example, this is applicable to any action you may be avoiding. Some examples people have worked through at our events include; asking a long-term partner to marry them, leaving an abusive relationship, leaving part time work, trying something new, starting a diet, taking on a new role, stopping breastfeeding.

This is a very powerful tool that will allow you to see past your fears and take action so you can transform your life and business.

ACTION STEP

What action are you avoiding?

Complete this fear setting exercise on the action to move past your fear.

What else might hold you back? You take action and you are transforming your life and business. What happens if you make a mistake? Great, you are learning. My best advice around mistakes would be to own them. They happen.

When you make a mistake of course you will feel horrible and there might be consequences for you and others. However, if you are hiding, it isn't going to help.

Admit to whatever has gone on and apologise. Work with your client or supplier or whomever to make right whatever has gone wrong as a result of the mistake. Learn from it, change things so it doesn't happen again and keep going.

Most people who are on the wrong end of a mistake just need the person who has made the mistake to acknowledge it. If your mistake triggers something in the person who has been impacted, then recognise this and do whatever you can to make things right without taking on their issues. Learn and keep going.

You want mistakes to be things that allow you to grow and be even better, not things that hold you back and keep you scared.

Rewards and consequences are also a key feature of goal setting. Many people set "black and white" or "pass and fail" goals. We prefer a methodology that allows you to have a staged approach, so you set a target and you add a minimum below it and a mindblower above it.

Say for example, you need more clients, so you are going to more consistently ring your past clients. You set a target of five calls a day. You would then set a minimum of two calls and a mindblower of ten calls. This way you have set up a range rather than a pass or fail situation, so can stay motivated and in action because the first level is more accessible and there is always another level to reach for. Once you have your minimum, target and mindblower goals, you would put in place a range of rewards and consequences to go with this. Remember, we want to reinforce good behaviours, so rewards and consequences are a way of letting yourself and perhaps others know what is working or not.

Your brain is like a puppy, it needs a metaphorical pat on the head when it helps you out, so it continues down the right path. Rewards are a great way of doing this. We're not talking about buying yourself large expensive gifts. The reward needs to be commensurate with the action or goal you have achieved. It could be taking a walk in nature when you have made a difficult call, or watching a movie with the family, or spending some extra time reading, having a bath, or a piece of chocolate. There are many different options, just make sure you set these up when you are setting up the goal or they won't happen when you actually achieve the goal.

Similarly, if for whatever reason you miss your goal, there need to be consequences. Obviously, if you had rewards in place then you don't get them and that might be enough. Or perhaps you need something else to support the right behaviours or outcomes such as a punishment you give yourself. We know one person who set as a consequence of failing to achieve his goal that he had to drive home in San Francisco rush hour traffic. He hated driving so this was his idea of hell. He failed to meet his goal once, forced himself to take the consequence and hated it so much he never missed his target again.

Another example is to make the punishment more of a visualisation rather than something real, as long as it hurts you emotionally so you want to avoid it. Remember my sharing his having a picture of Karene and Mya on my desk and visualising telling them I didn't love them enough to take uncomfortable actions such as phoning past clients. This was a massive incentive to stay in action and achieve my goals. What could you use for yourself?

Accountability

You are now clear on your 'Why', you have your goals clear and written down, you have worked through your fears and you are committed. Even with great intentions, sometimes life gets in the way. This is where having some form of accountability is key to keeping on track.

Accountability can be in many forms from simple to complex, formal and informal, paid and free. What you choose comes down to how important whatever you are trying to achieve is to you. Whilst we can't answer how important being in action and achieving your goals is for you, we can let you know what options you have and when you might opt for more formal and paid options vs an informal route. We can certainly share what we have chosen and why at various points in our journey.

Most simply, accountability is sharing your goals out loud. The very act of sharing what you want with another human (animals don't count here), means it's real. You have called them into existence through language. This can be as simple as telling a friend what you intend to do by when and then asking them to check in with you. Or posting your goal on Facebook for all your 'friends' to see.

You might get an accountability buddy. More than just a friend, this is likely to be someone who is on a similar journey to you and provides an opportunity for mutual support. You might meet up or talk once a week or fortnight to share what your key goals and actions are and then talk through whether you completed them or not. In effect this is an informal coaching arrangement and can be very powerful. The issue with this arrangement might come if your level of commitment differs compared to the other person, or when life gets in the way. This is when a paid accountability coach might be a better option. When you pay, the person you pay has a vested interest in the outcome. This means their level of commitment doesn't waver and if life does get in the way, you have a lever to make sure things are rescheduled and happen.

We provide a Focus and Accountability Coach for our clients to ensure they maintain their momentum and have someone to talk to when things don't go right. All of our Coaches have also completed our Mentorship Programme, however, a coach doesn't need to have done the journey you're on. A coach's role is to hold up a mirror to you and ask good questions that allow you to understand what might have stopped you or created a great result. Their job is to bring out the best in you. The most obvious example is sporting coaches. All Olympic athletes or professional sports persons have coaches. Typically, these coaches haven't performed at the level they are coaching, and they don't need to have. They need to identify blind spots, technique deficiencies and provide guidance as to where or how or what the athlete needs to do to improve/change.

The next step up from a coach is a mentor. A mentor, unlike a coach has performed at the same level or higher to that which they are guiding you on. They have experienced success and ideally failure as well in the areas of life or business you are looking to change. If there is an area of your life you want to change and you are committed, a mentor is going to be your quickest route to achieving success.

Mentors have made the biggest difference to our journey. For me in property for example, I had read the book *Rich Dad Poor Dad* and bought one house. I got further educated and with more knowledge I knew enough to be cautious and my progress stalled. Then I got a mentor and built an entire investment portfolio. Having someone who had experienced my journey and knew where the pitfalls were, was essential. And yes, my mentors cost me a LOT of money. In fact, Chris and I have invested well over £300,000 in our personal and business development so far. However, we've made more than a 12 times return on this investment so it has been more than worth it.

A mentor is also able to tell you what you need to know whether you like it or not. I am very grateful to Chris' mentors for providing some very tough love to sort out his clinic business. I know if they hadn't, we wouldn't have the life we now have. More importantly, we wouldn't be making the difference we are in other people's lives. Several years on, we still use mentors today in our businesses because when something is working why change. We change mentors when we need to focus on different aspects of our businesses and as we have changed. You may find you have mentors for a short time or a long time depending on what you are trying to achieve and the experience they have to offer.

As mentors ourselves, being direct with love is the difference between someone succeeding, or having to quit and get a 'real' job. That said, a mentor can't do it for you. As we've said a number of times now, you have to want whatever change you want enough to go through the pain, the fear and the effort required to get to the other side. And with a mentor, you greatly increase the likelihood of this happening.

Setting Yourself up for Success

One of the common attributes between ultra-high achievers is they don't leave things to chance. As you are a key part of your business, you need to have a way to set yourself up for success each day, no matter what happens. Hoping and praying you'll be alright on the night, is not the path to consistent success!

Karene and I have a couple of systems for this which we use everyday to ensure both we and our Team are functioning at the best possible level.

The 0-10 Scale of Energy

We discussed this in Chapter 6, Confidence. Maintaining high energy is vital to creating any sort of success. However, when we were discussing confidence we focused on high energy in order to have a bigger impact. Now we would like you to consider raising your energy in order to live life on whatever terms you want. The more you want to succeed, or enjoy, or participate in, or have in your life, the more energy you are going to need to both make it happen and keep it happening.

Every single high achiever we've spent time with; the millionaires, the billionaires, the olympic athletes, the serial entrepreneurs, the global philanthropists; all of them bring huge amounts of energy to whatever they're doing. This high energy is essential to be able to perform at any level that goes above and beyond that which most people live their lives by. So focus on raising your energy and keeping it high to make possible the life you want to live.

ACTION STEP

Use the 0-10 energy rating every day to keep yourself on track

Anything below an eight means you need to take action to get yourself back on track.

Get in State!

As discussed above, your energy level is everything. Getting in the right state is how you raise your level. Before any phone call, client conversation, presentation or one of our events, we get ourselves in the best possible state using one or more of the list below depending on the time available and the social expectations of where we are.

Move!

We usually start with our body and get it moving. Dancing, jumping, sudden movements, anything at all to get our blood pumping, our muscles engaged and our brains more alert. Movement wakes us up literally and figuratively. When you start moving, not only will you have more energy and feel more awake, you will find yourself thinking more clearly and with more purpose.

Posture!

Stand up tall and you raise your energy and your emotions. Slump over and you lower them. It's pretty much that simple. Pretend there's a bit of string connected to your head lifting you up and you'll gain a few centimetres in height as well as coming across more powerfully to everyone you speak to. Practice this standing up and sitting down so no matter what position you're in, you boost your energy and come across with presence.

Music!

Play some music that lifts your mood and you'll find your energy increasing. Allow your body to move at the same time and you amplify the effect. Karene and I play different songs depending on the situation.

For example, to keep us connected to the high energy and mindset of training our clients while we write this book, we're currently sitting here at our dining room table writing on our laptops listening to *Try Anything by Shakira* from the movie *Zootropolis.* We love this movie for many reasons and play this song at all of our events because of its energy and its lyrics. We'll both play this song before any important call or client meeting for exactly the same reasons.
For family times, we usually play a song from a Disney movie - Frozen II is a big favourite right now for all of us. This connects us as a family and we all get excited for whatever we're doing together.
If it's date night, either Karene or I will put on, *All of Me* by John Legend. This reminds us of many previous dates and the love we share together. Find your playlist for different situations and use it to raise your level!

Light!

Bright light tells the brain it's day time and time to wake up. Get out in the sunlight whenever possible to raise your energy levels. Artificial light doesn't wake the brain or the body up in the same way as sunlight. Stepping outside, or standing at an open window letting the sunlight wash over you will calm and relax you whilst also releasing endorphins in the body that energise and make you feel good. Obviously, please use effective eye protection and sunscreen if you're going to be out in the sun for any length of time, but remember, the bright natural light will wake you up and raise your level much more effectively than being inside under artificial light even if it's only for a few minutes.

Air!

Breathe. So important and yet most people tend to subconsciously hold their breath or breathe shallow when they are going into client situations. Lack of oxygen is not going to help you function well. Practice deep abdominal breathing and flood your body with oxygen and you'll both relax and feel more energised. Ideally, step outside and into nature and breathe the fresh air and this will massively enhance the effect. The Japanese even have a name for this and call it, Forest Bathing. It refers to the effect that walking in nature has on us to rejuvenate and relax our mind, body and emotions.

ACTION STEP

Get in the best possible State everyday.

What area of State change would you find most beneficial to raise your energy and increase your focus?

Start implementing this in your daily work routines.

Create the Win:Win before the Conversation even starts!

Take the time before any sales conversation to plan how you want the conversation to go. Not just in terms of what you want to cover, but more importantly what outcome you want and the benefit to both parties if that happens. The win:win component is essential to heart centred sales. Without it, it's just used car sales.

Chris often draws this out on the whiteboard in his office before making a sales call. He writes 'Us' on one side of the board and 'Them' on the other. Then he brainstorms what is in it for both parties if a successful sale occurs and we progress to working together. He ALWAYS starts with them first and only moves onto the other column once he has at least five benefits written for the other person.

For example,
The benefits to them of our working together might be:
Increased clients

Increased revenue
Staff training system
Happier staff
More effective staff

The benefits to us from working together might be:
Exciting new client to work with
Increased income
Explore new training techniques for increased results
Testimonial and success story from a new business
More work for our Team

Getting clear on the win:win before you speak gets your mindset focused in the right way and a much better conversation and better result is likely to ensue.

ACTION STEP

Write down the win:win scenario for every conversation before you have it.

See what a difference this makes to your mindset going into the conversation and the different results you create.

Find a Community

Having a supportive community is key to staying the course, whatever that is for you. You may have a loving family and community already who love you as you are. If you start to talk about change they might start to get concerned. This is perfectly normal. All of our loved ones want to keep us safe and we know the status quo is safe because we are already surviving it. Change however, is scary, as it might not be something we can survive.

Despite our evolution, the reptilian part of our brains, the bit just above the base of your spine that controls most instincts and impulses is all about keeping us safe. To do this, it usually avoids change. Right now, no matter how uncomfortable you might be, you are alive. In an attempt to keep us alive and 'safe', our brains equate change with threat. The brain doesn't have any evidence if you change you will survive. Therefore change is bad. This is why it can be hard to break habits and also why our loved ones sometimes keep us stuck or encourage us to stay the same. Recognise their actions for the love it is and also recognise not everyone will remain with you on your journey of transformation. This is ok.

Rather than getting rid of everyone in your life the minute they express resistance or question what you are doing; work with them to understand where their concern comes from them. Take the time to let them know what you want to achieve. Sometimes we assume people know what we are doing or thinking, and yet we haven't explained it to them. If they are still resistant, that's also fine as they will have their own beliefs etc to work with. Just recognise you might need to augment or supplement your current friend group with people who challenge and support you and your growth so those who are resistant have a diluted influence.

We shared how important having the right community and support has been for our journey. It's part of our 3 Step System for Success: Knowledge, Mindset and Community. Our Mentorship Programme and Wealth Mastermind follow this principle and provide our clients with a ready-made community for support, encouragement and challenge precisely because it makes such a massive difference. So if you don't have a community to support your journey, now is the time to go and find one, or perhaps join ours?

www.heartcentredbusiness.com/book-offers

ACTION STEP

Review your current community - the people you spend most time with.

Do they reflect your values and goals?

Are they helping you grow or keeping you stuck?

Explore adding more positive influences into your life and find a specific community who will support you growing in the direction you want.

Chapter Highlights

- ✓ Get clear on your goals and the action steps you need to take each day to move towards them. Create a clear reward and consequence structure
- ✓ Identify what fears are stopping you from taking action and explore what's the worst that could happen. Connect with the pain of inaction and use that to motivate you.
- ✓ Be Accountable to what you say you are going to do. Have someone else, either formally or informally, hold you to the standards you set for yourself.
- ✓ Spend every day in the best possible State for success.
- ✓ Surround yourself with a community that supports you moving forward.

In Closing...

Congratulations, you made it. Thank you for sharing this journey with us. We're excited for what's now possible for you. We said at the beginning, you need three things on your journey to ensure your success: Knowledge, Mindset and Community.

This book has given you some of the Knowledge. You're now clear on how to grow your business and what order to do things in. However, in many ways we've only just scratched the surface. Once you start taking action, things will change, so you will need to re-read and re-apply different components as your business grows. Learning and growing is a never ending process so keep reflecting on what you need to move you forward to the next Phase.

As for Mindset, we've explored the impact your mind is having on your life, your business and your finances. You now know your external reality is a reflection of what is happening for you internally and how you chose to react to life. This book has started shifting your mindset and belief patterns. Keep working on these one step at a time and consider additional support if you want to shortcut your journey.

Now, as proud as we are of this book, we have to reluctantly admit, there's no way it can contain all the answers to every situation you're going to encounter as you grow your business. This is where a supportive community who shares your values and can help you find answers is so important. The right community is the last piece of the puzzle that makes transformation a reality and we would gladly provide this for you through our community of heart centred business clients.

If you want to further accelerate your journey, take advantage of a FREE Coaching Call with one of our Coaching Team (valued at £1,000). By now, you're aware of the difference the right support can make and we'd love to fast-track your journey to success. We promise this free Coaching Call will give you three things:

1. You'll get energised, motivated and have a clear plan of action!
2. You'll have clarity on the three key areas you need to focus on to grow your specific business!
3. We'll explore if we're a match to work together to make your goals a reality.
   If we're a match to work together, we'll get started right away. If we're not a match, we'll advise what other types of support might be a better fit for you.

Whether it's best we work together or not, the call is FREE and you'll find it massively powerful. However, our Coaching Team has limited time, so this call is only for you if you are serious about growing your business and want our support in making that happen.
Please now visit

www.heartcentredbusiness.com/book-offers

to book your call.

We would love to hear what difference this book has made for you so please share your success stories with us so we can celebrate with you.

Connect with us via our public Facebook Group

www.facebook.com/groups/HeartCentredBusiness

Via email hello@heartcentredbusines.com

Or via phone +44 (0)333 987 4245

We're excited to be on this journey with you and thank you for making a bigger difference in the world!

Chris & Karene

www.heartcentredbusiness.com/book-offers

BONUS CHAPTER
100 Ways to Get More Clients

We're sharing the top 100 strategies of Attraction Marketing we teach to our clients. Once they implement our systems, our clients typically increase their income by £50,000-£100,000 within 12 months.

Obviously just getting more clients through the door won't magically make all your business challenges go away, but it's a good start, right.

Since we teach the right things in the right order, we've separated out the different Attraction Marketing strategies into Online and Offline actions. A successful and sustainable business needs to utilise both these areas. However, for most practitioners and experts earning under £100,000 per year, offline marketing will deliver the quickest return on your investment. We recommend our clients start offline and then progress online once they are getting results. We've followed that same format here covering all the offline strategies first before moving onto the online strategies.

Focus on the strategies that are easiest to implement first and then move onto ones that require a little more thought and input. Some strategies may be obvious, some less so. However, every one of these strategies has been tried and tested and collectively they've helped our clients earn millions in extra income. You'll also notice occasional repetition between online and offline strategies. Until you have tested each or asked your clients what works best for them, you won't know whether the offline or online approach works best in your business. Sometimes, you may need to try multiple different ways until you find what works best. For example, some clients may love text messages while others will prefer email or a phone call.

Have fun using these strategies to get more clients and grow your business. We'd love to know the results you get from implementing them. Send us an email to **hello@heartcentredbusiness.com** and let us know your successes and we can perhaps then teach you the next step which is how to have all those new clients happily paying you at least double what they do now.

Of course if you would love to just jump straight to that step, register here for a FREE Business Strategy session with one of our Coaching Team and let's explore what's possible in your business if we were to work together. Please now visit

www.heartcentredbusiness.com/book-offers

to book your call.

OFFLINE MARKETING

Offline Attraction Marketing is the place to concentrate if your business is earning less than £100,000 a year.

Why?

Because it's the area of marketing where you will have the biggest impact and get the best return on your time and money investment. Karene and I are fans of what works rather than what's popular, which is why our clients typically grow by £50,000-£100,000 in the first year of implementing our systems. By focusing initially on offline marketing, you get to find out what works with your particular target market. This means you get to test things out with real people in a simple way, such as by having a conversation with someone and asking their opinion, which doesn't cost you any money. Once you have refined what works for you and what doesn't, you can transition this into online marketing. This saves a fortune in time and money, and creates something that works, rather than gets lost in the noise of thousands of other experts shouting about their services in a very overcrowded online world.

Once you are earning over £100,000, you will have a better handle on your message, what works, and you'll have the money to invest in online marketing.

In Person Attraction Marketing Strategies

We all tend to forget, people buy people. The best form of marketing available to you is YOU. Connecting with people in person will build up trust, connection and knowledge of what you do far more quickly than any other marketing modality. It is definitely something to make time for as you plan your weekly business activities.

1. Get to know your local community

Most of our clients come to us from the local area, so taking the time to become known in the community is time well spent. Make a regular practice of leaving your place of business and going out and meeting other local businesses. Focus on understanding their business and how you could refer them to more clients. This 'give first' attitude will ensure you create a positive impression with other business owners and will encourage them to take a similar interest in helping you with your business. Fundamentally, the more people who know what you do in your local area, the more potential referrals you're going to get.

2. Attend Business Networking Groups

Business networking groups are events and meetings that are specifically set up to help you and other business owners to connect with each other. The relationships that can develop from these events often result in the mutual benefit of referring clients to each other and therefore supporting each other to grow your respective businesses. Some business networks are very structured and have set agendas. Other groups avoid any structure and simply provide a meeting place for business owners to mingle and get to know each other. We suggest trying out all forms of business networking to discover which style works best for you and your business. Perhaps one of our personal favourites and one we have found to be most useful for the majority of our clients, is BNI - Business Network International. However, to find a local business networking meeting in your area simply use Google and type in your postcode followed by Business networking. You'll be amazed at how many different groups are running in your area, no matter where you live.

3. Offer yourself as a prize to local groups or schools

Lots of schools and even charities run raffles or auctions or offer prizes for their internal competitions and are always looking for donations of prizes. Why not offer your services as the prize. It could be a one off consultation, or a series of sessions depending on how much value you are prepared to give away. If you are trying to enter a school community and have no current clients from there, working with someone for free who then becomes a referral source might open up all sorts of possibilities. Even if it costs you, it could be worth it right?

4. Social networking

Say Yes, to those social invitations. Hiding in your business and waiting for clients to walk through the door is not going to get you more clients. And yet it's what many practitioners end up doing. The reality is, unless you have a perfect shop window for your business with high foot traffic and a service that will appeal to a mass market, most of us are not going to get many clients just show up unannounced.

So what's the alternative. Get out there and meet people. The more people you meet the more people in your local area will get to know you and understand how you might be able to help them and/or the people they know. Enjoy having a social life where you go out and meet people and you'll be amazed at how many clients you can get just from having casual chats when you're at social gatherings.

Obviously, it is a social event so you should not be hawking your wares and trying to 'sell' your services to everyone you meet. However, if someone asks what you do, or if you meet someone you could help, it's only polite to share what you do in terms of problem:solution and let the other person decide if they want to know more.

5. Join a club

Becoming a member in a sporting or community group is a great way for people to get to know what you do whilst having fun and building relationships at the same time. Some great examples are sailing, golf, chess, ballroom dancing, bowling, craft and many more.

Anywhere you can connect with other human beings and have a conversation is a good place to start because where do people turn when they want a recommendation for something. To the people they know. Being a part of their club means you are automatically a more trusted part of their life compared with a stranger they find on the internet.

Obviously, though, pick a club or a sport where you want to go and enjoy being a part of. If you don't actually want to be there, you're not going to turn up regularly and you won't build lasting relationships.

6. Attend a MeetUp Group

Meetup.com is a great way to find groups of people with similar interests. It's simply an online directory that allows people to advertise groups and meetings they are running. There are thousands of meetups happening every day across the planet so there really is something for everyone and every possible interest or hobby.

Find a meetup you think you'll enjoy, register your attendance online and then turn up in person and see what it is like. Make sure to be social while you're there so along with having a good time, perhaps learning something new, you also get to increase your network by making some new connections with people who share similar interests as you.

How do you know they have similar interests. They wouldn't be at that meetup if they didn't. Remember, people like people who are like them. Starting to hang around more with people who share the same interests as you is a great way to increase your chances of having more like-minded clients start using your services.

7. Create a MeetUp Group

Alongside attending other people's meetups, what if you created one of your own specifically targeted towards your ideal clients?

Let's say you're an expert at resolving neck pain. What if you created a meetup group specifically called, "How to resolve your neck pain". This is likely to be attractive to people who actually have the challenge or problem you are perfectly equipped to support. Which means by offering your knowledge for free or low cost, you get exposure to your ideal clients and they get to understand who you are and how you're different from other experts in the neck pain field.

Obviously, this is applicable to everyone who has an expertise, not just you neck pain specialists. The key is to narrow down your focus to a clear problem:solution so it is immediately attractive to a certain group of people. The meetup itself should be informative and relatively light-hearted. Definitely NOT a 60 minute pitch of your services and how great you are. Just like networking, focus on giving first and providing useful information and you are much more likely to build the trust needed for people to start asking you how you could more specifically help them with their particular challenge.

8. Attend local community events

Being a regular part of your community at local events is a great way to build relationships. Attending these events is good as you can start to get to know people. However, even better is volunteering in some way to help out at community events. Yes, this can be time consuming so needs to be managed carefully to ensure it doesn't negatively impact other areas of your life. However, giving your time is a great way for people to understand more about who you are, and what you are like outside of your work role. The better people know you, the more trust they have in you and the more likely they are to make referrals to you when appropriate.

9. Sponsor a local sports team

Pick a sport you enjoy and actually have an interest in and get to know the coach and the manager. Ask them what they need, is it money in the form of sponsorship or advertising; or would they actually benefit more from your expertise. Either way, by first understanding what they want, it will create a better relationship that will be more mutually beneficial. Obviously, the upside for you will be exposure and getting known for what you do. This could be as simple as having your name or business services emblazoned on the players jerseys so you get advertising; or it could be by serving the team itself with your expertise, you start getting the team members and their families starting to see you as clients.

10. Visit your local colleagues who work in the same industry

Go and visit your local competition and build a relationship with them. Too many business owners never meet their local competitors to the detriment of both parties. Yes, on one level you might be competing for the same clients. However, I guarantee people who like you will not be the same people who like someone else. We are all different and unique individuals and therefore will appeal to different groups of people.

Getting to know your local colleagues could be a useful asset for when you go on holiday, or maybe need to make a referral for a client you can't support yourself. It's far better customer service to refer your clients to someone you know than just a random stranger and it works both ways - you may also get referrals out of it.

It can be a great way to do CPD (Continuing Professional Development) and build each other's skills. It can also be a great way to learn what your colleagues are doing in their business: the good, the bad and the ugly. Obviously, you can copy the good and implement what they are doing well in your own business. However, learning what other people are not doing well is just as valuable as it helps prevent you from making the same mistake. Chris used to keep both a TO DO list and a NOT TO DO list for things he saw when he visited other businesses.

11. Have a stall at the local fair or community event

Having a stall where you can showcase your expertise for your local community is a way for people to realise you exist, understand what you do and perhaps even try out your services in a mini 'taster' session. The more opportunities people have to experience your expertise and talk with you in person, the more likely they are to either become a client or recommend you to their friends and family.

One of the things you'll notice most when you have a stand at a local event is the number of people who comment they had no idea you did this, or no idea you were based in their local area. We are mostly all victims of being the world's best kept secret so having a stall dramatically increases your visibility in the community.

Does the stand have to be elaborate or particularly fancy. The key here is professionalism. It's not about spending a lot of money on marketing materials or fancy signage etc. Simply invest in some professionally designed and printed roll up banners, as well as nicely printed flyers or give-away materials for people to take with them. This will go a long way to build up your credibility and professional reputation.

One last point to consider is how you can get people to experience what you do personally (if appropriate) or what added value could you give them because they visited your stand. A free gift or a prize draw is always a good addition.

12. Have a stall at your local school summer or Christmas fair

Schools are great places to network and are very tight-knit communities where everyone knows everyone. Start working with some people from school and do a good job and you are almost guaranteed to get more clients from the school community as word will spread.

By hosting a stall at the school events, you contribute to the community, because you are paying money for the stall and you (hopefully) are making a difference for people who visit your stall, rather than just trying to sell your services. This 'give first' attitude is what drives school communities - think of the PTA (Parent Teacher Association) that every school has.

Something to be aware of is that just as a good reputation will spread rapidly around the school parents, so will a bad one. Make sure to go above and beyond in your service, quality and in taking care of people in that community and you will massively benefit.

13. Mentor in local schools or community groups

Local schools are always looking for contributors at their careers fairs and some have set up mentoring programs in senior schools so that the children have the opportunity to gain from knowledge and skills that goes beyond what they can learn in the classroom. There are also local charities that work with schools to run different careers days that may similarly allow you to build a relationship with the local school community.

Karene mentors Year 12 and 13 girls (sixth form for us older folk) at our daughter Mya's school. Providing guidance and support for these teenagers in their career aspirations has been fulfilling personally, as well as useful professionally as many more people in the school now know who she is as well as what she does in her businesses.

14. Create Referral Partnerships

Identify what types of additional services could be useful or interesting for your clients. By this we specifically mean services that would complement and support what you currently do with your clients rather than compete in any way. For example, if you are a Personal Trainer and you help people lose weight, additional services that would be useful for your clients could be: a nutritional assessment, a structural alignment consultation with an osteopath or chiropractor, a mindset session to work on removing 'bad' habits, or even a style or image sessions to help your clients create a new look to go with their new physique and lifestyle.

Once you've identified what additional services might be useful, take the time to locate and get to know local experts who specialise in these skills and build a referral partnership with them. How it works is you co-promote each other to your respective clients and because you offer complementary and non-competing services everyone benefits.

15. Advertise on your local Radio

Although radio does not have the same allure as it did in the past, it is still a great way to get your name and business known in your local community. Avoid national radio and focus on local stations only, as this is where you will connect with people in your area who are able to become your clients.

With radio commercials, it's worth investing in an expert to help you do it properly as you want to make the most of your opportunity and investment.

There are five key areas to consider in order to have the greatest impact:

- Make sure your commercial is short: it needs to be under 30 seconds

- Informative: think problem:solution so your listeners can immediately identify you as an expert and determine if you are relevant to them.
- Entertaining: you don't have to have jazzy music and special effects, but your commercial does need to be interesting and worth listening to. Just listing where you trained, your qualifications and that you are based at xyz address does not make for interesting listening.
- Have a call to action: People need to know *why* they should be contacting you and perhaps most importantly, *how* to do that. Do they phone you? Email you? Just pop into your office?
- Have a special offer: sometimes people need a little something extra to get them to take action. This could be a discount for the first five people, or perhaps a bonus for everyone who quotes xyz code.

16. Contribute to a magazine relevant to your profession

Identify some magazines that have a readership that you would describe as your ideal clients and ask them what type of articles they might like to feature in their upcoming editions. By asking what they are looking for before you start writing, you don't waste any time writing things they don't want, and you have much more chance of your articles being accepted.

Remember, to be interesting to the magazine's readership, and therefore interesting to the magazine editors, your articles need to be focused on providing solutions for common problems. Avoid making the typical mistake most of us experts make of going into too much detail and/or using technical jargon when explaining things. Remember, most people aren't as interested in this topic as you are, they simply want to understand what is going on and how to fix it. If you can provide simple to follow advice for a challenge that many people are struggling with, you will interest both the magazine editors as well as a lot of their readership who might then consider becoming a client.

An added benefit of contributing to a magazine is that you can then use their name and logo in any marketing you do which increases your credibility. For example, Chris and Karene Lambert-Gorwyn, as featured in Money Success magazine.

17. Volunteer

Give your time whenever and wherever you can. This is not about just becoming busy and overworked, nor about filling your diary with distractions so you don't have enough time to do the things you know you should do but are secretly avoiding... like making phone calls!

However, volunteering in some shape of form will benefit you and your business in many different ways. From building relationships, to expanding your network, to increasing your sense of fulfilment, to generally just having a good time. These are all good reasons to volunteer in any capacity you can. And because of the laws of karma, you never know when it's going to come back to you

18. Shop local and speak to people

Spending your money locally is a good idea economically as well as from a business networking perspective. Keeping money flowing in your local community is a good way to support other business owners to survive. Statistically, the more local businesses there are, the more every business earns as people can shop local for more of their needs. Therefore, doing your own shopping locally both helps the business community and indirectly your own business as well.

The added benefit is that by shopping locally, you get to know the other business owners and can start to build the type of relationship where you are all actively looking to support each other and will refer potential customers to each other.

19. Smile and start conversations wherever you go

Smiling is one of those universally contagious actions guaranteed to break down barriers no matter where in the world you use it. However, too many of us resist the simple act of connecting with people because of modern social norms of don't make eye contact and pretend to be busy looking at your mobile phone.

And in a way, it's no wonder, as we all grew up with the message of "Don't speak to strangers" When we're children, this is good, safe advice. However, does it really serve us as well when we are adults. Meeting strangers is the only way to develop the connections and community that makes success possible in any area of life or business. If you're not sure of this, let us put it another way, consider that every friend or romantic partner you have in your life was once a stranger?

Perhaps a more effective mindset for meeting people could be to consider a stranger to be a friend you just haven't met yet. And smiling at people is a way of starting that connection.

Now we don't advocate wandering around grinning at people like a crazy person. Perhaps consider situations when you have an opportunity to connect with someone, such as the person you're sitting next to on the bus, or someone standing next to you in a coffee queue, smile and start a conversation. It doesn't have to be anything profound, simply start with smiling at them and see where it goes.

20. Contribute to a local Radio Show

Become a guest speaker at a local radio. Local rather than national radio so you are speaking to people who could become your clients rather than the entire nation, which although is good for credibility, isn't useful for most professionals at building a client list. Also choose a radio station with a focus in your particular area, such as a health radio if you are in the health or wellness profession.

Radio stations are always looking for interesting topics and guest experts so come up with something that their audience might find interesting and get in touch with the radio to see if they will run with it.

As always, to have more chances of people finding it interesting and perhaps consider becoming a client, (and to have a chance of the radio featuring you as their expert) focus everything you say around the concept of problem and solution. People want to relate to what you're saying and feel they learn something that could help them immediately with a problem they are struggling with. This doesn't mean you have to solve the problem entirely with a few simple tips. However, it does mean there should be some solid advice you can give during your section that goes further than saying, "Pick up the phone and book a consultation with me to solve this problem"

Text Message (SMS) Attraction Marketing Strategies

Yes, this could be argued to be an online activity, however, it fits the grey area between online and offline. Partially this is because of how we access text or SMS messages. Nearly always it is via our mobile phones and the act of having something appear on our phones makes it more personal and more accessible. Texts by their very nature have to be short and to the point. No one wants to read a multi-page text message. The key, with text, is to use them effectively and in a way that encourages action rather than just interrupting people's days.

21. Text message Appointment Reminders

It's frustrating when a client doesn't show up for their appointment isn't it?!
The NHS calculates the cost of no-show patients in the billions. Even though your business might not be quite the same scale as the NHS, we're certain that any no-show hurts a little.

When you look at it more closely, a client missing their appointment is a lose:lose scenario. The client misses out on making progress that day and could be frustrated at the lack of results. On the other hand, as most practitioners and experts charge per session rather than in programmes or packages; if a client doesn't show up, the practitioners income for the day has just decreased significantly. This is a precarious way to run a business!

Send an SMS reminder the day before and one hour before someone's appointment. This will ensure they either show up; or they'll let you know they're not coming so you're not hanging around waiting for a client who doesn't show. Keep the SMS short, to the point and polite and your no-shows will definitely decrease. Most online scheduling tools will offer SMS reminders as part of their system so if yours doesn't, it may be time to get a new system.

22. Send out SMS check-up Reminders

Reconnect with past clients at regular intervals such as three or six months and remind them that a simple check-up, like getting your car serviced, or going to the dentist, could help prevent problems from building up. As always with SMS messages, keep it short and direct and include a booking link for the client to click on so they can easily schedule their follow up appointment. The simpler and easier you can make it, the greater the success rate of re-engaging your past clients.

23. Send an SMS special Offer

Send all of your past and current clients (providing they have agreed to be contacted this way), an SMS message that gives them a limited time promo code. This could be a discount on their next session for the first 5 people to respond. It could be a half price session of something that could support their work with you, such as massage or nutritional advice, if the link is clicked within the next 24 hours.

The quick and easy format of text messages means short term bonus offers are usually well received and well responded to. Either have a time limiter, such as 24 hours only, or a numbers limiter, such as the first 5 people and you'll enjoy a much better response rate.

24. Text Your Clients a Question

Ask your clients a simple question, such as, "Name one thing that could be done to improve this business or service" This question will generate engagement with your client base and also give you invaluable information about ways you could improve your business to better serve your clients. Not all the suggestions they make will be viable or doable yet pay close attention. If your clients tell you what they want and feel listened to, they're much more likely to remain your client and will bring many more of their friends and contacts to you as well.

As a way of saying thank you for their suggestions, enter all entries into a prize draw where they could win something, such as a free session, or a voucher for coffee/cinema/gift... anything at all just as a way to say thank you.

Phone

Picking up the phone and calling people is a massively underrated form of communication nowadays. Primarily, this is because we all fear rejection and therefore come up with all sorts of excuses such as we're too busy, or it's difficult to get a hold of people, or no one has time to answer the phone. And yet, if you knew that you would get at least 5 times more clients from phoning people compared with having the same number of people read a social media post, would that change your mind about whether getting on the phone could be a useful part of your marketing strategy?

Why does phoning people work so well? Remember, people buy people. If they connect with you online, there is a very superficial level of human interaction. However, when people hear your voice, there is a much deeper connection between you, meaning you have the chance of creating a better relationship. This is the start of someone either becoming a client, or referring someone they know to come and see you.

How many companies actually take the time to call you and see how you're getting on? Not many right? So getting on the phone is a great way to stand out from your competition and have people feel special because you made the effort to call them. As the world goes more and more online, it is these personal offline interactions that stand out and create long term brand loyalty

25. Personally call every person who has a Consultation within 24 hours

This courtesy call needs to happen within 24 hours of any consultation, whether or not that person has become a client. It is simply a call to say you enjoyed meeting them, to answer any questions they may have and to ensure they understand the best next steps.

If they have become a client, the next steps might be the details of their next session, checking they have the correct payment details to ensure they can make payment, or making sure they understand any exercises or homework you gave them. Speaking to people within 24 hours of the consultation is the best way to ensure they stick as a client, rather than being one of those who says they'll turn up for the second appointment and then you never hear from them again.

If you have a consultation with someone and they don't become a client, still follow up with them within 24 hours. This could be to check that they have the details of the person or service you have referred them to. It could be just to make sure they are ok and understand what their next actions steps are. These follow up calls are what will build up your reputation for outstanding customer service and ensure you become someone's go-to person for any challenges they or their connections have.

26. Follow up with people who had a Consultation but didn't become a client.

Staying in contact with people who didn't buy your services to make sure they are getting the support they need is one of the best ways to generate referrals. Looking after people who don't spend money with you shows people it's not just business, it's personal. Few companies ever provide this level of service and you will instantly stand out and build a reputation as the go-to expert.

To put this in perspective, in Chris's clinic, some of the people who provided him the highest number of referrals are people he never worked with. During the consultation, he determined he wasn't the best person to work with them and referred them to somewhere else. He then followed up to ensure they were getting the outcome they desired and generally made sure they were happy. This has meant those clients he never worked with, would send him everyone they knew because they understood Chris would give them exactly what they need whether he worked with them or not.

27. Follow up with all past clients at regular 3 - 6 month intervals.

Simply checking in with your past clients to see how their doing is a massively underrated activity in generating clients. The phone call is unexpected, always appreciated and often leads to the old client becoming a new client again, or in them passing you a referral. How many of your competitors offer this level of aftercare.

A simple courtesy call will go a long way to reminding your clients how much they value working with you. Obviously make sure you have their consent to call them by setting this up during the consultation. This way they know it's part of the service you offer your clients to ensure they keep making progress even after your initial time of working together is over. Most people would happily give you their consent to be called when it's presented in this fashion.

28. Phone a Friend

Phone your friends and family and tell them you're expanding your business and taking on some new clients. Many of them may not realise they can refer people to you and that this is a key way you run your business. Ask them who might they know who might like to solve xyz problem, where the challenge you describe is exactly what you specialise in resolving. Many of your connections will not have heard you describe your business in this way before so it is a great way to help them better understand what you do and how it might be relevant to the people they know. With only six degrees of separation keeping you from speaking to anyone on the planet, you'd be amazed at who your connections are able to introduce you to.

29. Reconnect with your contact list

Phone people you haven't spoken to for years and find out what they're doing in life and business. By reconnecting and being genuinely interested in what they're doing, they in turn will have an interest in what you're doing. It might be they have no idea you've started your own business. Or if they do know about it, they may not understand exactly what you do or who you might be able to help. Make it a priority to try and help the other person by thinking about connections and introductions you could make to them, or other types of support you could offer. By giving first in this way, it ensures people will also try to do the same for you, so the conversation is much more likely to end up as a win:win for both of you.

30. Ask for Opinions

Ask your friends and family for their opinion on your marketing message. Tell them you're expanding your business and testing out a new way of marketing and would love to get their input. Most people love to give their opinion so they'll happily give you a few minutes to tell them what your marketing message is. You then say your person:problem:solution message so they properly understand what you do. Once they've heard it, and given their opinion, you can simply ask, "Do they know anyone who might be curious?"

Post / Direct Mail Attraction Marketing Strategies

Remember what it was like to receive a letter or a card when you were little? It was exciting, wasn't it? Post was associated with something good such as our birthday or Christmas. This good feeling towards post stays with us even if nowadays we only receive bills or junk mail through the letterbox.

Sending people things through the post is a great way to grab their attention and reconnect them with what it feels like to get nice surprises in the mail. And is this digital world where everyone communicates online, going old school and sending out postal mail is guaranteed to help you stand out from everyone else and show more of a personal touch than just sending an email that will get lost with hundreds of others in an overcrowded inbox.

31. Send out a letter to all of your past clients

Write to past clients and simply ask them how they are doing. No other purpose than a simple courtesy letter just checking in is a great way to reconnect with your past clients and bring the great work you did with them back into their consciousness. This extra and unexpected customer service will go a long way to move them from past client to becoming a current client again (if that's appropriate) or could easily lead them to make you a referral.

Make sure the letter is short, clear and professional looking and include your professional photo in your letterhead to reconnect them with you as a person rather than just as a business.

32. Send out a thank you card

Let your clients know you appreciate them. A simple thank you for being a client card will go a long way to creating loyalty to you and our business and more referrals. A handwritten Thank You card is something almost nobody does nowadays.

Think about it, when did you last handwrite a thank you card. Probably after a birthday party when you were a child and your parents made you sit down and write thank you cards to everyone who attended. The message doesn't have to be long but the extra effort people know you have gone to write it personally will ensure it is well received. You will stand out from ALL of your competitors.

33. Remember Special Events

Birthdays, anniversaries, new babies, new jobs etc are all great opportunities to get in touch and show people that you care. You might just focus on celebrating the event with the client or you could also offer them something to get in touch in some way, such as a free MOT or call or similar that would add value to them.

34. Create a special offer flyer and deliver it to your local residents

Letting your local community know what you do is key to a small business. We all forget that most of our customers are locals and so we need to nurture our local community in order to be known as the go-to person in your area. Create a flyer that lets people know simply and clearly who you are and what you do, as in person:problem:solution. Avoid using medical or professional jargon!

To make it stand out even more and improve the likelihood of people taking action and coming to see you, your flyer needs to have an irresistible offer or free gift to entice people to come into your business. What constitutes an irresistible offer? It could be anything at all, such as a free consultation for the first 5 people who respond? It could be a free nutritional assessment for the first 10 people who book a massage. It could be a cinema or coffee voucher for anyone booking an exclusive half price consultation? As long as it seems like great value and appeals to your target market, it'll work. However, just so you know, a 10% discount does not count as irresistible and will just end up in the bin!

35. Create a special occasion postcard

Whether it's Christmas, Easter, summer holidays or whenever, send your local residents a postcard wishing them well and letting them know something you have going on in your business. It could be you just share that your team is expanding as you take on a new member of staff? It could be that you have a special offer available? It could simply be wishing them seasonal greetings and letting them know that you're around in case they need your services. Postcards like this, help make people curious about who you are and because you're now on their radar, they'll be more likely to think of you when they have a problem that needs fixing. Real Estate agents are great at this and staying on people's radar just by sending out seasonal cards.

36. Send your clients a letter gifting them and/or a friend a special offer

We all like to receive special invitations and gifts through the post. Send your clients an offer for a bonus or half price session and let them know that they can use this voucher themselves or they can gift it to a friend. Making sure that they can choose whether they want to use it themselves is a key part to the magic here. Normally most companies only make special offers available to new customers so by opening this out to your existing clients, you reward them for being part of your client family and continue to build their loyalty.

37. Connect with charities

Send a letter to local charities introducing yourself, thanking them for the work they do and offering them your services. This assistance could take many different forms ranging from giving some of your client slots to the charity for free for their staff to use; to coming into their offices and manning the phones, cleaning up, organising or whatever you feel you could do to help them.

Charities are great places to network, build a good reputation and simply give back. And as we all know, what we put out there always comes back to us in some way, somehow - if nothing else, think of giving to charities as karma in action!

38. Send a reminder letter like your dentist does

Why is it that we all accept that we should service our cars every year and get our teeth checked every 6 months but don't get any other regular check-ups?

One of the reasons why tooth health has improved so much and why dentistry practices have become so much more lucrative is the simple premise that we should all get our teeth checked every 6 months. What if you started advising the same to your clients, using whatever timescale is appropriate for your work?

Do you think people might have less mental health issues if they had a mental health check-up and tune up every 6 months?

What about Osteopaths or Chiropractors? Would their patients benefit from having regular realignment sessions to prevent problems from building up?

Every single profession could better serve its clients by suggesting regular sessions to head off problems before they start. Start introducing this in your own business and send a simple letter reminding your clients of the benefits of this. You'll get a lot more repeat clients who get better results and therefore are happier to be working with you

39. Write to your local Councillors offering your services

Whether we agree with their politics or not, being a Councillor often requires a lot of thankless service. Imagine how it might feel for them to receive a letter thanking them for what they do and offering your support and assistance. Local councils are a great place to build your network and establish connections that could prove very useful in promoting your services in the local area. Councillors, because of the very nature of their job, have a very wide network and a large degree of influence on the people that speak with them. Having your local councillor recommend your services is a sure-fire way to build a good reputation and get more clients!

40. Write to local celebrities or business heroes

Is there someone in your local area you admire or who has achieved something special. Write to them and let them know you admire what they have done and would like to offer them your support and some complimentary sessions with you. Whether or not they take you up on your offer, your letter will make them feel good and puts you on their radar as a like-minded professional. You never know where this kind of relationship could progress.

41. Write to your local Schools

Could you offer any form of your services to either educate the children or to help the school itself. Schools are a very powerful place to network and market yourself, but just like any networking, it only works if you give first. If you help the school in some way, they will probably be happy to mention you in their newsletter which suddenly means you have access to an entirely new database. Whether or not you have children yourself, becoming part of the school community will suddenly open you up to a previously unassessed group of people who all turn to each other for recommendations, support and advice.

42. Send your clients a thank you gift

Imagine how your clients might feel to receive an unexpected card or letter from you that contains a free coffee voucher or perhaps a book or some other simple gift. Small tokens of appreciation for your clients will work wonders in creating a stream of loyal clients and referrals.

It doesn't mean you have to spend a lot of time or money on this. Just consider what your clients might appreciate and perhaps combine it with the time of year. Such as a small Easter egg, or maybe a Christmas Tree decoration. It could be a printed voucher included in a simple card, or it might be a small package or parcel depending on what you send. The key here is that it is an unexpected physical token of appreciation that will go so much further to make someone feel appreciated than any email or social media post.

Attraction Marketing Strategies Inside your Business

Your business itself is perhaps one of your best forms of marketing you have available.

Why? Because everyone there has an interest in what you do, otherwise they wouldn't be there. However, too few of us use our biggest resource effectively. Now we know some of you will work from home, or even work with your clients online so you might not have a business premises per se. However, most of these strategies could be used in many different ways so start thinking creatively about how you could apply the following strategies and you'll be amazed at how many more clients you'll have 'walking through your door'.

43. Create a Special Offer Poster

Launch a special offer where your regular clients can purchase a bulk number of sessions in advance for either a discounted price or to get a bonus gift included. If these clients come in regularly they are going to purchase these sessions anyway, so by allowing them to purchase in advance and either save money or get something extra, you are doing them a favour. The benefits to you are:

- You get a more guaranteed commitment that the client is going to keep coming, because they have already paid for their sessions.
- The upfront commitment means the client is more committed to the work they are doing with you which means they will follow your advice more closely and get better results. Better results equals a happier client which is definitely good for business!
- You get an upfront injection of money into your business

Advertise this offer to your clients by creating a poster that is clearly visible in your waiting area or consulting room. If you don't have a specific place you work, or if you work virtually with your clients, then simply tell all of your clients about this offer as well as perhaps creating a flyer you could send via email. No offer will work if people don't know about it, so make sure to tell people so they can choose whether they want to take advantage of it.

44. Create a FREE Consultation flyer and ask your clients to give them away

Free consultations might seem like they cost you money, but they are a great way to get new people through your door. As most of your clients probably see you for at least a couple of sessions after the consultation, by giving away your time initially, you gain a new paying client which is worth more than the cost of the consultation. You can also work with donating this initial consultation to charity as a way of giving more to charity and if the consultation doesn't become a client then you are less likely to have to deal with refunds or concerns over what they got from the initial consultation

45. Identify your key referrers and nurture them

Ask every client for a referral and ensure you reward people who give referrals. People who have referred clients to you are invaluable and should be continually nurtured and made to feel special. Why. Well, if you want them to keep doing what they are doing, let them know you appreciate it. Saying thank you, acknowledging them, asking them how you could help them in return, touching base with them on a regular basis are all good ways to continue to strengthen the relationship and create even more referrals

46. Create a competition that all clients can get involved in

Depending on what your practice is, some examples could be:

Most increased flexibility (such as hamstrings, or hips, or shoulders etc)

Best 10 second video presentation

Most inventive way to describe why someone should attend your practice

Most weight lost

Most number of referrals

Best time to complete xyz challenge

Best photo demonstrating a value that's central to your business

47. Make sure everyone knows your business is based on referrals

A lot of our contacts don't know that it is ok to refer to us. Make sure they all know that because your business is based on referrals you don't need to advertise which means you can keep the session price as low as possible. Letting people know that referrals are your main source of clients is also a great way of promoting the quality of what you do. Automatically when people hear this, they know that your clients must be happy with your service otherwise they wouldn't refer you to other people.

A simple way to promote this, and create more referrals, is to put a simple sentence at the bottom of your emails and on all your marketing materials such as business cards and flyers. Anything that goes out to the public should advertise the fact that your business is based on referrals.

48. Create a family policy

Offer your clients the chance to bring in a family member and they'll both receive sessions at a family special discounted rate. If you're supporting and helping one member of a family, rest assured there's someone else in the family unit that would love to experience similar benefits.

By creating a family policy, you make it easy for more family members to access your services and even if they enjoy sessions at a reduced rate and you make less money per session, you have still increased the number of people using your services overall which means a bigger business and more people out there singing your praises

49. Provide flexibility of appointments

This doesn't mean working every hour God sends. Yet your clients need a variety of different appointment times available as they all have different needs. Some people will want appointments early in the morning before work; some will want appointments after the morning school run; some people will prefer lunchtimes; and some will prefer the evenings after work.

Having a variety of session times available throughout the week, helps your clients fit your services around their existing work and life commitments. A simple way to do this without sacrificing your own work-life balance is to adjust your diary so that all these times are covered throughout the week.

For example,

Mondays you might do an early shift and work from 7am - 12pm.

Tuesdays, you might work 12pm - 5pm

Wednesdays, you might work 3pm - 8pm

Thursdays, you might work 7am - 12pm

Fridays, you might work 12pm - 5pm

A schedule like this provides a variety of sessions throughout the week without having to work more than 25 hours per week. In addition, the sessions are spaced out so a client could attend twice during a week at the same appointment time. Of course, if your clients prefer evening sessions rather than morning sessions, you could adapt this schedule accordingly.

50. Limit your hours - set clear boundaries

If you're always available to your clients, you'll end up with no life outside your business and this is not sustainable in the long run. It also sets unrealistic expectations for your clients of you always being able to fit around their schedule which counter-intuitively means you downgrade your value.

This might seem a strange concept that being more available is perceived as less valuable. However, think about what is considered more valuable, things that are readily available or things that are more exclusive. The more exclusive something is, the more limited the access and the higher the price all leads to a perception of higher value. It's not about playing 'hard to get' to your clients and deliberately limiting your diary. It's about setting clear boundaries around your existing hours and limiting yourself to only working during these times and not taking on additional clients outside your set hours.

This means your clients have to fit around your diary rather than you fit around theirs. You'll also be pleasantly surprised how often clients who say they couldn't possibly come in at a different time, manage to free up their diaries when they have no choice. Something to note is working fewer hours while earning the same amount of money, is the equivalent to getting a pay rise, and with your free time you could always set aside an extra hour each day to see a new client as well.

51. Set up a loyalty scheme

Loyalty is what keeps clients returning to a business. Statistically, clients who return more often are the clients who are more likely to make referrals. Recognise your clients loyalty and give them treats and rewards when they've had a certain number of sessions. Sounds simple but you'd be amazed at what people will do to get a free cup of coffee.

We all know how much we like to get something for free, so think about what your particular client base might most appreciate. You could give people a coffee voucher, a free session, a book, cinema voucher, absolutely anything at all that you feel might help incentivise people to commit to turning up to their sessions. Greater commitment to sessions will get your clients better results and you have a better functioning business

52. Make referrals yourself

You can't expect people to refer to you if you don't refer yourself. It's like being told to brush your teeth by a dentist with bad teeth and halitosis. Put another way, it's just karma. We get back what we put out there!

Worried you don't know how to give referrals or that you don't know enough people. Start with your clients and listen to what they say. If they mention a particular challenge they are having and you know someone you think might be able to help, ask their permission to introduce them, if you think it's appropriate.

Adopt a habit of paying attention to what people are saying and listening with the concept of, "How could I help this person and who could I introduce them to that might make a difference?" This attitude of giving will foster the same attitude in the people you speak with and lead to your receiving more referrals just because you give more yourself!

53. Invite a local colleague to see your practice

Getting to know your competition is the best way to turn them into your colleagues rather than your competitors. Cross referrals will only happen between professionals who know and trust each other.

By inviting a colleague to see your business you're starting the process of building trust. Be open with them about what you do and how you do it and forget any worries about them stealing your ideas. Your clients come to you because of you. They will not abandon ship and go to your competition just because they start to do some things the same way you do.

By being completely open with your colleagues, they are more likely to be open with you and you might be pleasantly surprised at what you learn and how this could help your business. As they say, a rising tide raises all ships, so share your success and allow others to share their success with you and everyone will benefit.

54. Expand your Team

By having additional team members, you can offer additional services to your clients. This makes your business more of a one-stop shop for everything your clients need. This makes it much more appealing and convenient for your clients.

Make sure the additional team members are complementary rather than competitive with what you do currently. For example, if you are a Personal Trainer and help your clients lose weight, taking on team members who provide nutritional support, structural alignment, mindset training or styling advice to support their new body shape; would all be good additions to your business. Taking on another Personal Trainer who has a different training philosophy who would contradict your advice, would not be a good fit.

When hiring new people, or collaborating with other experts, we always advise it is better to hire based on personality and values rather than expertise. Of course you want someone who is competent so that they can help your clients. However, more important is how they make your clients feel when they are working with them and this comes down to their personality and their values.

An averagely skilled 'expert' with a great personality will make their clients feel great and they will come back time and time again. A great 'expert' with an average personality will make their clients feel good yet they are not that likely to come back.

Skills can be learnt. Personality cannot.

55. Offer additional services

What extra support might your clients need? Is there anything extra you could do for them, or is there any other service that could support your clients and complement what you're currently doing?

For example, if you currently work with people to improve their confidence, could you also offer them advice or support around their dietary choices?

If you currently help people lose weight, could you also help them create a new style to match their new physique?

If you work with people to resolve their back pain, could you also work on their mindset so they create better habits?

The more support and service you can give your clients, the more they will buy from you and the higher the lifetime value of each client. Lifetime value is the average amount that each client is worth to your business, as in, how much money do your clients typically spend with you when they engage your services. It is the lifetime value that determines if your business is sinking or swimming and how much marketing you need to do. A low client lifetime value, means you need a large larger number of new clients walking through your door to make ends meet. The higher the lifetime value, the fewer clients you need to make the same amount of income.

56. Host an evening or lunchtime drinks

Inviting your clients, their connections and your local community to your place of business for a social gathering is a great way to let people know what you do and build a sense of community around you. If you don't have a premises where you can invite people, consider using a local venue such as a coffee shop. In this situation consider hosting your drinks at a time when the venue is not usually open. This way you create additional revenue for the venue at a time when they don't usually have any, and you are not conflicting with any of their existing business. An example of this might be that most coffee shops close in the evenings as their busiest times are during the day. If you hold an evening drinks, you are using a space not otherwise being used and so creating a win:win for you and the owner.

Decide if you're serving alcohol or not and make the drinks free as it's very rare for someone to abuse this at an event like this. Usually we would suggest non-alcoholic during the day and alcoholic in the evening but it depends on your client base. The drinks serve as a chance to network and mingle and by inviting your existing clients as well as new people, you build a sense of community. This in turn creates loyalty to you and your business. Allowing your clients to bring friends and family means you widen the group of people who know you and so people who are not yet your clients get the chance to meet you and understand what you do.

57. Share your knowledge

Hold a small seminar or workshop either in your business or somewhere local to where you work and share your expertise for free. By sharing your knowledge in a person:problem:solution format, people get to:

- Understand what you do. With this knowledge, they can refer you to other people.
- Learn something useful. They can hopefully use this to improve their life in some way. This, generates goodwill and increased likelihood of them either becoming your client or making you a referral
- Know you as the go-to expert in your area. This increases your chances of referrals as an expert is always in higher demand compared to a generalist.

If you don't want to hold your own workshop, you could offer this service to any groups who meet in your local area, such as the WI (Women's Institute), the Rotary Club, Church Groups; as these groups are often looking for interesting topics and speakers.

58. Bring in an expert

Hosting a talk or workshop for an expert who is non-competitive to what you do is a great value add for your clients. Make sure the person you invite to speak to your clients is an expert in a topic that would be of interest to your clients and is complementary to your services.

For example, if you are a muscluo-skeletal practitioner, such as an Osteopath or Chiropractor, some great experts for you to bring in would be Nutritionists, Mindset Coaches and Personal Trainers.

Hosting a talk like this for your clients is a great win win all round:

- Your clients are happy as they get to meet someone useful and/ or interesting.
- The expert you bring in is happy as they get the chance to meet some new people they otherwise wouldn't have met and they might get some new clients.
- You're happy as you get all the reflected glory and everyone loves you as you made it all happen

59. Review your services

Spend one hour each month reviewing your business services and exploring ways you could improve or upgrade the experience and outcomes for your clients. The more you can increase and improve your level of service, the happier your clients will be, the better results they're going to get, the more you'll stand out from your competition and the more referrals you'll get!

It might be that the changes you make each month are minor things, such as, updating the magazine collection in the waiting room, or providing a range of different teas for your clients to choose from while they wait for their appointment. However, continuous improvement is what the Japanese call Kaizen and is the reason why companies like Toyota have been so successful. Kaizen means continually looking for improvement, no matter how small, in every area of the business. Adopting an attitude like this is a sure fire way to improve your business, get more clients and earn more money.

60. See what your clients see

When you finish work one day, exit your business as you normally do and then stop. Turn around and approach your business as a client would. Understanding what your clients experience is the best way to understand how you can improve it for them. Improve their experience and you'll automatically improve the chances of getting more referrals.

If you have physical premises...

What do they see as they stand in front of it? What does the front door look like? Where do they go when they are waiting for their appointment with you.? What is the waiting room like? Are the magazines new or old?

What is your Consultation room like? Where do they sit or lay down? Is the ceiling freshly painted or are there cobwebs in the corners?

How do they pay, who do they pay and where do they pay? Is it consistent every time?

If you work online…

What is the set-up of the meeting? Do you call them or do they call you?

If you are on video, what are you wearing when they see you? What is in the background of your picture?

What is the sound quality like?

Do you make notes for them or record the call? If you do, when and how do they get access to this?

How and when do they pay?

61. Put up a sign outside your place of work

This could be a Board you put up and take down whenever your business is open. It could be a sign that is attached to the wall - either sticking out perpendicular so it catches the eye, or laying flat like a poster. It could be a simple bronze plaque beside your doorbell.

Whatever version you decide on, make sure it ticks the three key advertising boxes:

- It needs to be eye catching. If people can't see it or don't notice it, it doesn't help you.
- It needs to have a clear message and be worded in terms of problem and solution. No one cares about your title or qualifications. They care about what you can do for them.
- It needs to be simple with no distractions. Make sure the words are easy to read, the pictures need to reinforce the message rather than distract away from it.

62. Use window signage

If you have windows in your place of work that can be seen by passers by, consider using one way signage where you can still see out of your window from the inside, yet from the outside people see an advert for your business. There are many different companies offering these types of window signs. Choose one that still lets a lot of light in and follow the 3 keys of marketing:

- It needs to be eye catching. If people can't see it or don't notice it, it doesn't help you.
- It needs to have a clear message and be worded in terms of problem and solution. No one cares about your title or qualifications. They care about what you can do for them.
- It needs to be simple with no distractions. Make sure the words are easy to read, the pictures need to reinforce the message rather than distract away from it.

63. Advertise your business on your car

Putting an advert on your car is a great way to spread the word in your local area about what you do. Make sure the message is clear, the writing large and your contact details very visible. An additional side benefit could be tax advantages as your car is now being used for work purposes. Check with your accountant to explore this.

Two things to be aware of:
Check with your insurance company to make sure they allow signage on your car under your current insurance policy
Make sure you know how to remove the signage when you no longer want it, or when you want to sell the car.

ONLINE MARKETING

Social Media Attraction Marketing Strategies

Social media is the key area where everyone puts their attention nowadays when trying to get more clients, however, much of what we see online isn't very effective. With so many people trying the same thing and using social media to promote themselves, the key is to stand out from the noise and give your potential clients something of real value and interest.

64. Start a competition

People love competitions and the chance to win something. Launch a competition that will engage people in a simple and easy way to participate. There has to be a prize at the end and make sure it is something people will want. When deciding on what to use as a prize, keep in mind, the larger your audience and the more people you want to get engaged, the larger the prize needs to be.

For example, you could ask people to come up with a name for your business with a prize for the winning suggestion.

You could have a competition for the most extreme picture taken of someone holding one of your flyers.

Be creative and most importantly, allow the people in your competition to be creative. Give people encouragement and feedback as the recognition is as important to your audience as the chance of winning the prize itself.

For a more basic option you can have people write their name on a list to guess the jellybeans in the jar

65. Post daily value pieces - Give first

Everything in your business should be about giving first. The late great Zig Ziglar said, "You can have anything in life that you want, if you just help enough other people get what they want first!" So start giving. On social media this means you make sure to post something every day that is useful or interesting for your audience. This doesn't have to be a massive post, in fact it's better if it's not. Short and simple posts educating people about ways they could improve their life, such as drinking more water, or standing up and taking breaks from the desk, will have much more impact and chance of people reading it!

The more you give, the more people will follow you and listen to what you say. The more this happens the more they are likely to reach out to you if they have a problem in your area of expertise.

66. Once a week have a special offer

You have to help your community know how they can access your services and the best way to do this online is by having a weekly offer. This could be for a discounted Consultation or package of sessions. It could be a 'bring a friend for free' offer. The offer can be anything you like as long as it provides value to your audience, has to have a limited number of places, and MUST have an expiry date.

If your offer isn't valuable, no one will take you up on it. For example, giving a 10% discount is rarely enough for people to take action. Make it what we call an irresistible offer. Something it's hard to say no to, or even better make it something they can't otherwise get.

You have to have a limited number of places otherwise you could end up working ridiculous hours earning very little money because more people than you expected took advantage of your offer!

There has to be a time limit, otherwise there is no incentive for people to take action. If the offer expires in 48 hours, people know they have to act today otherwise they miss out. While some people will feel this is too 'salesy', just ask yourself, if you know you have a month to get something done, when do you usually do it? At the end of the month right? Whereas if you only had 24 hours, you'd take action straight away. So by putting a time constraint in place, you make sure people take action if they are serious about taking advantage of your offer.

67. Start a podcast sharing your knowledge

In today's world, it is not enough to just be an expert. People want to know that you care about them. What better way to demonstrate that than by giving your knowledge and expertise away for free in a podcast. Podcasts can be long or short and can cover whatever topic you feel could be interesting. The key is that by hosting your own podcast you are automatically positioned as an expert and can build a large community of people who specifically turn to you for advice. The concept is to teach without expectation of return and you'll be pleasantly surprised at what does come your way because of the reputation you build.

68. Create a daily video

Start sharing your knowledge and experiences on a daily basis. This will help your audience connect with you as a person and give them a daily dose of something useful, interesting and perhaps entertaining. These videos should be a combination of candid selfie videos showing what

you're up to, along with more professionally staged shots where you will use a camera and tripod rather than just a camera.
Keep all videos under 3 minutes and ideally record them using software that transcribes your words into text so people can watch your video with the sound turned off and can just read what you're saying.
With the selfie style videos, these aren't about being perfectly presented. However, you do still need to come across professionally as you are building your brand and how you dress, speak and what you say will influence whether people view you as an expert or not.

69. Start a podcast interviewing other experts

Interviewing other experts automatically positions you as an authority as you are the one doing the interview. Not sure how well this could work to make you successful?
Let us ask you, what is Oprah's expertise?
All she does is interview people right. Of course, this is an oversimplification, however you get the point. And yet, whether or not you rate her as an authority, no one can deny she's been phenomenally successful.

How do you pick who to interview. Create a list of all the people you rate as an expert in their field and who your clients might be interested in. Then simply start reaching out to these people. You can also ask your connections who they know that might be a good interviewee. Guaranteed someone you know knows someone who's up to something interesting!

70. Join LinkedIn and Facebook Groups where your ideal clients hang out and start posting useful content, give advice and answer questions.

By becoming known as the Go-To person in the Group for answering questions on a certain topic you get a reputation as being an expert. By giving this advice and support for free you build up a large community of people who respect and value you. Then if they ever experience a challenge in your area of expertise, who do you think they'll reach out to? Your competitor down the road who they have no relationship with? Or you, the expert from their online community who gives free high quality advice?

71. Search through LinkedIn and Facebook for connections.

Identify people who could be advantageous to your business. Perhaps they are in contact with your target market. Perhaps they are well-respected in your field so linking with them will raise your credibility. Perhaps they are someone you could learn from, collaborate with or form referral or joint venture partnerships with.

Connect with these people, share and comment on their posts and suggest you get on the phone and have a chat to explore any potential business collaborations

72. Create an online JV Partnership

A JV (Joint Venture) is a partnership with a non-competitive business who serves the same target market as you. You collaborate so you can promote each other's services to your respective database of clients and create a three way win:win. A win for your clients - they get to meet another expert who could help them. A win for your JV partner - they get introduced by a trusted expert to a warmed up group of potential clients they otherwise wouldn't have access to. And it's a double win for you as you are seen by your clients to be offering additional support and your JV partner will subsequently promote you to their client base!

73. Do a live video a couple of times a week

Follow the same format we have already discussed about making your content valuable and interesting for your ideal clients; however, these sessions are live and therefore even more valuable. Giving people the chance to interact with you live and ask questions will massively increase your connection to your potential clients and build quicker relationships .

This could be done via Facebook Live, a webinar provider or any other social media platform that allows you to present live and have people interacting with you. Nothing quite beats the experience and the authenticity that comes across from a live presentation. Because there is no chance to edit the raw footage, there's a lot more 'realness' that comes across and people will feel that they've gotten to know you more personally than from a recorded video. The better people feel they know you, the more likely they are to recommend you and use your services.

74. Get interviewed by other experts

Being interviewed is the perfect way to position yourself as an expert in your area. Just by being the person sharing knowledge on the interview, you're automatically viewed as a higher authority on that topic. This adds to your credibility meaning people are more likely to come to you rather than your competitors down the road who have not been interviewed.

Search for podcasts and shows that would be of interest to your clients, approach the organisers and offer your services. Most organisers are continuously looking for new experts and new content so providing you can offer their audience something interesting and relevant, then chances are they'll happily interview you and it's a win:win for both of you.

75. Be prolific and strategic!

Make use of as many different media channels as possible to promote your services. The more you can make your profile and your business visible, the more people become aware of you. We always advocate having a primary platform where you focus most of your attention but make sure you have all the other bases covered. If your ideal clients mostly find you through LinkedIn, this definitely needs to be your primary focus. However, make sure you still get exposure on all the other main social media platforms, so you get maximum brand presence and recognition. If you don't know which platform your clients use, ask them.

76. Sanitise your online profiles

Update and sanitise your Facebook and LinkedIn profiles so you look professional
What is the first thing people do when they consider working with someone. They check them out on Google. No matter how good the SEO is on your website, the chances are Facebook and LinkedIn profile will come up first on any Google search. Why? Because they spend millions more than you do to make sure they come up first!

So if we know that your social media profile will probably come above your professional website, consider if you really want potential clients seeing those holiday snaps of you topless on the beach. Or what about those drunken pictures you're tagged in with your friends. It's time to untag yourself and remove pictures or content that you don't want clients to see. This doesn't mean you can't share your personal life online - just be aware of who could be looking at it and only share what you're comfortable with everyone knowing.

77. Connect with every person who likes, shares or comments on your social media posts

If people are engaging with your content, you have built a connection with them. Take this to the next level by connecting with them directly and get to know them. What's going on in their life? What challenges are they experiencing? What other interests do they have?

The more you understand who connects with you and what drives them, the better you can target your marketing to create better engagement.

Always remember that one of the most important human drivers is recognition. By reaching out to people who comment on your posts, you help them feel validated which reinforces their connection with you and increases the chance of progressing the relationship.

78. Ask your audience how they solved a particular challenge

Every problem in the world has at some point been solved by someone else. Therefore start using your database and get them to share their experiences. If you combine this concept with the reality that everyone's favourite subject is talking about themselves, you'll be amazed at how much people are willing to support others by sharing their own experience.

Start a post asking for suggestions on how people have overcome a certain challenge that you know your clients might be curious about. Or it could be something you want help with yourself? Simply starting a conversation like this is a great way to connect with people and build a relationship.

79. Create a Group

Create your own group on LinkedIn or Facebook that will bring together people of similar interests. Obviously focus this conversation on topics that your potential clients would be curious about. Such as, if you work with people with neck pain, then create a group that will help people to solve their own neck pain. Now I know you might be thinking that if we teach them how to solve their own challenges, then they won't ever come into your business and become a client. The thing is, there are two types of people in this world: DIY and DFM.
DIY refers to Do It Yourself. These are the people who want to figure out how to solve their own challenges and so they'll love free advice and would be unlikely to come into your business anyway.
DFM refers to Done For Me. These are the people who just want you to fix them so they can get on with other things. These people have no interest in following advice and doing it themselves, but they will still be interested in a group that promises to teach them how to solve their challenges. These are the members of the group who are likely to reach out and become clients and every DIY person who participates in the group is likely to know at least one DFM person that they'll mention your details to if they find the group useful

Email Attraction Marketing Strategies

We all get far too much email these days, however, it is still a VERY good way to build your client list if used effectively. Obviously, with the data protection laws, you can't and shouldn't just spam people indiscriminately. However, staying in touch with your clients as part of doing business with them (as long as you have permission), is just good customer service.

80. Send out a Welcome Email to all new clients

Saying Thank You to all new clients is good customer service. If you combine this with a short piece about how you work, the community of clients you have created and the values that underpin your business, you'll start to build a deeper connection with this new client

Make sure it's a short email so people don't drift off. Always remember that people are busy and less is so much more!

81. Send your Clients a Gift

Sending your clients the occasional gift via email, such as a link to something they might want is a great way to reinforce a positive relationship. It could be as simple as a link to a YouTube video that they might find interesting. Or a discount code for a show you know they'd enjoy. Anything like this is going above and beyond for your clients and it'll help you stand out from your competition while building loyalty with your clients. You may or may not combine this with the seasons, special events in their lives or just because you were thinking of them.

82. Voucher for a free session for them or a friend

Sending your clients the occasional voucher they can use themselves or give to a friend is a great way to reward them for being one of your clients. By making it a voucher they can use themselves or give away, it makes it extra special as a lot of companies only give promotional sessions to new clients which excludes their existing clients and makes them feel less valued. Always remember that your existing clients are much more likely to spend more money with you compared to with new clients so they should always be offered the same benefits as new clients and perhaps even better offers to say thank you for their loyalty.

83. Start a regular email newsletter that delivers great value every week or month

A simple email newsletter that engages your audience does wonders for building your community. Vary between providing useful and practical information, thought provoking ideas and general interest pieces. Short and sweet is definitely the key here. This could be weekly if less than 100 words, or if you want to make it longer then perhaps aim for fortnightly or even monthly. We usually find that more frequent, shorter newsletters are much more likely to be engaged with. Whereas the longer, more elaborate and traditional style newsletters generally wind up being deleted as people don't have time to read them

84. Send all your clients a special booking code

Let your clients know that this code gives a free Consultation.
The code is personal to each of them so if they give the code to someone who uses it to book a consultation and become a client, they

automatically get a free gift, such as a free session themselves, a coffee voucher, or anything else that you feel your clients might appreciate. Making the voucher a win:win for both parties dramatically increases the chances of getting your clients to make more referrals as they feel recognised and appreciated.

Website Attraction Marketing Strategies

Did you know that having a website is not essential to running a successful business, despite what everyone would have you believe.
How do we know this. Because Chris grew his clinic revenue over £100,000 revenue in less than a year without having a functioning website. And we have trained thousands business owners how to do the same.
However, this doesn't mean having a website is wrong. A good website will definitely help you get more clients, the key, as always, is if you're going to have something, make sure it is done well so it attracts clients rather than putting them off!

85. Write a blog and post it weekly on your website

Consider what information your clients and potential clients might find useful and write a regular piece that you post on your website. Consider always focusing on things that are useful for your clients rather than going into great scientific detail or jargon that could overwhelm people. The more interesting and engaging the content, the more people will read it and you build up a community that regards you as the go-to expert in your area.

Note: Post these blogs onto your website rather than a social media platform and then promote them on social media. This way when people click on them on social media, it is your website that gets better Google rankings rather than Facebook etc. Something to note as well is that all blogs also need to be over 500 words otherwise, they won't rank well for SEO purposes. Writing less than that is not a good use of your time as you'll miss out on the wider benefits.

86. Rewrite your website content so it positions you as an expert

People don't wake up thinking, "Today I need to find an Osteopath/ Coach/Massage Therapist/Accountant (insert your profession here)".

Instead they wake up thinking, "I have XYZ problem and I want to get rid of it". Then they start looking for an expert in that area.

A website that focuses on your titles and qualifications isn't what people are looking for. Re-write your website content so it focuses on a specific set of problems and the solutions you get for your clients in these areas. By being more specific we attract more clients as we are seen as an expert rather than just looking like everyone who has the same qualifications as you.

87. Update your About Us section.

No one cares when you graduated or what qualifications you hold. Sorry to say that after all the years and effort you've put into your studies. People assume you're qualified - it's an expectation. What they want to get from your website is to better understand who you are and why you are the best person for them to trust to solve their problem. Consider sharing how many clients you've worked with, what types of results you typically get clients and how your extra-curricular activities make you even better at your career. This is the point to share things about yourself such as whether you have children or not, whether you engage in any particular sport, perhaps even what your long term aspirations or goals are. Remember people like people who are like them The more you reveal who you are (professionally, of course), the more chance people have to connect with you and decide you're the expert for them.

Something to note is to especially avoid using jargon or professional terms when you describe your expertise or problems you like working with because if people don't understand what you're talking about, they're not going to trust you. Use the rule that a 7-year old has to be able to understand what you do. If they can't, your marketing isn't simple or clear enough and you risk people not properly understanding who you are or what you do and therefore they will choose a different expert to work with.

88. Add a behind the scenes section

Let people understand what really happens in your practice. Have pictures of where you work, pictures showing you working with a client (obviously get permission from the client before using their image), pictures of you and your team engaging and perhaps relaxing in between clients.

Show your workspace, let people get a feel of what it will be like for them to visit you as a client. Show lots of smiling photos of your team interacting with clients. Have a picture of the outside of your building so it's easy for people to find. The more your potential clients feel they know you and understand what will happen when they start working with you, the safer they will feel and the more likely they are to want to work with you than someone else.

89. Create an App

This is definitely an activity to consider only when you have a steady stream of clients and are looking for a way to streamline their booking process, build a community and take your business to the next level.

An app can be a great way to demonstrate your business is going places while providing high levels of service and something few of your competitors will be able to match. Consider features such as online booking, direct access to one of your team for immediate support, a news and updates section, some sort of tracking function where your clients can record their progress and achievements. The key is to start simple and add extra features as you go rather than trying to make it all singing and dancing from the very beginning

Unless you are a tech wizard, this is definitely something best to outsource while you stay focused on serving your clients. Use your time to create the concept and outline of what you want the App to do, and then pass it across to the experts to build.

90. Add an instant chat feature

Having the functionality on your website to engage people in conversation is invaluable. The chat feature makes you seem more accessible to your potential clients and gives them a risk free way to ask questions. There are lots of applications that allow you to add a 'bot' to your website. A 'bot' is like an online robot that will handle a lot of the standard questions without needing to involve a human. Therefore nurturing potential customers without taking up any of your precious time.

However, make sure the chat feature moves people as quickly as possible to a phone call as speaking directly to a live person will start the process of building a relationship far more effectively than communicating via instant chat. To put it very simply, the more people you get onto a phone call, the more new clients you will get into your clinic!

91. Add an opt-in feature

Giving people a reason to give you their contact details is a vital part of your website. Once you have their contact details and permission to contact them, you have the chance to build a relationship with them. And it is this relationship with people that will lead to more clients and more business.

The opt-in box is simply a way of offering a gift to people in exchange for giving you permission to communicate with them. A lot of websites have this opt-in box appear as soon as people have landed on the home page, however, this is not helpful. When someone has only just arrived on your website, they don't have enough information to know whether they want to learn more from you and so we all instantly just hit the cancel button and the opportunity is wasted. Instead, have your opt-in box appear either after a certain number of minutes that someone has been on your website, or timed to appear when they click away from your site. This has a much higher likelihood of uptake as now the person has a better idea of who you are and what you do and therefore can make an informed decision if they want to receive anything else from you. Doing it this way dramatically increases the chance of people staying on your list and not immediately opting out

The other thing that will make a difference to whether people opt-in will be based on the perceived value of your free gift. In exchange for giving you their details, people quite rightly have an expectation that they will get something in return. Always make your giveaway high value so it's a no-brainer decision for people to register to receive it.

92. Create a high value give away

Make sure everyone who connects with you online has the chance to get something super high value for free. This could be a free eBook, or video series, or downloadable PDF, or a white paper. Whatever your potential clients might find interesting and useful.

Remember, if your giveaway isn't perceived as valuable, people are not going to give you their contact details or permission to contact them. When we say make the giveaway super high value, we don't necessarily mean high monetary value. Instead it's about providing them with something that will be useful or valuable for them. A lot of websites make the mistake of offering low value items and all that happens is people unsubscribe from the database and the chance to build a relationship is gone. Give high value free content and you'll stand out from everyone else and build a database of people who love and recommend you.

One concept to consider is that you should give away your best content for free. Sounds counter-intuitive doesn't it as why would people still pay for your services if they could just download a free product and learn what you do for free? However, most people will download the free product, be impressed by it, not use it and then want to become your client. Not convinced on this? Have you ever downloaded a free eBook or video and not watched it? We've all done this, and your clients will do the same. Just focus on producing something your clients will find valuable and whether they read/watch/listen to it or not, you'll start generating more clients!

93. Create a Client of the month section on your website.

Recognition is a fundamental human drive, so create a space on your website where you can give credit to clients who go above and beyond in any area. Updating this monthly gives people a reason to visit your site and creates a community feel within your clients. It also allows you to support some of your clients causes and things that are dear to them which will make them feel special and recognised far beyond just being your client.

This could recognise people for progress they have made through working with you, such as how much weight they have lost, or how many miles they have been able to run (depending on your expertise). Or it could be to recognise them for achievements outside of your business, such as raising money for charity; or helping their children accomplish something; or organising a community event. The possibilities are endless, just focus on acknowledgement and you'll be amazed at how positively people will respond. If you don't have a website, you can also do this on social media groups.

94. Create a charity section

Share what you do both in and outside of the business to support causes and charities near to your heart. Share why you are passionate about these causes and what actions you're taking, what money you've raised and what support you'd like to generate to achieve something extra.

This lets people get to know another aspect of you and it will reinforce their decision to work with you because you care. The more people who understand other sides to your personality the better. This means they get to connect to you as an expert, as well as a heart centred human. The greater the connection, the less concerned they are going to be about paying you for your services because they recognise you are focused on bigger things than just making money.

95. Make it easy for clients to contact you and book a Consultation

This could be simply making sure your phone number is clearly shown on every page of your website and you state something along the lines of, "Call me now for a free 15 minute chat to explore resolving xyz issue"

Or it could be setting up an online booking process so clients have immediate access to your diary and can book their own sessions. Whatever route you go, the easier you make it for people to see you, the more likely you are to have lots of clients.

Too many websites are so complex they put people off. Everyone is busy nowadays so the easier you can make it for them to get the information they need to make a decision, the better. And once they have made a decision to work with you, you want to simplify the process of booking an appointment.

96. Optimise your website and all landing pages for mobile

More and more people are using a mobile device for all their online activities. If your website or landing pages are not optimised for mobile, you are not engaging with an ever increasing number of people. A mobile responsive website creates a far better user experience which is the start of a potential client building a relationship with you.

Remember people will judge your competence and expertise based on their experience on your website. This isn't fair or even accurate, yet it's what we all do. Make sure your reputation is enhanced by your web presence rather than diminished.

97. Take your prices off your website

Everyone thinks they should have their prices displayed on their website, and the usual argument is that everyone else does this, so we should do it too. However, the main focus people have when searching for an expert to help them is whether this is the right person for them to get the results they want.

How do we all make this decision. Because most websites are not clear on the concept of problem:solution (as in what is the expertise and what results do clients typically get), the usual ways people make their decision as to whether or not you are the expert for them, is to check out your photos and your price. They look at your photo to make sure you look normal, professional, and most of all safe. And then they check out your price. If you're more expensive than your competitors down the road, most people will not book a session with you.

However, if your site is a very clear problem:solution conversation and it's targeted to exactly what the person is looking for, by not having your price, you are more likely to have them ring you to enquire. Once you have someone on the phone, they are much more likely to become a client. Yes, you might have a higher percentage of people visiting your site and not making enquiries. However, those that do enquire, are automatically self-selecting for being people who are more serious about getting their particular problem resolved and so are better clients overall.

We know that the usual objection to this approach is that if we are too specific in stating our problem and solution, then we are actively putting off all the people who that might not be relevant for. So what?!!!

Do any of us have the time or the capacity to help everyone on this planet. There are over 7 billion of us!!. We need to narrow down our marketing to appeal directly to the people we are best suited to help rather than trying to be a catch all for everyone out there. By being more specific, you'll attract more clients and they'll be exactly the ones you want to work with rather than trying to work with everyone and not having enough people walking through your door.

98. Contribute articles to an online publication

A great way to increase your visibility and credibility in the marketplace is to be seen as an expert. One way to do this is to be able to say, as featured in xyz publication. Now we would all like to have an article published in something like the Times newspaper. However, the chances of that happening are slim for most of us. However, virtually all these great publications have an online version where they have many more articles and much more content than the paper version.

These online publications have a much higher demand for articles and therefore they are much more likely to accept something you submit as long as it seems credible and meets the golden rule of focusing on solving a problem that their readers might be facing.

The benefits to you are two-fold:

- If they accept your article, you can now say, as featured in xyz and you don't have to say it was the online version as they do not have different names or logos ;)
- Your name and expertise is now visible to a whole lot more people and some of these might want to become your client so make sure they know how to contact you!

99. Get professional photos

Website photos are an area that most of us let ourselves down on and it's mostly because of the misleading name we give them: headshots.

The main thing people are looking for when they look at a photo of you is to know that you are not a threat to them. In other words, that they'll be safe with you. This might sound a bit simplistic, however, consider that not that long ago evolutionarily speaking, we were living in caves and everyone who wasn't part of our tribe was a potential danger to us. Part of our brain is still always scanning for danger and threats and it hasn't evolved yet to understand the difference between a photo and reality. So how can we demonstrate that we are not a threat to them if they can only see our head?

Obviously, any image needs to be professional with you dressed smart and exuding confidence, experience and kindness. However, the key way that we humans know that someone is not dangerous is by seeing they don't have a weapon in their hands.

Sounds a bit dramatic we know, however, think of the universal ways we humans greet each other. It's often an open hand wave, or by shaking right hands. Both ways say very clearly," I have no weapon in my hand, I am not a threat."
Now, just to be clear, this is not something we are consciously thinking every time we meet someone new or look at a picture. However, our subconscious brain is always working in the background looking for danger.

We need to be aware of this in our photos. If the hands cannot be seen, the subconscious brain will be thinking there might be a weapon out of site and so the person is considered less safe. No one is going to voluntarily work with someone who they feel 'unsafe'. So make sure rather than a headshot, you have a picture that shows you from the waist up with both hands visible and empty. This might just be a small change, yet it can have a big difference in how you are perceived by your potential clients.

100. Create a free video series

Create a simple yet informative series of videos that people can download for free. Make sure the videos are clear, easy to follow and provide clear value such as actionable things to do or thought provoking concepts that will help them tackle a problem or issue they're challenged by.

Always aim to deliver high quality free content as possible. It doesn't mean you have to spend a fortune getting professional videos produced. Focus instead on what people would most benefit from and share from your expertise and experience. The easiest way to get started is simply to get a tripod or mount for your smartphone and use it to record your videos. You can then download the videos to your computer and use free editing software such as iMovie or Windows Media Player to make it look professional. Yes, obviously professionally filmed and produced videos will look better, however, they are definitely not needed initially so save yourself some money and try doing it yourself. Uncertain if you can do this? Chris is definitely NOT tech savvy and yet he managed to film and edit the entire Online Training of our 7 figure Mentoring Company using his iPhone. If he can do it with his tech challenges, so can you!

How will people access these videos. Get an opt-in box set up on your website for people to register their details in return for the free series and this way you can serve and support them over time through your blogs and newsletters.

How did you get on?

Have you implemented many of these marketing strategies?

If not, go back and progressively test them out and see what works best for you

Thanks for reading Grow Your Heart Centred Business and we hope to hear soon about the amazing success you're creating

Best wishes,

Chris and Karene Lambert-Gorwyn

www.heartcentredbusiness.com/book-offers

Red Flag Sheet

- Describe what thought has come up, as best you can.

- What is the emotion associated with this? (e.g. sorrow, fear, anger, sadness, despair, hopelessness etc.)

- What do you feel in your body? (hot, cold, pain, nausea, tiredness, a need to run screaming from the room etc)

- Where in the body do you feel this? (Chest, stomach, head, throat, neck, jaw etc.)

- Summarise the thought in one sentence.